KIRSTY

KIRSTY

A Father's Fight for Justice

Charles W. Pearce

iUniverse, Inc.
Bloomington

Kirsty
A Father's Fight for Justice

iUniverse books may be ordered through booksellers or by contacting:

iUniverse
1663 Liberty Drive
Bloomington, IN 47403
www.iuniverse.com
1-800-Authors (1-800-288-4677)

ISBN: 978-1-4697-4638-8 (sc)
ISBN: 978-1-4697-4640-1 (hc)
ISBN: 978-1-4697-4639-5 (ebk)

Printed in the United States of America

iUniverse rev. date: 02/27/2012

In memory of

Kirsty Jayne Pearce,

And two special ladies in her life:

Konon and Mama Sin.

*These two very special aunts
shared so much love with Kirsty on earth.
They are now sharing that love in heaven.*

Introduction

I AM WRITING THIS BOOK IN HONOUR OF MY BEAUTIFUL DAUGHTER, Kirsty Jayne, who was cruelly taken from us on 29 August 2003, at just seventeen years and six months. The care given to her in the hospital after she was taken ill can be described only as terribly amateurish from a medical point of view, a total indictment of the medical services in my country. People in my country have always stated that the medical care in the United Kingdom is better than that offered anywhere else in the world. Unfortunately in some areas, it is not.

Kirsty lived in one of these areas of inadequate medical care. When Kirsty died, it was the most numbing effect that my body had ever felt. My precious little girl was honest, funny, and very brave. She suffered so much pain in her short life but never complained.

The most awful thing about Kirsty's passing was the manner in which it occurred and the absolute complacency shown by the doctor responsible for her care.

It is so easy to complain about medical care when something appears to have gone wrong and a life is lost, particularly if it is that of a child. When the authorities disclaim any responsibility, knowing full well that they are partly to blame, the pain of the loss is even greater.

When you lose a precious loved one, it is normal to go into denial mode. I did, to such a degree that I found myself going to the medicine cupboard and taking out Kirsty's medicine, ready to give it to her when she was due to wake up from her sleep—but then I would find myself crying at the reality of the situation that Peggy and I were in. I just could not believe Kirsty was gone, and this continued for a very long time. Even today, I often tell Kirsty that what happened could not be and the bad nightmare I am going through will come to an end. It never has, of course. This is obviously the state of denial that everyone goes through and depending upon the circumstances, continues to go through for a very long time.

The main question that is always asked with unexplained death is simply, "Why?" That simple question is never answered in a case of negligence. Nobody wants to get involved in cases like Kirsty's. For those involved in the negligence, keeping a low profile is the order of the day.

The strange thing is that after almost eight years of Kirsty being gone, I still expect her to come through the door with a big smile on her face and then a hug. I think of the times she would say to me, "When I get my new hips, I will run into your arms and give you a big kiss." Sadly this will never happen.

When I say my prayers at night, I pray for all the young children who passed away as Kirsty did. I know that they are all together, and that makes things a little easier.

Love is beautiful, binding, and everlasting; you cannot live without it. My wife, Peggy, and I love our daughter so deeply and miss her tremendously, but the one consolation we have is that we will be together again someday—though when that day comes, others will shed tears for us. Love is all around us. To find love is not very hard, though to find it, you must first give it. This story shows how vulnerable we all are and how much we depend on others as we attempt to wend our way through life's difficult times. We cannot do it alone.

Depending upon others during a crisis can sometimes be a complete waste of time and energy; though people mean well, they sometimes don't understand and don't know how to help. Quite often you are left on your own by the people who have promised the support you need. Usually this is because they feel that they are intruding upon your grief. In the long run, of course, this tends to make you much stronger and able to cope with all that comes your way. It teaches you that depending upon yourself is the way to go.

PREFACE

THIS BOOK HAS BEEN WRITTEN IN AN ATTEMPT TO SEEK JUSTICE for my daughter, Kirsty Jayne, who died as a result of poor medical care in a period of only thirteen hours from the time of admission to the paediatric ward.

The procedures needed to keep Kirsty alive were in place but not used. If they had been, then things would have ended up much differently than they did. Had the medics only used simple common sense, then the outcome for Kirsty would have been much different, but they were complacent and indifferent to my daughter's needs.

The General Medical Council (GMC), which claims to be the regulator of the medical profession in the United Kingdom and boasts, "Our purpose is to protect and maintain the health and safety of the community by ensuring proper standards in the practice of medicine," failed to honour its pledges and give Kirsty the justice owed her. When I first made a complaint to the GMC, I firmly believed that its claim about fairness in dealing with the general public would hold true; but after three years of fighting, it became apparent that fairness goes only one way. I would call it a completely biased organisation on behalf of its own members, with no interests in the well-being of the general public.

The GMC was as complacent and indifferent as the doctors treating Kirsty. Even though the council agreed that the doctor concerned with Kirsty had shown negligent behaviour and the parliamentary ombudsmen found him severely guilty in administering poor care to my daughter, he was never punished. As the GMC put it, "Though the doctor's behaviour can be considered as negligent, it was not negligent enough for him to face a hearing in front of his peers." This statement beggars belief considering that a young girl died in part because of that negligence.

It is impossible to have meetings with the people who count in England because the public is told that it is inappropriate for ministers or their officers responsible for public departments to get involved. I am sure that the people I wrote to, such as the prime minister, minister of health, and the lord chancellor did not see the letters I sent; I believe that they are screened from such annoyances.

I really worked hard in seeking justice for Kirsty, but to no avail until over seven years after her death, when the coroner for County Essex agreed to give me the inquest I had been seeking for so many years. This is the same coroner who refused my request for an inquest in 2005.

On reflection, I do understand the coroner's reluctance to grant the inquest in 2005; she had not seen the ombudsman's report at that time, and so it was difficult for her to agree to my request. That did not stop me for being angry at the whole situation, and I would hope that anyone reading this book would understand my anger. To gain respect, you must first give it; but of course, many people do not live by this.

As I write this book, my hopes are that anyone who reads it will understand my frustration at the total refusal by the medical profession to face up to their responsibilities with regard to the doctor responsible for Kirsty's care on the night she died.

Kirsty's story is not unique. There are many, many families that have had the same traumatic experience that we had, and like us, failed to get the justice they were entitled to.

Acknowledgements

So many people knew and loved our daughter that it would be impossible to list them all, even if I could remember all of their names. So, whoever you are, thank you for making Kirsty's short life as happy and memorable as possible. Peggy and I will be eternally grateful.

Kirsty was loved by many people, and she returned that love. As far as she was concerned, there were no bad people in this world. That helped her to believe that her world was perfect, when in fact it was far from it. The following story will explain what I mean.

I would like to thank some very special people who tried so very hard to help Kirsty obtain some form of normality in her life:

Professor Patricia Woo, Professor Mike Dillon, Dr. David Taylor, Dr. Kevin Murray, Dr. Robert Dinwiddie, Dr. Lucinda Carr, Dr. Karen Davies, Dr. Graham Derek, Dr. Kjell Tullus, and Dr. Clarissa Pilkington. They never gave up searching for answers to Kirsty's problems, and we are grateful for their efforts.

Mr. Zdenek Gregor, Dr. David Easton, Dr. Jackie Askwith, Dr. M. Rajah, Dr. Shariff, and Dr. Ramanan, also were very important in Kirsty's life.

Thank you to all the physiotherapists, speech therapists, teachers, and nurses involved in caring for Kirsty over many years. Without you, there would have been nothing to help Kirsty through her everyday routine. You all made life more bearable for her.

A very special thanks to the staff of St. Clouds Hospital and the Arnold Palmer Hospital for Women and Children in Kissimmee, Florida. The unstinting efforts of the staff there over many hours brought Kirsty back from the brink. God bless you all.

Val Richards, Kirsty's community nurse who had such an impact on her life, provided many visits and general support over the years. She was a good friend and continued to visit Peggy and me for three years after Kirsty's passing. We wish her the best of luck with her new life in Portugal with her husband, Dave.

To my very special son, Tim, brother to Kirsty, who had great difficulty in coming to terms with her passing. He loved her deeply and misses her tremendously.

Thank you to the aunts, uncles, cousins, and Magic, the wonderful dog in France that did not understand her but seemed to understand her needs. Magic gave Kirsty some very happy moments.

Thank you to John Baron, MP, a man that Kirsty was proud to call her friend. No matter how busy he was in parliament, he would always find time to reassure and support us. I thank you, John, and your team for your support.

Many thanks to Diane and Jim, the parents of Christopher, a young man who passed away six months prior to Kirsty, at the age of twenty. You have been such wonderful friends over the last eight years, and your support has been the rock that we have always and still do lean upon. It is a privilege to have you as friends; our love goes out to you.

I am so proud of Peggy for the dedication and love she has shown to Kirsty, Tim, and me, but also for the way she ran the house and ensured we were all loved equally. I salute you, Peggy, and thank you for being the lovely person you are. You know I love you deeply and am very proud to be your husband. You made Kirsty's short life as comfortable and enjoyable as it possibly could be, and that was why Kirsty considered you to be her best friend. You are a true example of what a wonderful mother and wife should be. Thank you, Peggy.

The one person above all we could not forget is Peggy's brother, Laugi, my best friend and Kirsty's favourite uncle. When we needed him, he was here, and he supported us as only he could. He still continues to do so; he misses Kirsty terribly. We can never thank him enough. We love you, brother.

There are many other people over the years that are too numerous to mention who helped to make Kirsty's life more tolerable, and they are to be thanked. These were people that were drawn to her from all walks of life. Even though they may have only known her for short periods, they were invaluable in providing Kirsty with many good times, and Peggy and I with many happy memories.

Last but not least, I would like to thank Gordon Smith, Britain's best medium, who gave Peggy and me a most memorable and unforgettable experience when he gave us a private reading. He was fantastic; the manner in which he picked up on things in our lives that he had no knowledge about prior to the reading was uncanny, and at the same time very comforting. Many people are skeptics with regard to psychic mediums; I admit I was one of these types before our meeting with Gordon. After our meeting, my view changed completely.

It is quite understandable that some people should mock my views, and this I quite accept as they have the right to do so. People have actually said to me that there is nothing after death and I should stop having these unproven thoughts. It has been suggested that I only believed Gordon because he had just happened by pure luck to bring me what I wanted to hear. I always try to make people understand that Gordon knew nothing of Kirsty before the reading. He certainly knew nothing of Chris, Diane's son who passed away six months before Kirsty, and yet he told us that Chris was brought through with her.

Chapter 1

THIS IS THE TRUE STORY OF A VERY SPECIAL YOUNG LADY, DEEPLY loved and cherished by her family and friends.

Her name is Kirsty Jayne Pearce, and she was born 22 February 1986, to parents Peggy and Charles. She was the only sister to Tim.

This is her story; it is one of courage and stubbornness that needs to be told.

Kirsty was determined to enjoy life to the fullest, even though she had so much stacked against her. She never complained or felt sorry for her predicament, but rather had much empathy for others she considered to be suffering more than she.

She loved life and attempted to get as much out of it as she could. She never gave up.

When Peggy found out she was expecting our second child, we were both over the moon and started to make plans for the new arrival.

Though we had no idea what sex the child would be, we began the expectant parents' game of trying to pick a name. This went on for weeks, but we knew it was pointless, so we decided to wait until the baby arrived.

At 01.40 hours on 22 February 1986, Kirsty arrived, weighing in at three pounds, twelve ounces. This was small, especially since she was a full-term baby. Nobody could understand why she should be so small because there had been no traumas for Mum during her pregnancy and she felt good during the whole of that time.

After Peggy had given her the usual mother's welcome, Kirsty was taken wrapped in foil to the special baby unit.

It was explained that because she was low in weight, all precautions had to be taken. For the following two weeks, all that happened was for Kirsty to be cared for as any mother would have done. Peggy would have loved to provide that care. She was sometimes allowed to feed Kirsty, but generally it was the nursing staff that dealt with Kirsty's daily routine.

Peggy and I were with Kirsty for most of the time, and as there was little we could do in actually caring for her, I decided that I would be the tea boy for the special baby care unit. This suited the nurses because they could then get on with their duties. Very often over the next few months, I served as their unofficial tea maker.

The change in Kirsty became obvious even to me. I could see that she was filling out and looking very well, even though she was still quite low in her weight.

Peggy and I began to relax about Kirsty as time went by; a lot of our anxiety started to ease.

After a fortnight, Kirsty's weight had risen to five pounds and the doctor felt she was fit enough to come home. We were very happy to take her home. I don't think I ever packed the car so quickly once it was time to bring our pretty little girl home. We had been praying for this over the previous two weeks.

I sang all the way home. When our son, Tim, had first met Kirsty in the hospital, it was not such a big deal to him. After all, he was only two years old himself and did not understand exactly what was going on. However, when Kirsty did eventually come home, he was captivated by her and amazed at how tiny she was.

Peggy and I could see that he fell in love with his sister. He immediately swamped her with kisses, an act that Kirsty was not particularly impressed with, but Tim was not too concerned. After all, he was only two years old, so why should he worry?

We all stood back and admired this tiny bundle in her cot.

Peggy and I agreed that we were lucky to have the perfect family and we wanted nothing to spoil it, but sadly, as so often is the case, this was not to be; dark clouds were looming on the horizon.

For two weeks, we enjoyed ourselves doing everything we could for this little bundle of joy.

Tim had gotten used to the idea of Kirsty being around and did what he could to help too.

Two weeks after Kirsty came home, on the twenty-second of March, she stopped feeding and started vomiting. We noticed that she had a blue tinge to her lips and a blue mottled pattern on her body. Her breathing was laboured, something we would see many times over the next seventeen and a half years.

I contacted the hospital to inform them of Kirsty's plight and was told to take her back to special care.

On arrival, she was placed into an oxygenised cot. Shortly afterwards, she was examined by a young doctor who said he thought Kirsty had ingested her feed. This meant that instead of the milk she was drinking going straight to the stomach, it would somehow go to the back of the throat and then on inhalation into her lungs, causing pulmonary oedema, which is the clinical name for fluid in the lungs.

Though this was the explanation given to Peggy and me, who are both trained nurses, we suspected that the pulmonary oedema was caused by other problems in Kirsty's body and it did not occur solely when she was fed.

The doctor told us that this was a possibility, but only time would tell. He then told us that he had detected a heart murmur and would have to discuss the problem with the consultant paediatrician.

This revelation distressed us both; we had only just gotten used to Kirsty, and here she was back in the hospital.

A week later, Peggy and I were informed that Kirsty would have to go to the Brompton Heart Hospital in London when fully stabilized for tests to find out what the problem was with her heart. And so on the fifth of April, off she went, happy and smiling.

Kirsty remained at Brompton for six days, where her blood was tested, scans taken, and cardiac tests carried out.

At the end of it, nothing was found, which did not surprise Peggy and me. This situation would be repeated over and over again over many years to come. Our view was that the problem was not her heart, but rather the crisis she'd had on the twenty-second of March, which had totally upset her system.

We kept these thoughts to ourselves because we did not want the paediatric team feeling insecure or thinking that we were being smart arses. After all, we were just parents in this situation, not nurses, so what would we know?

Kirsty was transferred back to Basildon Hospital from the Brompton on the fifth of April and remained there for four days before being discharged.

We were so happy to have her back and hoped there would be no further problems. Little did we know that much more was to come.

We were very concerned about the problems that Kirsty had had to contend with and decided that if I were to retire from nursing, it would be good for her to have me around. As the only driver in the house, I could take her to the hospital in any emergency. I did retire, and Peggy continued working as a night nurse.

As the years passed, Peggy and Kirsty became real friends, not just mother and daughter. It was such a shame that illness interfered so much and hospital admissions were so frequent.

Peggy originates from Mauritius, which is an island in the Indian Ocean. The people there are generally gentle and friendly, and that is the way she is. Peggy is also a very loving person, particularly toward her family.

Peggy has had her share of losses in her life. Two elder sisters, Kam and Sin, were so good to Kirsty and Tim; they always were the first to remember birthdays and all other days when gifts were given.

Sadly they have both passed. Kirsty called one aunt "Mama Sin" and the other "Konon," which means "Aunty" in Peggy's mother tongue. She loved them so much. I am sure they are all together now, and they will get plenty of songs from their niece.

Kirsty's admissions were many during the first year of her life. She had eleven more to the local hospital in that year.

On one occasion when Kirsty was admitted after being discharged home for only one day, the consultant paediatrician told Peggy and myself we were being neurotic and should let the nurses teach us how to care for our child. We were shocked and told him that I'd had four children from a previous marriage and Peggy was bringing up her second child, but he was not interested and discharged Kirsty at the end of the day anyway. Peggy would remind this consultant of his very poor judgement quite forcibly many years later.

Three days later, Kirsty was readmitted and had to be ventilated, so from then on there was no further talk of neurosis. The medical team started to take Kirsty's situation much more seriously.

The stupid remark from the consultant was very damaging to the relationship we had built with the nursing staff because it was made within earshot of medical students and nurses. We were shunned for some time after that until they realized how ill Kirsty really was at times.

During this very bad period, it was hard to understand how the staff did not support us; they could see how distressed and worried we were.

I believe the reason was that none of them were willing to confront the consultant. It is a well-known fact that medical personnel become more rigid and aloof the higher they reach in their careers. This, of course, does not apply to all doctors, but it did with ours. Understandably there are very few nursing staff that would risk problems with their careers by questioning the consultant's attitude even though they would realize how unprofessional he was in his behaviour.

On 16 March 2004 as part of the internal investigation with regard to the causes of Kirsty's death, we had a meeting with the investigation team of the hospital that oversees complaints against the hospital by the next of kin or carers. At that meeting amongst others was the consultant paediatrician that had been so rude to us eighteen years previously.

Peggy was absolutely livid and proceeded to remind him of how he had intimated to all and sundry how neurotic and poor parents we had been; he was totally nonplussed as to how to handle this sudden onslaught on his name and professionalism.

As for me, I just sat there saying to myself, "That's it, Peggy, go for the bastard." When she was able to let up, she just could not stop crying. The consultant had nothing to say, but I doubt very much if he'd had such an experience prior to that day.

After Peggy's outburst, the investigation collapsed, and the members of the panel were up and out as fast as their legs could carry them. Suddenly we were in an empty room. We just hugged each other, and I said, "Well done, darling." Then we left for home.

Two days after the meeting we received the following letter from the consultant; I think he had regained his composure after Peggy's verbal attack.

Dear Mr. and Mrs. Pearce:

I just wanted to drop you a brief personal line about something that particularly upset me at our meeting on Tuesday.

I am very glad that you told me about these feelings you have had about me all these years. I only wish you had told me about them sooner.

I take a great pride in my relationships with parents, but clearly I got it badly wrong this time, and I could hardly have been further out in my assessment of Kirsty's symptoms when she was a baby.

I am deeply sorry for the distress and anxiety I caused you then and since, but at the same time I am really glad that this is now out in the open. I hope you can find it in your hearts to forgive me.

Yours sincerely,
Paediatric Consultant

We consider ourselves lucky that we did get an apology for some of the wrongs done to Kirsty over the years, even though it took over eighteen years to come to fruition. Other people have not been so lucky and have never been apologized to at all.

After doctors failed to find any answers to Kirsty's problems, such as seizures, repetitive respiratory distress, and of course the constant episodes of pulmonary oedema, which on at least one occasion required ventilation, she was transferred to Great Ormond Street Hospital in October 1986 to see if they could find some answers. Kirsty was nine months old.

After many tests and scans, the consultant paediatrician informed us that the brain scans showed that Kirsty had a strange phenomenon called cerebral calcifications, which may have been caused by toxoplasmosis. This disease can be caught if in contact with a cat's faecal matter, but we had never had cats. After three years of constant scans and blood tests, the doctors agreed it was not that problem, though they still had no idea of what Kirsty was suffering from—absolutely no idea. Even after her death, they failed to find any answers.

For over seventeen years, many nationally and internationally renowned doctors tried to diagnose Kirsty, always without success.

Peggy and I became very frustrated because of the failure of doctors around the world to give answers that might have led to a cure for Kirsty. Internationally renowned doctors in various parts of the world attended seminars led by Professor Mike Dillon, who was Kirsty's nephrologist, and Professor Patricia Woo, who was her paediatric specialist, but all they had to offer was agreement that she was unique and the only person known in the world to have suffered the combination of problems that she had.

A paper is being written at this time by Professor Woo, who was Kirsty's main paediatrician in Great Ormond Street Hospital, London, to be presented to the medical fraternity. It will also be used as a teaching tool, in hopes that this may be a help if other cases like Kirsty's appear.

Many children in the world have serious problems with no obvious medical answers, and their parents must suffer with them the same way that Peggy and I did. We really do feel for them. It is so hard for parents, and mothers in particular, to watch their young children suffer day after day, while the doctors are unable to resolve their problems. The doctors treating Kirsty could not understand her problems because she was truly unique in the medical world and they had never been presented with such a case previously. They were out of their depth and should have called for help from the on-call paediatric consultant.

I watched this with Peggy for more than seventeen years; it was so upsetting for her. The most awful time was for her to stand by Kirsty's bed on the night she passed away for thirteen hours and watch her slowly die because of poor medical service. The indifference shown to Kirsty's needs by the medical staff made it even more terrible for Peggy.

Peggy will never gain full recovery from this chapter in her life because Kirsty was her life.

I shall never forgive the people responsible for Kirsty's care on the night she passed away. Though Kirsty was obviously dangerously ill on her last night, she was for the most part ignored. The doctors were complacent; their attitude appeared to be that this was a regular occurrence for Kirsty, and so there was no need for concern because she always got over it. This time they were wrong and just did not realize the seriousness of her condition.

For every medical condition, there is a specified treatment. In Kirsty's case, that would have been immediate admission to the intensive care unit and standby for ventilation, but the doctors on duty that night had never seen a case such as Kirsty's (it must be remembered she appears to be the only patient of her type in the world) and they were floundering from the time of her admission. They just did not know how to begin, and so Kirsty died in a most awful situation, frightened and without dignity.

There was one man that might have saved her, but he was at home tucked in his bed; nonetheless, he was on call and should have been made aware of the situation, but of course he was not disturbed.

CHAPTER 2

KIRSTY WAS DUE TO START SCHOOL IN JANUARY 1991. AT A preschool medical examination during the previous October, the doctor discovered what he thought was a cyst in her right eye and suggested that we take her to the local eye clinic, which we did. After an extensive examination of Kirsty's eyes, the ophthalmologist apologised because he could offer no treatment. He informed Peggy and me that there was more than one condition in the eyes. He said this was rare and he had no choice other than to refer her to the general hospital in Romford. Since that hospital was only fifteen miles from where we lived, it did not take long for us to get there.

At the hospital, we were directed to the ophthalmology department, where Kirsty's eyes were once again fully examined. The ophthalmologists also informed us that Kirsty had more than one problem in her eyes and said they would refer her to Great Ormond Street Hospital for Sick Children in London.

Kirsty was first seen by the ophthalmologist in London on 7 November 1991. That doctor confirmed that there were problems and these would become more serious as time went by.

Kirsty's eyes did not improve, and after a couple of months, she was referred to Moorefield's Eye Hospital in London.

On 22 January 1992, when she was examined first by an ophthalmology registrar, he was totally baffled and just mumbled, "Oh dear, I'd better get the boss." The "boss", as the registrar called him, was an ophthalmology retinal surgeon, an expert in many serious eye conditions, such as the ones Kirsty was suffering from.

The surgeon at Moorefield's examined her eyes for what appeared to us to be an eternity, though in reality was only thirty minutes.

After the examination, the surgeon informed us that Kirsty had suffered a retinal detachment in her right eye and had other problems in the left eye that needed treatment with laser surgery.

Apparently this retinal detachment was caused by the separation of the inner layers of the retina from the underlying retinal pigment epithelium. Exudative or serious detachments occur when subretinal fluid accumulates and causes detachments without any corresponding break in the retina. Exudation of material into the subretinal space from abnormal retinal vessels occurs in hypertension, retinal venous occlusion, and of course vasculitis, which Kirsty suffered from. Apparently the exudates were dripping onto the retina of the left eye, and these had to be stopped.

I knew that one cause of this serious eye problem could be toxoplasmosis, and we retained this suspicion even though doctors did tell us this was not the cause. My thoughts have always been that medicine as a science is still a very mysterious field and the experts do not always get it right. I am not claiming that I know better than those experts, but I am just suggesting that toxoplasmosis could perhaps be the cause of Kirsty's problems.

The laser treatment was carried out on 18 March 1992. The surgeon that carried out the laser treatment told Peggy and me that the exudates had slowed as he'd hoped in the left eye and with luck would stop spontaneously. Slowly this did happen, though the damage already done to the eyes could not be rectified.

Peggy and I were hoping that this would be the last of Kirsty's troubles, but unfortunately this was not to be the case. She ended up permanently blind in the right eye and badly damaged in the left one by the time she was only six years old. It was never established at what age Kirsty lost the sight in her right eye.

The sad part to all this was that Kirsty had never complained about her eyes, Peggy and I could see no problem, and it was only because of a medical examination that anything was seen at all. It was only then that we really understood that there were very serious problems with her eyes and we should be concerned as to what the future held for her with regard to her sight.

Peggy and I were terribly sorry for our daughter's eye issues, but Kirsty was the least bothered and just got on with life the best she could by doing her main thing, watching television.

Schooling for Kirsty was normal during primary school, and generally she had very good attendance.

Kirsty enjoyed primary school, which was for a period of two years. Apart from her eye problems, she seemed able to cope even though she could not keep up to the normal standards expected for a child of her age.

This was partly because of her eye problems, but also because of her lack of growth, which appeared to hinder her coordination.

Tasks that were easy for the average child became major ones for Kirsty, though during her short school life, the other children would help her as much as possible; they were so caring towards her and enjoyed helping her, and she enjoyed being helped by her little friends. There are, of course, exceptions to the rule. With thirty young children in one classroom, there had to be the odd one or two that would tend to be a little on the cruel side.

On one occasion, one sweet little cherub informed Kirsty that she could not play with her and her friends because she was too small and would not be able to keep up with them. On another occasion, they mocked her for not being able to see properly, with taunts of "Hey, one eye, which is the blind one?" Of course, Kirsty took these rare cruel spates in her stride because she just loved being at a school where generally everybody looked out for her.

After leaving primary school, Kirsty was sent to a couple of schools that were specifically designed for disabled pupils, but unfortunately she was often too unwell to attend. She usually only attended school for no more than three weeks in any year from the age of twelve on; though this was the case, she tried so hard to learn what she could at home with Peggy and myself.

A lot was made of the size factor with Kirsty, and this was explained by the doctors as being that of a condition that was known as being below the third centile. This meant that Kirsty was in that third of the population that was affected by growth and developmental retardation. She certainly was small, and to put this into context, at the age of eleven, she had a bone growth test, which showed her to have the bone structure of a six-year-old.

When Kirsty became seven years old, it was time for her to go to junior school. Because of her poor eyesight, the education department agreed that she should go to a school where the corridors were very wide and easy to get around. Kirsty was happy there, settling in very quickly and making many friends. She was there for four years, though her attendance was pretty irregular because of illness.

On 22 February 1997, Kirsty reached her eleventh birthday. It was then discovered that she was suffering from polyarticular junior chronic arthritis, which is a condition where more than one or two joints are affected. In Kirsty's case, over that year all of her joints were affected, and she suffered much pain. As usual, though, she never complained.

During her eleventh year, she started to attend senior school. She was so happy and excited at the thought of joining other children of a higher age group, but unfortunately her arthritis kicked in with a vengeance and she ended up going to senior school in a wheelchair. From then on, school became almost a nonevent; invariably she could not attend very often.

Seventeen days at school in a year was considered very good attendance for her, as illness always tended to interfere with her schooling. Although she could hardly read or write, she became very articulate by listening to things and watching television. She would ask for explanations to anything she did not understand, and her memory was so good that she was able to retain most of what she learnt. Kirsty taught herself and became very clever in the process. Peggy and I are very proud of her achievements.

Whenever she could not attend school, she would get her books out and practice her reading and writing at home with the help of Mum or Dad. When Kirsty did manage to get to school, it was as enjoyable as she could make it. She was very popular with the other pupils, and they were always there to help her; she had many friends.

Like all children, Kirsty could get herself into a little trouble at school, not major problems but enough to cause disruption in class. The problem was that she tended to talk when a lesson was in progress, and this would upset the teacher. On one occasion, Kirsty was sent to the headmaster for being noisy, and he immediately punished her by giving her a lollipop and allowing her to eat it in his study. All he said to her when she left his study was, "Tell your teacher you have been punished." The above anecdote shows just how nice people could be towards her, and it was nice to see.

Kirsty's party piece was to spell Mississippi to whoever would like to hear. What she could achieve with only half the sight of one eye was truly remarkable. The Mississippi spelling game was her favourite, though in reality she found it difficult to spell any word that had more than three letters in it and she would get very frustrated over this problem.

When she turned sixteen on 22 February 2002, Kirsty talked about going to college. This was something she really wanted to do, and we encouraged her with her hopes and ambitions. It was so heartbreaking that college was never to be.

As previously stated, whenever Kirsty could not attend school, she would get her books out and practice her reading and writing at home with the help of Mum or Dad. She learnt quite a lot doing things this way, and because she had her own methods, you could say she taught herself.

CHAPTER 3

Though Kirsty had many problems over the years, it was from February 1997 onwards that events became much more severe for her.

Initially she complained of a stiff and painful neck and found it impossible to turn her head from side to side because of very bad pain. Because of the severity of the pain, we took her to the accident and emergency department of our local hospital. This is the first point of contact in hospitals when an emergency occurs and treatment is urgently required.

The registrar there sent us to the consultant paediatrician in children's services. This was an absolute farce as far as I was concerned because the consultant hardly looked at Kirsty and appeared totally bored. He eventually said, "There is nothing wrong. Take her home and give her a hot bath." This was the same consultant that nine years earlier had called us neurotic because of our constant concern about Kirsty's well-being. This useless man totally lacked people skills and had no idea of how to interact with parents.

Peggy and I were furious and told him so, but he was not moved. We did go home and gave Kirsty Calpol, which is a pain relief and anti-inflammatory drug for children. It did ease the problem a little.

Peggy phoned her sister in Paris, France, and explained what had happened at the hospital.

Her sister suggested she make an appointment for Kirsty to see a doctor in Paris. We agreed, and so she made the appointment for a week later. The thing about the medical intervention in Paris was that we had to pay the costs of the consultation, X-rays, and any other tests that needed to be done in order to diagnose Kirsty's problems.

If the National Health Service doctors in the United Kingdom had done their job, then it sure would have saved us a lot of money. After all, Kirsty's appointments would have been free in this country; and on top of that, we would not have had to go to the Continent to find the answers we had been searching for.

So Peggy and Kirsty went to France, where she was seen by a well-known professor of paediatric rheumatology. The rheumatologist gave her a thorough examination and had X-rays taken of her neck and spine. He then told Peggy that Kirsty had arthritis and he was surprised that the doctors in England had not realized this.

After the examination, Peggy was handed the X-rays and a report to be given to our family doctor. The rheumatologist emphasised that this should be dealt with as soon as they arrived back in England.

Peggy and Kirsty arrived back home a few days later and made an appointment to see our family doctor, who listened to our story, viewed the X-rays, and then told us he would make an appointment for Kirsty with a different doctor at the hospital. We took Kirsty to see the new doctor two weeks later. He also examined her and said he would refer her to a consultant rheumatologist.

After about a week, we went to a different hospital to see another rheumatologist. Kirsty was very pleased because the consultant was a female; I think she had seen enough of male doctors by that time. The consultant who saw Kirsty was a very nice lady, and Kirsty liked her; she did not mind being examined by her in the slightest.

After the doctor completed her examination of Kirsty, she commented that she was very concerned with the fact that one so young should be suffering with this arthritic problem. She ordered blood tests and asked us to bring Kirsty back to see her in two weeks for the results.

When we returned with Kirsty for the follow-up appointment, the doctor informed us that the results confirmed the diagnosis of arthritis; she wanted to refer Kirsty to a paediatric professor of rheumatology at Great Ormond Street Hospital (GOS) in London.

We were happy with this because we knew of Great Ormond Street's reputation as one of the great hospitals; it was known throughout the world for its treatment of children. If it meant there was a chance of this problem being eradicated, then we and Kirsty were all for it.

We all had great hopes, but little did we know that this eradication would not happen; things would get much worse over the next few years. We all trundled off to GOS and made the acquaintance of the rheumatology professor. She was a very pleasant Chinese lady with an extremely soft voice, which immediately put us at our ease. She organized more blood tests and X-rays.

We were then given an appointment to take Kirsty back two weeks later for admission so that she could have physiotherapy and hydrotherapy to help with her joints.

Over the years, Kirsty would have to endure many painful periods in many different hospitals, but not once did she complain; she would just comment that there were children much worse off than she was. Kirsty had so much empathy for others that it was a pleasure being with her; she was a total joy.

Kirsty loved singing, and on one occasion she was invited to the boardroom at GOS for a Christmas party. She met the cast from the London musical of *Saturday Night Fever*.

The female lead singer asked her if she would like to sing a song with her. Of course, Kirsty did not need to be asked twice. She sang "My Heart Will Go On," from the film *Titanic*.

I cried as I watched and listened to her, and it would not be the last time there would be tears in my eyes.

Chapter 4

April 1997, and it was time to return to the hospital for sick children at Great Ormond Street once again to find out what the blood tests and scans had found. When we arrived, we were seen by the rheumatologist.

She told us that Kirsty had polyarticular junior chronic arthritis; this is the type that affects more than two joints. In Kirsty's case unfortunately, it was affecting all of her joints, and most of the time she was in a lot of pain. As usual, she made no complaints.

This admission was the first of fifty-one at Great Ormond Street that Kirsty would endure. Overall, she would have 101 admissions to various hospitals. These hospitals included the Moorefield's Hospital in London, the London Hospital in Mile End Road, London, the Paediatric Paris Hospital for Children, the Arnold Palmer Hospital for Women and Children in Florida, and the Florida Hospital Centra Care in Kissimmee, Florida, where the emergency room in particular saved Kirsty when she was on the brink in December 2002. We love them so much for what they did; and if I am able to get this book published, then they will most certainly be given a copy. The Florida Hospital Centra Care was just about the best medical establishment I have ever had the good fortune to be involved with, and for Kirsty it was just perfect; it was professionalism at its best. They were so great that night, and we appeared to be in the right place at the right time, thank God.

Much research was carried out over the years in an effort to find the causes for Kirsty's problems, but nobody could come up with any answers. Even though the doctors treating her were internationally known and she was discussed at many seminars around the world, she remained a puzzle to the medical world until the end of her days. A paper is being written by Professor Patricia Woo, who is the head rheumatologist at Great Ormond Street Hospital, regarding Kirsty's problems. This will eventually be presented to the medical fraternity, in the hopes that it will help other children in the future.

At this time, Kirsty is the only case of this type in the world to have turned up presenting with this particular combination of illnesses. She was, and still remains, a true enigma.

Many different treatments were tried in an effort to help Kirsty. One of these was Indomethacin, a nonsteroidal anti-inflammatory drug. Like all drugs, this has side effects, one of which is depression; and this is what happened with Kirsty. I had to take her back to Great Ormond Street Hospital in April 1997 and have them take her off the drug. She was back to her normal self within thirty-six hours. Amazingly the doctor said that she did not know this particular drug had this effect, so I advised her to read about it in the British National Formulary, which lists all drugs that are used in the United Kingdom by registered doctors, or the *MIMS*, which is the book that doctors use for prescribing drugs that are in current circulation.

Another drug that caused Kirsty terrible distress was Cyclosporine, which doctors described as being useful in the treatment of arthritis though it was never specifically designed for this problem. In fact, it is the drug of choice for counteracting rejection of organs after major transplant surgery. Patients treated with this drug are more susceptible than usual to infections, and it can also cause kidney damage. The effect on Kirsty was awful; she started with terrible tremors, which then developed into grand-mal seizures. She was initially treated in the paediatric ward in the local hospital, where they had great difficulty stabilizing her.

The doctor said she would have to be transferred to Great Ormond Street Hospital in London. So Peggy accompanied Kirsty to London on 4 October 1997, with a doctor and nurse in the ambulance. Once there, she was admitted to the rheumatology ward after first being assessed by the neurologist.

Kirsty remained in the hospital for five weeks. During that time, she was very ill and suffered a left ischemic episode. This is a minor stroke. It is usually short-lived, but the effects can be quite traumatic and very frightening for a child. The symptoms presented in a way that caused Kirsty to droop at the right side of her mouth, with quite severe spasticity down the right side of her body. This was a very distressing episode in Kirsty's life, and for a while she was quite depressed. Eventually the episode reversed itself, though it did take a few weeks.

The doctors refused to believe that Kirsty's latest problems had been caused by Cyclosporine, the drug that they had prescribed (though it is common practice for some doctors to not admit their errors), and so a lumbar puncture was performed. They then said the drug was one of four possible reasons for her troubles, but they still could not believe that Cyclosporine was the main cause.

Six weeks after the event, the neurologist admitted that the stroke was caused by the Cyclosporine, just as Peggy and I already had realised even before their tests were carried out; as nurses, we had seen evidence of this previously in other patients. I reminded the neurologist that Cyclosporin was not a drug designed for arthritis and she should have been more cautious. She informed me that they could try any drug they thought would be of benefit for conditions other than that for which it was designed. I term this as absolute arrogance by the medical profession. It is what I call "unofficial drug testing", using children as guinea pigs.

A drug that helped her but also caused her a lot of distress was Pamidronate, one of the bisphosphonate group of drugs, which was used to encourage new bone structure and to ensure healthy bone growth. It had to be given by infusion and required careful monitoring because of the danger of severe side effects. Unfortunately the side effect attributed to this drug was exactly what Kirsty did not need, which of course was pulmonary oedema. Because of the Pamidronate, she suffered quite often with this problem. In fact, it happened every time Kirsty was infused with that particular drug. All the medics that dealt with Kirsty were well aware of how susceptible she was for suffering from drug-related problems. If anyone could suffer from these side effects, then Kirsty most certainly would. The Pamidronate appeared to be having the desired effect on her bones, and after about eight months, there appeared to be a stronger bone structure with a little more density, though the pulmonary oedema was persistent. Pamidronate worked in thickening and strengthening Kirsty's bones, but the side effects of this drug caused problems.

The Pamidronate was given and Kirsty was to be treated every two months for two years, at which point the treatment period would be extended to every four months. It appeared that the Pamidronate was working the way it was hoped. Kirsty's bones started to thicken and get stronger; but on three occasions, the drug caused pulmonary oedema, a buildup and retention of fluid in the lungs. Kirsty had suffered with this problem for a number of years, and so it did not take much to trigger an episode.

Pulmonary oedema would turn out to be the bane of Kirsty's young life. It first showed itself on 22 March 1986, just one month after she was born. This was the beginning of hell for Kirsty, as the ensuing years would show. Although it would usually take only a couple of days to rectify this problem, it was damaging to her lungs. Watching her struggling to breathe during these episodes was most heartbreaking; she was a very brave young lady. The more episodes Kirsty experienced over the years with pulmonary oedema, the more difficult it became to manage the problem; and this caused her much distress. On one occasion, this caused left ventricular failure, which took ten days to right itself.

The one drug that did help Kirsty's joints was brought in from the United States. The drug was called etanercept (Enbrel). After only three subcutaneous injections of this drug, the pain in her joints lessened, and the inflammation and swelling of the joints started to subside. This drug made Kirsty feel much better, though a lot of damage had already been caused to her joints by her arthritic condition.

CHAPTER 5

As Kirsty had always wanted to go to college, we made enquiries about enrolling her, with a view to commencing in September 2003.

The Southend College of Adult Education in the county of Essex invited Kirsty with me and Peggy to visit, with a view to her being enrolled for the next term. After we had a look around the college and viewed their facilities, the principal said she would be happy for Kirsty to start there in the new term, which would commence in September 2003. Peggy and I were very pleased because it meant that Kirsty had the opportunity of perhaps learning with good-quality tutors who had a reputation of being ideal in the tutoring of disabled children. The teaching staff was reputed to be as good as any to be found elsewhere in the county. We enrolled Kirsty in an education block to try to catch up with what she had missed over the previous years through illness. Little did we know that this would be snatched away from her in the most terrible way imaginable.

As Kirsty's general health appeared to have improved, the Middlesex Hospital's senior orthopaedic surgeon believed that Kirsty would benefit from a double hip replacement. So in June 2003, when we took her to see him, the surgeon told Kirsty what he would like to do for her. She was so happy that tears rolled down her face. After composing herself, she asked the doctor, "What if I don't wake up after the surgery?" The surgeon thought for a while and then reassuringly told her that would not happen and that all her other consultants would be in the theatre to ensure that things went according to plan.

The surgical plan was uplifting for Kirsty, as she really did want to get away from her wheelchair; this was the best news she'd had for many years. It really was just a matter of ensuring that her sockets were strong enough to take her new hips. A provisional time was given for eighteen months in the future to carry out the surgery so that the Pamidronate would have longer to strengthen her bones and make the surgery less of a risk. Sadly and very unfortunately, this surgery did not take place because two months after meeting with the surgeon, Kirsty died as a result of very poor medical care; she never had a chance of survival, because that chance was never given to her.

Peggy and I were quite as excited as Kirsty over the possibility of the double hip replacement. We, too, wanted to see her back on her feet once again, but we were very concerned about her being able to cope with such an operation. We felt relieved to a certain degree and happy for her, but there were still nagging doubts at the back of our minds. Kirsty was not concerned in the least because all she was thinking about was the possibility of getting back on her feet again. She also made me a promise: "Dad, when I have had the operation, I will run into your arms and give you a big hug." Sadly for us both, this was never to be.

Kirsty very much enjoyed going on holiday with Tim and us, and she had great fun when she visited Disney World in Florida twice. We also visited Mauritius, because this was Mum's place of birth, and we made many trips to Paris, where Peggy's family all lived.

Kirsty was a very small seventeen-year-old and retained that childish innocence she'd had all her life. She firmly believed that the Disney characters were real and that Father Christmas existed. We never tried to change her beliefs. To watch her holding conversations with Cinderella, the Fairy Godmother, Mickey Mouse, and Father Christmas at the Disney resort in Florida was both heartrending and a joy to behold. The characters quite happily joined in to what they could see was a very important part of Kirsty's day-to-day existence.

Before Kirsty contracted arthritis at the age of eleven, she could do many things. Even with arthritis, she tried to remain active, though she was not that strong. Doing things that other children took for granted was not that easy. So when she went roller skating with Peggy, care had to be taken to protect her against accidents that could cause problems with her brittle bones. She and Peggy would hold hands and gingerly find their way around the local roller-skating rink at zero miles per hour. Kirsty herself was not concerned about danger because she feared nothing, but Peggy was not so fearless. Thankfully the expected accidents did not happen.

Another thing Kirsty loved to do when she was younger and before the arthritis affected her was ride her bicycle. One day she was peddling away, singing her heart out, when I realized she was on a downward slope and moving rapidly away from me. Very quickly I chased after her because I realised she could not pull on the brakes because her hands were too small and weak. To my horror, I noticed she was out of control and heading for a brick wall. Somehow I got there first and saved the day. Kirsty called me her hero and I loved it, though of course I realised that I should have been paying more attention. As usual, she was not fazed in the slightest; to her it was just a great laugh.

We set off on holiday to Paris on 1 August 2003, and we were all looking forward to having a nice time with the family. August is the holiday month in France, and therefore we knew that all the family would be there. Kirsty just wanted to get there and go to Euro Disney and, as she put it, "see Mickey and all my other friends". This would turn out to be her last holiday.

We spent two weeks in Paris during the first fourteen days of August 2003 and had a great time visiting relatives, sightseeing, and going to Euro Disney. That summer was very hot, and on the day we visited Euro Disney, the heat was very intense. The heat did not bother Kirsty because all she wanted was to see her friend Mickey and all the other characters. Nothing else really mattered to Kirsty. Her wishes were to be fulfilled, and so she was a very happy young girl.

Kirsty enjoyed herself, and she had no traumas at all over that period. That was the first time she remained well for the duration of any holiday she'd had. Usually she would spend part of her holiday in the hospital, and we were so pleased for her. If anybody deserved a pain-free period in her life, it was our princess.

The weather remained beautiful for the whole of the holiday, and we were all well and truly refreshed; the heat of the sun made Kirsty's joints less painful.

Time sped by, and soon it was almost time to return to England. Before that, we were to have one more surprise. Peggy's brother Laugi, Kirsty's favourite uncle and my best friend, who lives in an apartment in central Paris and owns his own hairdressing salon, had arranged a surprise dinner party so that all the families could be together, which was a rare feat considering we lived in England and the others were in different areas of France.

The night of the party arrived, and everybody met at Laugi's apartment dressed in their best bib and tucker, summer style. They all looked very smart.

Kirsty herself looked lovely in a pink Chinese-style dress, with her hair specially styled for the occasion by Laugi. Sadly, he would never do it again. She really was beautiful, and looking at her made me so proud that I had her for my daughter. Glancing at Peggy assured me that she was as proud of Kirsty as I was.

The dinner was a beautiful occasion—great company and lovely food. We ate outside on the very large balcony that encompassed three quarters of the apartment and overlooked the glittering lights of Paris. It really was a breathtaking sight and one that we would never forget. There was a distinct French cosmopolitan feel about the whole evening, and everybody had a whale of a time.

I think it would be true to say that Paris has an aura all of its own. I would defy anyone to sit and have a meal on a balmy warm evening there and not feel the romance wafting around them.

It was a rare occasion for the whole family to get together in this manner. Unknown to everybody was the fact that the next time we would meet as a family, both Kirsty and her beloved Mama Sin would have left us.

Kirsty felt well and was able to really enjoy herself. She sat at the table with everybody, and we stowed her wheelchair for the evening. I don't think I had seen her eat so well for ages; she certainly made short work of the chicken drumsticks.

Many snapshots were taken that night, and Kirsty was in quite a few of them. We often look at them and reminisce about that particular night, remarking how lucky we all were to have been together for that occasion.

The evening passed quickly, as it always does when you are having fun, and too soon it was time to leave and return to our hotel. Kirsty kissed everybody good-bye, not realising that other than Peggy and myself, everybody there would never see her alive again. That was the very last time she ever saw or spoke to them.

We arrived back at the hotel at 1.15 a.m. and were totally bushed, but not Kirsty. All she wanted to do was talk about the great time she'd had, so we talked and gradually fell asleep.

We were due to be going home two days after the party, so most of our time was spent getting organized and buying last-minute presents, one of which was a glass with Disney characters around the outside and a packet of Hubba Bubba gum. These were for big brother Tim, who had not come on the holiday with us because of work commitments. He never drinks from that glass and has not touched the gum; they are sacred to him.

Kirsty had one last visit to Aunty Ram's house because there was a special friend there, Magic, the biggest Labrador retriever I have ever seen. Magic was so big that he could hold two tennis balls in his mouth simultaneously. I think he sensed that there was something different about Kirsty, and he was amazingly gentle around her. It was as if he knew he should not be rough with her. She loved him, and when we returned to France about a year after her death, he was looking for her, whimpering at the closed door.

Saturday the sixteenth of August arrived, and we knew we had to return home. The holiday had been brilliant, and we did not want to leave. Even now I wonder at times whether or not things might have turned out differently if we had stayed. We knew we couldn't stay because Peggy was due back at the hospital where she worked as a night nurse, and I had to organise Kirsty's hospital appointments.

We left for the Paris Nord train station to catch the Eurostar train. On this trip home, Kirsty met her final new friend, whose name is Orietta. She is a travelling manager on the Eurostar train. Orietta is of Italian descent and based in London, working for the Eurostar train company. Because Kirsty was in a wheelchair, she and Peggy were transferred to first class, which is the Eurostar policy for wheelchair-bound customers. Of course, poor old Dad had to rough it in second class. The concern that Eurostar has about the comfort of disabled people such as Kirsty pleases me. I will always be grateful to them, and especially Orietta, for making Kirsty's final train journey so very special. That trip was the only time that Orietta was with Kirsty before she died, though after her death all our relatives came to know her and we are still firm friends.

I heard all about Orietta from Kirsty when we arrived back home. She fell in love with this charming woman, who gave Kirsty all her time on the two-hour journey back to England. Sad to say, they would never meet again. When we informed Orietta of Kirsty's death, she broke down and at first refused to accept that this lovely young girl that she had met on only one occasion was gone and she would not see her again. We see Orietta regularly each year when she joins us at the memorial service that is held at Great Ormond Street Square Church. The service is in memory of all the children that have been patients at the hospital and sadly passed away. We see Orietta at other times, and she comes home occasionally for lunch.

We have also met Orietta's mother, who sometimes visits from Italy, in London and spent a pleasant time having a chat over a meal together. Like Orietta, her mother is an extremely charming lady; Kirsty would have loved to have met her. Of course, the topic of conversation is always Kirsty, someone we never ever get tired of talking about. Peggy and Orietta spent much time going over what happened to cause the sudden death of Kirsty and have always agreed that the events on the night Kirsty died should never have been allowed to happen. Oh, if only the medics had done their best! Had they done so, then Kirsty would be here today—we know this, and so do the hospital and medics responsible for her care. So many times we have asked why and how, but there is never an answer. There never will be, until all the investigations possible have been carried out.

Attempting to find answers to situations such as Kirsty's is very difficult because of the reluctance of some medics to stand up and be counted, to simply tell the truth in investigations of this type. It is very noticeable that there is absolute silence from the police and the director of public prosecutions.

My duty to Kirsty is to find justice on her behalf. I shall never stop until that is achieved. I swear to you, Kirsty, that I will succeed. Everybody is out for survival and will "duck and dive" in order to escape their responsibilities, as has been shown by the sleazy behaviour of members of parliament, who have been caught with their hands in the cash till. They escape judgement on their wrongdoings because they make the laws, but if the ordinary members of the public were to do the same as they, then prosecution would be swift. It is no wonder that the General Medical Council allows doctors to escape their responsibilities. Parliament allows this to happen by setting down antiquated laws to run the system. The country goes into meltdown, and then they call themselves good representatives of the people.

I suppose it must be termed poetic justice as each day brings a wave of MPs running away and leaving their jobs because of their indiscretions. Some of these people are members of the cabinet. At the moment, the newspapers are having a field day.

CHAPTER 6

AFTER OUR VERY NICE TRIP AND SPENDING VALUABLE TIME WITH the families in Paris, we arrived back in England, said our good-byes to Orietta, promising that Kirsty would see her again, and headed off home to Pitsea, Essex. Though we were sorry to leave Paris, it was still nice to be home again. I think everybody has the same emotions, and my view about that is simply that holidays are a part-time of life. Similar to when you do part-time work, they are not forever.

We arrived home, and everybody started to settle in. For Kirsty, that meant going to her room, which is an extension to the lounge and encroaches into the garden by fourteen feet. Kirsty loved her room because it was en suite and really expansive.

Entering Kirsty's room was like taking a trip to Disney World because it had so many stuffed toys. These toys were replicas of those seen on holiday at the Disney Park in Paris, and to her they were all part of her home, a wonderful place for Kirsty to relax. There were also more than 250 DVDs and videos, a thirty-two-inch television, which she needed because of her poor eyesight, video and DVD players, and a CD player. She had everything she needed, and rightly so.

A number of people said to us that we spoiled Kirsty, which was untrue. She was granted certain benefits by the state because of her various disabilities, which meant that she was able to come shopping with Peggy and me and spend her own money, which she was entitled to. She was very proud of this.

None of these shallow people stood back and reflected on their thoughts or showed any empathy for Kirsty's plight. They continued to believe that Kirsty was spoiled. They were the lucky ones, not her.

Kirsty required round-the-clock care, and this meant that Peggy went back to her stint of working four nights weekly and I looked after Kirsty while she was away. She would come home in the morning and take over caring for our lovely daughter for the next five hours and then grab five hours sleep before returning to work. Peggy carried out this routine for all of Kirsty's life and never complained because it was a pleasure for her to do things for her daughter. On her nights at home, Peggy would juggle the housework with her time caring for Kirsty. To her it was a pleasure looking after this very special young lady.

I would deal with any emergencies that might crop up with Kirsty over each twenty-four-hour period, and there were many of these over the years.

Whenever anything happened, it was always at night, and it was always the same pattern. Usually Kirsty would call out between three and four o'clock in the morning. I would go into her room and almost immediately would hear the rasping sounds in her lungs. This, of course, meant to me that there was a real danger of Kirsty going into respiratory distress, leading to another episode of the dreaded pulmonary oedema. In fact, the rasping indicated that this was already happening.

The first thing I would try to do was to reassure Kirsty that we would soon get the problem sorted out, so that she would be as comfortable as possible in a very short time, though I did know, of course, that this would depend on the severity of the attack and how she responded to the prescribed treatment, which was nebulised Ventolin, Frusemide, and Amiloride. Most times Kirsty responded very quickly to the nebulizer, but of course there were times when things did not go according to plan.

If the indications were that Kirsty was going into full-blown pulmonary oedema, I would take her to the hospital, where she had direct access to the children's ward. This saved her having to go through accident and emergency, which would have been the normal procedure and would have caused unnecessary delay in her treatment. If Kirsty had not the benefit of this special arrangement, she most certainly would have suffered much more. There were other children who had the same access as Kirsty, and their families were very grateful for this.

That first week home from Paris sped by, and Kirsty was pleased to hear that Laugi, her favourite uncle, was arriving on the twenty-third of August to spend his annual holiday with us.

We picked up Laugi from the Eurostar station at Waterloo London, and we were all very pleased that he had come. Kirsty was over the moon; she really loved that special man and chatted to him all the way home. Laugi was very kind and extremely considerate to her and would do anything to please her.

On Monday, 26 August, we all went to Great Ormond Street Hospital because Kirsty had an appointment to see Dr. Tullis, who was her nephrologist. He was a very nice Swedish specialist that Kirsty took to immediately. Before he was allowed to carry out his consultation, Kirsty made sure he was introduced to her uncle; once that was done, he was able to do his job. Once Kirsty had told the doctor all about her holiday and he had finished his consultation, he told Kirsty that as far as he was concerned, she was fit for hip replacement surgery and he would inform the orthopaedic surgeons at the Middlesex Hospital. Kirsty was ecstatic when he told her that she could go ahead and have surgery for hip replacement, and because of this she just could not stop smiling.

It is shocking that Kirsty should be so happy at that moment, but then within three days be dead. The world is such an unfair place for some people, as it turned out to be for her. I am still bewildered as to what happened on the fateful night she passed.

It seemed as though one moment she was there and the next she was gone. Even now whilst writing this book, I just cannot believe what happened.

CHAPTER 7

THE MORNING OF 27 AUGUST 2003 WAS NO DIFFERENT THAN ANY other day. Kirsty was still excited about getting new hips. Since it was Wednesday, it was also the first night of Peggy's working week. How we now wish that day could have turned out totally different.

The day was relaxing for us all, and we enjoyed it in our usual way: plenty of laughter, Kirsty singing, Peggy and me sorting things out in the house. Soon it was time for Peggy to go to work. Just before she left, Kirsty asked her to stay at home. This was quite unusual, as normally she liked Peggy to go because she knew she would be allowed to stay up a little later. Kirsty had never done this before, and I believe she knew something was happening within her but could not explain what it was. She was not her usual self by the time Peggy left, though she did settle and watch television with Laugi and me.

In her room, Kirsty had a sofa bed made especially for her. It was very comfortable, and she slept very well in it. Peggy and I slept on a double-size sofa bed in the lounge. This worked well for us all because if Kirsty needed us, we were close by. Since almost all of her bad episodes were in the early hours of the morning, it was the correct thing to do; we were proud to deal with her needs at any time of the day or night, including bathing, toileting, feeding, and dressing. The arthritis had made such simple tasks that a normal child would cope with just impossible for her. We continued in this vein up to the point that Kirsty died, and how we wish we could still be doing it. Kirsty was happy, of course, that her mum and dad were the ones caring for her.

As I have stated previously, we were with Kirsty every minute of every day for seventeen of the seventeen and a half years she lived. That night, as usual, Laugi slept in Kirsty's old bedroom upstairs; this was the room that she was determined to return to once she could get back on her feet. We all kissed each other good night and went to bed.

At 4.00 a.m. on 28 August 2003, Kirsty called me complaining that she was suffering with fluid in her chest. This was her normal way of letting me know that she was having one of her bad episodes. She was never wrong about this because she understood her own body pretty well; she knew exactly what was happening at these times, as this had happened many times in the past. I got up and checked her with my stethoscope. It was not too bad, but it was there, a distinct rattling in her chest.

I gave Kirsty her usual treatment at times like these: Amiloride and Frusemide to encourage fluid out of her body, and nebulised Ventolin through a face mask to help with her breathing. After forty-five minutes, she settled down and fell asleep again. The rasping had eased a little in her chest, and I was hopeful that she would manage to get a decent rest.

Kirsty was awake again at eight o'clock. I asked her how she was, and she said fine. Her chest sounded clear at that time, so I gave her medication as routine, but she did not want breakfast. This did not worry me too much because she was not a great eater at the best of times. From then on, I kept a very close eye on her. Though I could not put my finger on it, I felt things were not quite right.

At eleven o'clock, I checked Kirsty's chest and detected a slight crackle, so I gave her another nebulised Ventolin treatment. Once again, it settled her down, but I still felt uneasy.

At three o'clock, Kirsty suddenly went into respiratory distress, with her breathing rate rocketing to forty-five per minute; normally fifteen breaths per minute would have been correct for her. I knew that I needed to get her to paediatric triage at the local hospital fast, so I phoned them and requested permission to take her to the hospital; they asked me to hold fire because they were overloaded with other sick children. When I went back to Kirsty, I knew she could not wait; it was obvious she was in deep distress and would need to be seen immediately. I phoned the triage unit again and told them I was bringing Kirsty there. We eventually got there at five o'clock. This was Kirsty's fiftieth admission to that hospital, but little did we know this was the beginning of her final illness and it would be her last.

In triage, she was immediately given a high dose of oxygen, and a complete check was carried out on her system by the sister in charge. Her oxygen saturation was sixty-eight, and this was an indication as to how severe this illness was; it should have been recording in the high nineties. Saturations of ninety-nine would be expected in any healthy child.

After a while a doctor appeared, and in time he organized blood tests and carried out the usual admission examination. At seven o'clock, Kirsty was transferred to the paediatric ward, and I went home to collect the medicines that I knew she would need. At that time, I felt that she would now be safe—what a mistake that was.

I arrived back at the hospital. I could see there was no change, but as we had seen Kirsty in this situation many times previously, I did not think there would be any outcome other than a slow improvement and her returning home within the next couple of days. Peggy asked me to go home to sleep and to take over from her the next morning. This had been our routine during many episodes of this type.

Laugi and I kissed Kirsty, and I told her she would see us the next morning, which unbelievably did not happen until she had passed away—what a terrible shock. She would never see us again in this life.

On the way home, I told Laugi not to worry as we were sure to see a dramatic change in Kirsty's condition within the next twenty-four hours. This had always been the end result in the past, and I could not believe it would be any different with this admission. The best thing we could do was to go home to bed and try to sleep.

I informed Tim, who had gone out with his girlfriend, about the situation by phone. He said to me, "Don't worry, Dad. You know Kirsty will be okay now." Like us, he figured it would not be too long before she would be back to her old self once again.

Peggy contacted the hospital where she worked and told them of the situation with Kirsty. She informed them she would not be at work for the foreseeable future as her daughter was very ill, and she was unsure how long she would be absent. As it turned out, it was five months before she went back.

CHAPTER 8

ON THURSDAY, 29 AUGUST 2003, I AWOKE AFTER AN AWFUL night's sleep, constantly twisting and turning and all the time thinking of Kirsty and wondering how she was. I did not want to ring the ward because it would have disturbed all the other children. I had this terrible feeling of foreboding, and I found myself calling to God to make Kirsty well. I am not a particularly religious person, but that day I felt the need for divine intervention. I was very scared of what the day would bring.

I called the hospital at seven o'clock to find out Kirsty's condition and was asked to go there immediately as she had taken a turn for the worse. I woke Laugi and told him what was happening, and he said he would come with me to the hospital. I asked him to stay with Tim, who was still sleeping, and promised to let him know what was happening as soon as possible. Laugi adored Kirsty, and in the immediate future he would prove to be our rock.

I arrived at the intensive care unit at 7.05 a.m. and proceeded to go into the ward. As I opened the door, I saw Peggy walking toward me with the consultant paediatrician and a nurse. I could see that she was totally distraught, and my heart sank. It broke my heart to see the absolute anguish on her face, and because of that I knew that the worst had happened. She came to me, put her arms around me, and sobbed, "Kirsty's gone." Upon hearing her words, I just sagged and burst into tears myself.

We were shown into a side room, where the consultant told us that we would not need an autopsy. He told us that he would furnish us with a certificate for cause of death. He was totally uncaring and unprofessional and did not have the common courtesy to even offer his condolences.

I informed him that I would decide on the autopsy and there most definitely would be one.

The thing that made me mad was that this person standing in front of me had not come to help my daughter when she needed his expertise. He was at home in his warm bed, though he was the consultant on call. I did not like being told to accept the death certificate and be sent on our way by an ignoramus. I was not happy with the night's events as Peggy had related them to me. I just could not fathom what the doctors had done for Kirsty whilst in their care. I was convinced that they were trying for an immediate cover-up, for which I was very angry. I felt I needed to make our feelings known. Peggy and I demanded an autopsy, as we could not accept the poor medical care given to Kirsty that night. The consultant was opposed to this and said, "You don't need an autopsy." I blew my top and told him, "Shut up. That is our decision, not yours."

It seemed to me as though nobody wanted to discuss what had happened during the night anyway and would rather we asked other people at a later date. The only person that gave any sympathy was the intensive care nurse; she herself was extremely upset at what had happened. The paediatricians, and there were two of them, said nothing. The intensive care nurse had tears in her eyes and asked me why Kirsty had not been sent to them sooner because then perhaps she would have pulled through. She could not understand how Kirsty was left in the paediatric unit for thirteen hours before being transferred to intensive care. I could not give an answer; nobody could. I asked Peggy what they had done for Kirsty that night, and she said, "Nothing." She had literally been left to stand by Kirsty's bedside and watch her die.

I wanted to see Kirsty and was taken to her bedside. I just could not believe this had happened. There was my lovely daughter's lifeless body in front of me. I could not control myself; the tears rolled down my face. I had an overwhelming feeling of guilt because I had not been there when she'd passed.

The one thing that I could not come to terms with was that children are supposed to outlive their parents. I know that this is not cast in stone, but it was our expectation.

Another myth is that men don't cry. Believe me, that morning I just could not stop crying; it felt as though somebody had thrust a knife into my heart, the pain was so intense. I do not believe I have stopped crying since Kirsty's death. I shed tears every day.

I was still at Kirsty's bedside when the nurse told me that Tim was on the phone. With a sinking feeling in the pit of my stomach, I went to talk to him. When I picked up the phone, all he did was to cry out and shout to me, "No, Dad, she isn't dead, is she?" Somehow I managed to say to him, "Yes, Tim, she is." At that point, the nurse told him we would be home shortly, but I could hear him sobbing as she put the phone down. Thank God his uncle was with him. As for myself, I thought this was just a bad dream and that I would wake up soon.

The nurse told us that Kirsty would now be taken to the mortuary and that we could see her whenever we wished. Peggy did not want to leave Kirsty, even though she knew there was no point in staying on the ward.

We kissed our precious little girl many times and then left for home, as we knew that Laugi and Tim needed us and we needed them.

When we got home, we just huddled into a little group for comfort and support. Tim kept asking how this could happen, but I could not give him an answer. Laugi said to me, "But Chas, you said she would be home today." I had no answer for that either. I just felt so very sick.

Peggy was very tired because she had been on her feet for two days and nights. We were able to convince her that she needed a rest, but she would not go without me. I lay down with her, and she gradually fell asleep, though as expected she was very restless.

Laugi told me that he had informed all the families in France and that they would be on the train first thing the next day. I was grateful for this, as I knew that Peggy would be able to cope with this awful situation a little better if they were here. We somehow managed to get through the day, though of course we were scared for life from that day on. It was terrible, but we did manage to see Kirsty later that day.

The most awful of places to visit is a mortuary; it is always cold and forbidding and perhaps even a little frightening. The most awful time is when you have lost someone you love, and it is even worse when that loved one is your child. Seeing your child in the mortuary is totally devastating. When I saw Kirsty in that place, I was close to being destroyed. But I had to be strong for Peggy, who needed all my support.

I noticed that Kirsty's eyes were slightly open, and I said to her as I kissed her and gently closed her eyes, "I know you can see me." I told her how sorry I was for not being with her when she left; I was so full of guilt. I have never managed to rid myself of these feelings of guilt, and I am sure they will remain with me for the rest of my life.

I knew deep down that there was nothing I could have done to save Kirsty, but it didn't stop me from saying, "What if I had gone to the hospital sooner? Would I have made sure she had gone to intensive care before she did? Would it perhaps have saved her life?"

I don't think I shall ever find the answers to these questions.

CHAPTER 9

THE DAY AFTER KIRSTY PASSED AWAY, THE FAMILIES ARRIVED FROM France. They were devastated and just sat together and wept. There was nothing else they could do. I did a lot of my own crying in private or with Peggy, and we were a comfort to each other.

On the first of September, Peggy, Laugi, and I went to register Kirsty's death and deal with all that is demanded under the legal system. How numb I felt sitting in the registrar's office, which was of course very austere and quiet; everybody appeared to be walking without sound. After all of the form filling and then collecting that awful document known as a death certificate, knowing that Kirsty's death was now officially certified within law, we got into the car, and I said to them both, "I can't believe this." This is what I have said every day since.

After returning from the registrar's office, we had an appointment to see the consultant paediatrician who had cared for Kirsty for the previous five years. She wanted to discuss the autopsy results. We met her in her office at the hospital, and she said that there was nothing on the report that explained the reasons for Kirsty's death. She was as shocked as we were.

I told her that I believed that the doctors caring for my daughter had botched up and were in over their heads with a case that the greatest experts in the world had been puzzled with for seventeen years. As far as I was concerned, the registrar had failed to contact the on-call consultant. To dig himself out of the hole he was in, he tried to give the impression of knowing what to do and decided to go it alone instead of calling out the on-call duty paediatric consultant. Kirsty's own consultant said that the registrar who was treating Kirsty had told her that he was in constant contact with the senior doctor on call. This would be proven to be untrue, and more would come of this later.

Even though we were in a mess emotionally, we still had family to care about and things that had to be done in the house. This is where Laugi came to the fore and took control. He was by our sides all the time.

We had to get to the task of organizing Kirsty's funeral and arranged for the undertakers to bring her body from the hospital to the funeral parlour. They asked if we would like them to arrange for a minister of the church to visit us at home in order to plan for the funeral. We were grateful for this, as we had no idea how to sort these things out.

The minister who came to see us told us her name was Brenda. She was a slight lady with a very gentle voice. She was kind enough to see us at home and gave us a plan for the funeral service, and we were quite happy with it. I wrote the eulogy, which was one of the hardest things I had ever done in my life, but it was the very least I could do for my precious daughter. Peggy selected music that she knew Kirsty would like.

We were able to visit Kirsty at the funeral parlour twice each day, so we were able to have our final precious moments with her. These we will cherish forever.

At the funeral parlour, Kirsty was resting in a room that was named Rose, a name Kirsty loved ever since she watched the film *Titanic*, whose main character was named Rose. Basically, it was the story of a lady called Rose who had survived the disaster. Since Kirsty's passing, we have met a number of people named Rose, who have made themselves known to us. Though I suppose that is just coincidental, I would have loved it to have been more significant.

The day before the funeral, a strange thing happened: half the wall plugs in the kitchen malfunctioned, and the light under the stairs flickered constantly. I called an electrician. He could find nothing wrong and said he would come back the next day. Suddenly midmorning on the day of the funeral, everything came back on. The electrician came back and left the house at speed when I told him that it was only my daughter's way of letting us know she was all right. There have been quite a few similar instances since then. I talk to Kirsty every day; perhaps this is how she responds.

Two hours before the funeral, everybody went to say their final good-byes, and all remarked that she really did look beautiful. Kirsty had long hair, which had been brushed to perfection and cascaded equally down both sides of her face and halfway down her chest. The salmon-coloured dress and bolero she wore was one that her aunties had sent from Paris. She looked gorgeous, and as much the princess as those she knew from Disney.

Kirsty's casket was pure white, appropriate for this innocent young girl. We put certain items in the casket that we thought she would want for her journey back home to God: the seven dwarf figures, her watch that had been a gift from France, a pearl necklace and diamond earrings that she was given when she was a baby, a family photograph, a *Titanic* CD, and the DVD of the film *The Guru*. She most certainly had beautiful things to accompany her on her journey.

Once our tearful good-byes were said, we went home to prepare for the ceremony.

The hearse arrived at the house at 12.30 p.m. My heart sank because I knew that Kirsty would be making her final journey from the home and those she loved. There were many flowers already around her casket, and as many more as possible were added. The remainder of the flowers were carried by mourners in their cars.

We started Kirsty's last journey on earth with very heavy hearts. The families walked the first mile behind the hearse, and other mourners followed in their cars. There were fifty-two vehicles in all.

A mile from the house, we reached one of Kirsty's favourite places, the local market. She loved us taking her there, so we stopped to give her a final look. After this, the families climbed into their cars, and we continued to the cemetery chapel. The chapel is a very modern, light, and airy building that fortunately does not give you that awful feeling of doom that you sometimes get when going into some places of worship.

Brenda, the minister, met us when we arrived. A short, slim, and very sweet lady, she led us into the chapel behind Kirsty's casket, with Celine Dion singing "My Heart Will Go On," a song that Kirsty knew very well and often sang to the family when she was in her room.

Once seated, I glanced around and was amazed to see the chapel was full, so much so that many mourners had to stand. More than three hundred people had come to pay their respects to our beautiful daughter. Peggy and I were so touched at what we saw.

The service for me was a bit of a blur. I remember saying to myself, *What are we doing here?* I was still hoping to wake up from the dream that I was having. I suppose I must have been in some form of denial; this is what people tell me, and I don't think I can argue with that view.

A neighbour's boy named Nick had written a poem for Kirsty, and that was being read out loud. Suddenly I was back in the real world again, and from then on, I concentrated on the remainder of the service, though I found it very difficult. For most of the time, I sat there in a daze with the picture of Kirsty's face firmly in my mind; at that time, that was what I needed. A prayer was said, tributes to Kirsty were read, and then the next piece of music, which she also loved, "The Swan Princess," was played. More tears flowed. I had written the eulogy for Kirsty but just could not read it, so it was read by Jackie Askwith, one of the many doctors who had treated her over the years. She read it beautifully. It is as follows.

Eulogy to Kirsty Jayne Pearce, 22 February 1986-29 August 2003.

On 22 February 1986, I became, and still am, the proud father of a beautiful girl, whom we named Kirsty Jayne.

In no way could we have known the pain and suffering she was to endure over the following seventeen and a half years and how she would accept this with very little complaint and certainly much dignity.

Peggy, Kirsty's mum, and I, with the help of her brother, Tim, tried to make her life as full and happy as humanly possible. For the most part, we succeeded, though being human, there were small errors along the way.

As a family, we are proud of the way Kirsty handled herself during her lifetime. She shared so much love with everyone she met and would find time to sympathise with others whom she felt were also suffering as much and sometimes more than she. She was, and remains, a total joy to us, and we have been so privileged to have had the opportunity to care for such a wonderful daughter. We thank God for ensuring that Kirsty was born into the right family for her.

I am sure that Kirsty will be looking down on us and saying, "Don't be sad because I am in heaven with my Aunt Kono, Mama Sin, and Frank Sinatra," the man she loved to sing along with, and boy, couldn't she sing well. She certainly did it her way.

Hospitals became a way of life with Kirsty, and of course she made many friends over the years with a multitude of doctors and nurses. This is what they were to her, especially the males. I often would pull her leg and say, "Anything in trousers." She would willingly agree and with a cheeky grin on her face say, "Yes, Dad."

I know that Kirsty would wish me to pay respects and many thanks to the staff at all the hospitals she needed to attend for the tremendous and constant efforts they made in order to help her through some very bad times in her life. She would expect me to do this, and it is done with many thanks.

Thank all of you that were there to help Kirsty; you know who you are, so I will not mention names.

Thank you to all within the family, brothers and sister, aunties and uncles, cousins—the support you gave was so important. Oh yes, and I must mention Magic, the big lovable Labrador that only understood French, though he did seem to understand Kirsty's sign language and it really was funny to see them together.

Everybody that Kirsty met became her friend, and most importantly, she knew they cared.

Kirsty, your spirit and love will remain with us forever, as will ours for you.

Thank you, God, for allowing us the privilege of having and caring for our beautiful daughter for so many wonderful years. We feel so much humility and will never allow ourselves or others to forget our little princess.

Bye-bye, sweetheart. We will meet again. R.I.P.

Love forever. xxxx.
Dad

After the final prayers and the blessing, the service ended. We slowly left the church to the song "How Do I Live Without You?" sung by LeAnn Rimes. We walked to the graveside behind Kirsty's casket, had one final prayer, and then watched her being lowered into the ground. Coupled with her death, this was definitely the worst moment of my life. As I watched Kirsty's casket being lowered into the ground, I heard myself sobbing. Peggy and I just held on tight to each other; neither of us could believe this was happening.

After laying Kirsty to rest, we released two beautiful white doves by the graveside. Up and away they went, only to come back and circle the grave once, and then they left for good. It was such a fitting final act. The whole service was so beautiful, though awfully upsetting.

The grave would not be filled whilst we were there, which is good because no way could I have watched that being done.

It was only after we arrived home that I realized that I would not be seeing my daughter again. I was so upset and felt in a daze.

Since Kirsty's passing, many times people have said to us, "You will get over it." I can assure them that just does not happen. Losing a child is the worst thing that can happen to a parent, and it is not something you ever get over.

We've also been told, "Time heals." Again, let me assure you all that this does not happen.

The worst expression of all is, "It is God's will." This is the one statement I will accept less than any other. I mean, how could God allow Kirsty to suffer for all those years and then commit the final act of cruelty by taking her from us? We are good people, and we love our daughter. She should still be here with her family. My faith has been challenged very much.

The poem that follows was written by Nick, Kirsty's sixteen-year-old friend. It is beautiful.

The Doorway to Heaven

As I look up to the sky,
I see her face but dare not cry.

As I see her in the ground,
I feel her pain but hear no sound.

I hear quiet voices everywhere,
But feel a shame I cannot bear.

With all my strength and all my might,
With all the darkness of the night,

Kirsty

I wish to see her just once more.
Oh look, she's waiting by the door.

A good friend, Diane, the mother of Chris, who died six months before Kirsty and is buried very near her in the same cemetery, sent the following poem:

I did not die though you cannot see me.
I am here, I am all around,
Joining in your tears and laughter,
Echoing your every sound.

I did not die, though my body faltered,
Weakened yes, and I drifted away.
But life, not death, has touched my soul now,
And I have come to a brand-new day.

I did not die to leave you lonely.
I would not leave to see you cry.
For one day we shall walk together,
And you will see I did not die.

CHAPTER 10

THE DAY AFTER THE FUNERAL, WE WERE STILL TRYING TO COME to terms with what had happened. As usual, Laugi was the strong one. Even though he was suffering as much as any of us, he just got on with what needed to be done. He was just fantastic, running around all over the place with me, arranging Kirsty's funeral, dealing with the registering of her death, and generally organizing whatever needed to be done. Without him, I would have been useless, and I can never thank him enough. He admitted to me in private that he finally found things getting tough when Kirsty's casket was being lowered into the ground. As I glanced at him, I could see the tears running down his cheeks as he whispered to me, as he had done on the day of the funeral, "She's gone." Up to that point, he had been the strongest one of all the family; but like everyone else, he had finally come to his breaking point. Even at the end, he had given his all for his favourite niece. When he did eventually return to Paris, he always kept close to us and never forgot the bond we had with him. Laugi came to see us every month for the next three years. He certainly is very special to us.

Eventually the day came when everybody had to return home to Paris. A house full of family and friends had at one stroke become a home for three.

Peggy was deeply depressed over losing Kirsty, and it took her some time before she could return to work. It was, in fact, five months before she felt able to go back.

I felt quite lost at times because, like Peggy, my whole routine had now changed. No longer would I get up in the morning, give Kirsty her medication, take her for hospital appointments, take her to therapy, or run to the shops to get something she might need. That was my life, and I missed it terribly. I wanted it back, though I knew this was not going to be. The final chapter in that part of our lives was over, and somehow we had to find the strength to live with it.

I used to play golf quite regularly when Kirsty was with us, but that stopped when she passed away. I don't think I shall have the inclination to play again, and I never have.

Peggy and I go to Kirsty's grave twice each day, not to mope but to look after her beautiful stone and tend to the small garden at her grave. We also send balloons for her to pick out of the sky on the twenty-ninth of each month, which was the day she passed, and the eleventh day of every month, the day she was buried. We do this every month of the year.

Tim goes to her grave only on special days, as he finds it difficult to cope with her passing. I am sure that Kirsty understands that he grieves for her in his own way, though I am sure she wishes he wouldn't.

Tim was an IT analyst at the hospital where Kirsty passed, but he had to leave because it was too painful working in the place that his sister died. He is now very successfully working in London.

The families in France got on with their lives, but we are able to speak to them every day on the phone, so they continue to support us from a distance.

Everybody misses our little angel, as we do, but we talk to her every day. We know she is with us forever.

Kirsty and I used to watch the soaps together, and in a way we continue to do so. The television is on all day in her room, as it was when she was alive, and I sit with her even today watching the soaps together as we always did. Whenever a new Disney film is released, we buy it, and Peggy watches it with her. It is never quiet in her room, and we are happy with that. That is how she would have liked it, because that's the way it was when she was there.

We have many happy memories of the time we spent with Kirsty, and we often go through them with both sadness and joy. What we had was beautiful, and nobody is able to take that away from us.

I look at the stars on clear nights and wonder which one is Kirsty. I know she is up there somewhere, looking down on us and protecting us.

CHAPTER 11

THE PROBLEMS THAT KIRSTY HAD WERE MANY, SO I WOULD LIKE to show what she was up against. The following is what I would show doctors that had never met her previously. This saved a lot of questions from being repeated on the many admissions to different hospitals she was admitted to around the world. This list that I compiled also shows the many problems that Kirsty suffered from and how resilient children are compared with adults when it comes to illnesses and how little they complain. They are all heroes.

My hope is that hospitals will attach this type of list to the front of all children's case notes in the future. I believe that the hospital where Kirsty received most of her inpatient care will be implementing my idea in some form.

Kirsty's problems:

Polyarticular junior chronic arthritis, with valgus to both ankles
Microcephaly
Micrognathia
Asthma
Intracranial calcifications
Complex seizures
Raynauds disease
Right bilateral retinal detachment
Below third centile in growth
Learning difficulties
Colitis
Anaemia
Generalised osteoporosis
Hypothyroidism

Vasculitis in the small and medium blood vessels, including renal arteries, and impaired kidney function.

In November 1997, Kirsty suffered a reaction to the drug Cyclosporine, causing grand-mal seizures, and was admitted to the local hospital. She was then transferred to the children's hospital Great Ormond Street in London for specialist care. Kirsty remained there for five weeks and during that time suffered a left transient ischemic episode; this affected the right side of her body and was very frightening for her at the time.

No unifying diagnosis was found up to the time of her death, though the following were considered but then discounted after extensive investigations:

Fahrs coats syndrome
Tolmes
Cerebral vasculitis
Pseudohypoparathyroidism
Hypophosphotasia
Chromosome 22q deletion
Toxoplasmosis
Noonans syndrome

The extensive investigations included testing of her deoxyribonucleic acid (DNA), which is a nucleic acid that contains the genetic instructions used in the development and functioning of all known living organisms and some viruses. Any particle of the body can be tested in this manner when looking for answers to a serious medical problem and even in a criminal investigations. It is also now widely used in proving paternity issues.

One of the big issues for Kirsty when she was growing up was whether or not there was an undiscovered malignant illness or syndrome that she could be suffering from; though there was regular testing of her DNA, nothing ever came to light. This was very frustrating for the medical teams and also for Peggy and myself, and of course Kirsty, who often said that she did not understand what was going on within her body. This need of understanding was with her all her life, though she was not going to let the small matter of knowing what her illnesses were upset her too much. Kirsty just got on with her life the best way she knew how, and it seemed that she was not going to let anything get to her. We are very proud of her.

The DNA profiling technique was first reported in 1984 by Sir Alec Jeffries at the University of Leicester in the United Kingdom. It is now the basis of many DNA databases around the world. As Kirsty was born two years later, it was a fairly new testing process, and so she was unable to benefit from it.

I am always amazed at the level of tolerance children have to a medication regime such as the one below. I would have hated taking them myself, though Kirsty seemed not to care at all. I suppose that was because she had been taking them for so many years that she never gave them a second thought. In all, Kirsty had to tolerate sixteen different types of medicine twice daily. It is not surprising that her appetite was so poor, having to stomach that amount.

Below are the medications that Kirsty needed to take each day:

Salbutamol

Tegretol Retard

Losec

Feldene Melt

Magnesium Glycerophosphate

Co-Codamol

Calcichew D3

Sytron

Enbrel injection twice weekly

Amiloride

Frusol

Pamidronate infusion twice monthly

Salamol Steri-Neb

Sodium Valproate

Omeprazole

Iron supplements

Lactulose

Ranitidine

Thyroxine

To make things easier to understand about Kirsty's problems and treatment, I've included a glossary of terms at the back of this book.

CHAPTER 12

MANY TIMES YOU HEAR OF PATIENTS OR RELATIVES COMPLAINING of the treatment received at hospitals by themselves or loved ones. It is not easy to address these issues when things have gone wrong, because all along the way, there are people and organisations that will block your efforts for fear of the public finding out how poor their service was.

It appears that it is politically incorrect to complain about officialdom, especially government departments, but my God, how it sometimes needs to be done! With regard to the care received by Kirsty during the night she died, the authorities continually refuse to take responsibility for their actions, even today, with regard to Kirsty's poor treatment, and that is almost eight years after Kirsty died.

What officialdom fails to understand is that not everybody wants to sue when mistakes are made. Most of the time, a simple apology will do when mistakes are made, even serious ones, but sometimes this can take a long time to materialise. This is what happened in Kirsty's case and was the cause of much unnecessary stress for Peggy and myself.

When Kirsty passed away, we were looking for answers, because she had been in this situation many times previously and within thirty-six hours had returned home. Why was it so different on this occasion? We believed that the doctors taking care of her were negligent and had just let her die. This has been labelled death by indifference by Mencap, an organisation that is involved with disabled people with learning difficulties. The doctors responsible for Kirsty did not have the skills to treat her and failed to summon help when needed.

Having obtained copies of the medical notes, Peggy and I, who are trained nurses, could see that the treatment on that night was lacking in the extreme, so we decided to go through the long, drawn-out National Health Service complaints procedure.

We sent letters and had two meetings with the hospital management. It was decided by the complaints panel that the care for Kirsty that night was as it should have been for somebody as sick as she. We were absolutely furious; we smelled the odour of a cover-up.

Once the hospital denied our claim, we decided to ask the Healthcare Commission to look into our complaint. The Healthcare Commission is the body that is there to ensure that all care given to patients is the best and most professional possible. They carried out a very limited investigation into our complaints, and after fourteen months, told us there was no problem seen in Kirsty's care and therefore no reason for them to investigate any further. This was another slap in the face for us, but we vowed to continue our quest for the justice to which Kirsty was entitled.

We had one final string to our bow, and that was the National Health Service Parliamentary Ombudsman. We complained to her about the poor hospital care for Kirsty and the failings of the Healthcare Commission in its investigation. We hoped that the ombudsman would be of some help, and after only seven months, she completed the investigation and sent us the report that I have included below, which was also sent to the Healthcare Commission and the hospital where Kirsty passed away.

The health minister also received a copy, and though we tried to get a comment regarding the report, we were told by letter, "Sorry, but it would be inappropriate for the minister or one of her officers to comment about the ombudsman report." We figured this was a standard reply to situations like ours. This was most likely sent by a person that had a pile of the same letter that would be sent to anyone else that had the temerity to complain to those ministers that are voted in to serve the public. We also sent a letter to the prime minister and the lord chancellor, but they sent their letters to other minor departments, claiming this was the appropriate action.

In this country, only the highest-profile cases get personal attention from the hierarchy; the lesser are ignored—the very people politicians depend on in an election.

The lord chancellor's departments were not interested in my complaint that the coroner was wrong not to give us an inquest; in fact, they agreed with the coroner's decision that Kirsty's death was by natural causes. This was absolute nonsense and a disgraceful decision, and they knew it. I do not believe that any of these people actually studied the ombudsman's report in detail.

I will not give up on my efforts to prove officialdom wrong and immoral. Writing this story on behalf of Kirsty is the only way of succeeding, and I am determined to get that justice for Kirsty.

Peggy and I love our daughter and are so angry her life was taken from her, partly because of incompetence resulting in what we describe as seriously poor medical care, and shocking complacency with regard to Kirsty's well-being.

The following is the report that the ombudsman prepared on my behalf. The names of people involved in Kirsty's care on the night she died have been omitted, as well as the name of the hospital in which she died.

The Ombudsman's Report.

Health Service Commissioners Act 1993

Report by the Health Service Ombudsman for England of an investigation made into a complaint by Mr. Charles Pearce.

Complaint Against: University Hospitals NHS Foundation Trust and the Healthcare Commission.

1. This is the final report of an investigation by The Health Service Ombudsman into a complaint made by Mr. Charles Pearce about the care and treatment that his late daughter, Miss Kirsty Pearce, received at the hospital in 2003. The Hospital is managed by the NHS Foundation Trust. Mr. Pearce has also complained that the Healthcare Commission failed to investigate his complaint adequately.

Background.

2. Miss Kirsty Pearce was seventeen when she was admitted to the Paediatric unit of the hospital on the evening of 28 August 2003. She had had multiple and severe health problems from birth and her parents were her full-time carers.

A great many different health professionals had been involved in her care over the years. As she required frequent hospital contact, she had direct access to the Paediatric unit at the hospital. On 28 August Kirsty was short of breath and coughing. This had happened before, and her parents first treated her at home with oral diuretics (Amiloride and Frusemide) and with Nebulized Salbutamol. When it became clear that she was not improving her parents contacted the Paediatric Triage Team, and Kirsty was admitted. Her condition failed to improve. At 6 AM on 29 August she was transferred to the Intensive Care Unit (ICU), but sadly she died at 7 AM.

The Complaint.

3. Mr. and Mrs. Pearce first complained to the Trust in January 2004. They believed that there had been a failure in care for Kirsty and that she had not been adequately reviewed by a senior doctor. They also believed that had she been transferred to the ICU sooner she would have survived.

4. The Trust took statements from various members of the medical and nursing staff and responded to Mr. and Mrs. Pearce on 9 February 2004. Mr. and Mrs. Pearce were not satisfied with this response. Further correspondence followed, and two meetings were held on 16 March and 12 July. The Deputy Chief Executive wrote on behalf of the Chief Executive on 4 August.

5. Mr. and Mrs. Pearce remained dissatisfied and wrote to the Health Commission on 25 November. On 16 February 2006 the HC responded, but Mr. and Mrs. Pearce remained dissatisfied. They wrote to the Ombudsman on 11 March.

The Ombudsman's Investigation.

6. The Ombudsman would not usually investigate a complaint before all stages of the NHS complaints processes have been satisfactorily completed. If she has formed the view that the HC has failed to carry out

an adequate investigation of a complaint, she would normally ask the Health Commission to review it.

7. I am critical of the HC's investigation of Mr. and Mrs. Pearce's complaint.

From the file records of the HC's investigation, it did not appear that adequate clinical advice was taken. There was a brief report of a discussion with a clinical adviser on file. This gave no indication of the qualifications of the adviser. It did not appear that the adviser had seen Kirsty's clinical records. The advice was extremely limited. On further enquiry, the HC has told me that the clinical adviser was appropriately qualified, had seen Kirsty's medical records, and had had an extended discussion with the case manager, of which only brief notes were kept, as much of his advice confirmed the explanations that had previously been provided to Mr. and Mrs. Pearce by the Trust. How such clinical advice is recorded has been the subject of discussion between the Ombudsman's office and the HC and I therefore make no recommendations in this regard.

8. However, despite my view that the HC's investigation was seriously flawed by the inadequacy of the clinical advice, I decided that this complaint should not be returned to the HC for reinvestigation, because of the additional delay and distress this would cause. In my investigation I have had access to Kirsty's records for the last five years of her life and to copies of all the complaints correspondence. I have consulted with one of the Ombudsman's professional advisers, a senior nurse with experience of paediatrics, and I obtained a full report from an independent Consultant Paediatrician. I have not included every detail of the investigation, but I am satisfied that nothing of significance has been overlooked.

The Independent Adviser's Report.

9.   The adviser has written a full report reproduced here:

The treatment and care of Kirsty Pearce (Date of birth 22/2/86; deceased 29/8/03) by the NHS Trust when admitted to hospital on 28/8/03, leading to her death the following morning.

This report is based entirely on a review of the hospital medical records of Kirsty Pearce and the health service Ombudsman's file of correspondence relating to the original letter of complaint from Charles W. Pearce (Kirsty's father), 5 January 2004.

Consultant Paediatrician MB BCh MA MRCP FRCPCH.

Foundation NHS Trust.

Background.

Kirsty Pearce suffered from a complex array of medical conditions associated with significant disability but without a unifying diagnosis. A large number of both national and international specialists had contributed to her care.

Some aspects of her condition, including the pulmonary oedema that led to her death, remain unexplained by medical science despite extensive investigation.

Her routine and emergency care locally was delivered by the hospital in the immediate area and co-ordinated by the Paediatric Consultant responsible for her care.

In addition to her problem list, Kirsty suffered recurrent, unexplained episodes of pulmonary oedema (fluid accumulation in the lungs causing breathing difficulty and a drop in oxygen levels). The episodes of pulmonary oedema were unpredictable and varied in severity. The first episodes appear to have occurred prior to 1998, and by 2002 it was recorded that she could suffer up to two minor episodes per week. Every one to three months she suffered a much more severe episode requiring hospitalization. These episodes responded to a combination of

Frusemide (a diuretic medication that causes the body to lose water and salt through the kidneys), nebulised Salbutamol (usually used for asthma), and oxygen supplementation.

Kirsty's condition required a complex regime of medication that on the whole was delivered by her parents. In addition, she required ongoing physiotherapy and orthotic treatments to try and help prevent joint contractures and improve her mobility.

From Kirsty's records, she did not appear to be able to walk from the age of ten and was then confined to a wheelchair. The family was considering the option of hip replacement surgery for her.

In December 2001 she had a multi-specialist review at the Great Ormond Street Hospital for Sick Children, which was thorough and extensive but which was unable to provide a unifying diagnosis and which could not explain Kirsty's ongoing episodes of pulmonary oedema. The report gives some insight into Kirsty's personality, describing her as being cooperative but quite a character that belied any developmental delay and who had a good grasp of many aspects of her illnesses and who was lucid with respect to the management of her problems.

In January 2003 Kirsty underwent a cardiac catheterisation (tubes inserted through blood vessels in the groin into the heart to measure pressures within the heart chambers) in a search for a cause for her recurrent pulmonary oedema. This reported that no abnormalities were found, and indeed during episodes of pulmonary oedema, echocardiograms (ultrasound images of the heart) had not identified any problem with her heart that could account for the condition. Kirsty's impaired kidney function was documented as early as 2001, but this was not to the degree that would normally cause fluid retention.

Between September 2000 and August 2003, Kirsty had numerous admissions to hospital, but eight of these, including her final admission on 28 August 2003, were due to episodes of pulmonary oedema causing breathing difficulty and hypoxaemia (low oxygen levels). Prior to Kirsty's final admission, all of the episodes had responded to treatment with intravenous Frusemide, oxygen, and Salbutamol. During some of the episodes, Kirsty also received antibiotics to cover the possibility of additional infection.

Kirsty's Final Illness.

Kirsty's final illness developed on 28 August 2003. Her parents had direct access to the Penguin Unit (paediatric assessment and observation unit), which is frequent practice for children with complex medical needs. It is noteworthy that Kirsty had been seen in a clinic at Great Ormond Street Hospital for Children just two days before on 26 August, where her Consultant Paediatric Nephrologist commented on how well she appeared.

On the day of admission, however, it was recorded that Kirsty had complained of vomiting and a cough from that morning and that she had failed to respond to doses of diuretics given at home by mouth (Frusemide and Amiloride). Assessment at 5 PM was undertaken by the sister on the unit, who recorded a respiratory rate of 60 breaths per minute, pulse oximetry of 66% in air (normal would be between 96-100%). Her pulse rate was not clear on record and her temperature was 36.8 (normal). Oxygen was administered. She was transferred to the paediatric ward (Puffin) at 7.40 PM.

The entry in the medical notes for the Penguin Unit was not timed and was followed by an entry that was neither signed nor timed recording blood test results, which identified a normal kidney and liver function and a low marker of inflammation (CRP). Her blood count, however, identified a very high white count (29.2), which was ringed in the notes. This can suggest infection. A urine dipstick result did not identify any evidence of infection.

At 6 PM the SHO (Senior House Officer) recorded her admission details in the medical notes. His examination recorded breathlessness with a respiratory rate of 40, a pulse rate of 130, and an oxygen level (pulse oximetry) of 96 per cent whilst receiving 10 litres of oxygen per minute. For a healthy girl of this age, the normal resting breathing rate would be 12 to 16 per minute and the heart rate would be 60 to 100 per minute. He recorded crackling noises when her chest was listened to. Her heart sounds were recorded to be normal and the pressure in her neck veins was not high (this can be a marker for heart failure).

Her abdomen was soft, with no abnormalities detected. There was no comment about Kirsty's circulation, such as blood pressure record, her peripheral temperature, or a measure of her capillary refill time (this is a standard part of clinical examination taught and used to assess the adequacy of the circulation by pressing on the skin for five seconds to cause blanching and then counting how many seconds it takes for the colour to return). Such tests would normally be part of the comprehensive assessment of any ill child. The SHO recorded a chest x-ray result suggesting a recurrence of her pulmonary oedema but also questioning the possibility of infection on the right side of her chest. His management plan proceeded in line with previous treatments to administer intravenous Frusemide, provide pain relief, to start antibiotics, to maintain a fluid balance chart (usually this means in and out volumes and is especially important in someone receiving diuretics and known to have renal disease), to check the urine and perform blood tests (which had previously been entered in the notes), and to discuss with the Registrar.

The nursing communication sheet recorded an entry on 28 August 2003 at 7.40 PM. The named nurse was recorded as "Alex" and the entry made by "Lucy". This recorded how Kirsty's oxygen levels improved to the 90s with oxygen and that when Kirsty was moved to the ward her oxygen levels were 78% in air, rising to 85% in oxygen, and that these subsequently came up slowly to 89-91%. This alone was indicative of a gravely ill patient. She recorded that Kirsty passed 175 ml of urine, her respirations were 60 per minute, she was coughing a lot but felt cold in a warm hospital environment. Feeling cold would imply circulatory compromise, which is seen in conditions such as dehydration, heart failure, or severe infection. There were no further nursing entries on the communication sheet until 5.30 AM on 29 August. In the interim her observation chart recorded high heart and respiratory rates, which both continued to rise during the night. Observations were done two hourly until midnight, hourly till 2 AM, and then at 4 AM and 5 AM prior to her transfer to ITU on 29 August. Pulse oximetry in high flow oxygen prior to midnight were between 94% and 96%, but by 2 AM had dropped to 92% and at 4 AM to 82%, which are pre-terminal observations that would carry a high risk of cardiac arrest.

The medical notes recorded an entry by the SHO at midnight detailing that Kirsty was still breathless, with a respiratory rate of 40 per minute (which was not in agreement with her observation chart) and a pulse rate of 130 per minute. Saturations recorded were 98% in oxygen (which was higher than any value recorded on her observation chart).

The paediatric specialist registrar was reported to have seen Kirsty at 10 PM. There was no clinical or nursing record of this, but in his statement to the Trust written five months after the event (21/01/04), he recollected the clinical findings of that assessment, recording that she was breathless in bed with three pillows, with a respiratory rate of 70 per minute (very high), a pulse rate of 130 per minute, and a blood pressure of 112/60 (this latter observation was entered onto her observation charts on admission and there is no record of it being rechecked between then and five hours later at 10 PM).

He recollected that his examination of her cardiovascular and abdominal systems was unremarkable. No changes to her management plan were made, and the outstanding components of the SHO's earlier plan were not expedited.

At 1.10 AM in the morning on 29 August 2003, at the SHO's request, the paediatric specialist registrar reviewed Kirsty. He recorded that she was breathless (tachypnoeic), that her breathing rate was 50 per minute, heart rate 140 per minute, and her oxygen levels between 92% and 94% in ten litres per minute of oxygen. His plan was to continue monitoring closely (no frequency specified). Both before and after this instruction, the observation frequency was not what I would consider close. There was instruction to administer a further dose of Frusemide. There was no record of Kirsty's conscious level, fluid balance, or of an assessment of her circulation.

The next record at 3 AM by the SHO reported that Kirsty was "still much the same" but with marginal improvement. Pulse oximetry was recorded to be between 92% and 94% and pulse rate 140. Crackles persisted, and his plan was to further discuss with the registrar.

The registrar reviewed again at 3.10 AM and reported that Kirsty was still breathless and in distress. But now that the pulse oximetry levels had fallen to 89-90% while still in high flow oxygen, this would imply dangerous instability in a seriously ill patient. There was no record of the state of her circulation, fluid balance, or state of hydration. His plan was to discuss Kirsty's condition with the Consultant on call and also to discuss with anaesthetics and to continue close monitoring. There was no record in the notes of contact with either the Consultant or anaesthetist at that time or of advice received.

Two hours later at 5 AM on 29 August, the paediatric registrar was requested to review Kirsty and recorded that she was not improving and that her oxygen saturation were in the 80s while still on oxygen. Her respiratory rate was 65 per minute and the heart rate 140 and she was sleeping in the propped-up position. She still had crackles in both lung fields and was documented to have passed urine, but her detailed fluid balance was not reviewed and the state of her circulation was not documented.

He recorded contact with his Consultant and recorded a suggestion to repeat a dose of Frusemide and to inform the anaesthetist to review and assess, but that if Kirsty were to deteriorate she would require Intensive Care. There was no specification of what change in observations would constitute a further deterioration.

The next record was by the specials registrar in anaesthetics, who assessed Kirsty at around 5.10 in the morning on 29 August 2003. His record reported that Kirsty was conscious and responding to commands (this was most likely indicating a moderately reduced level of consciousness in the traditionally used AVPU scale: Alert, responds to Voice, responds to Pain, and Unconscious), that she was breathless with shallow, rapid breathing (implying exhaustion), and a fast heart rate. He

71

recorded that Kirsty had poor circulation, appeared dehydrated with a poor capillary refill (this was the first mention of this clinical parameter from the time of admission), and that her oxygen levels were between 83-84% in high flow oxygen (15 litres per minute). He discussed with his Consultant on call and made arrangements for Kirsty to be transferred to Intensive Care for ventilation.

It appears as though on intubations in Intensive Care, Kirsty collapsed and went into cardiac arrest, and despite resuscitation efforts she failed to recover. Her death was recorded at 7 AM.

Post-Mortem Examination.

Kirsty underwent a post-mortem examination at the request of her parents, and this confirmed the presence of pulmonary oedema without any obvious precipitating factor. The report suggested that Kirsty had a normal heart, and although the final report suggested that her pulmonary oedema was due to left ventricular failure (a failing heart), the reason for her condition remained a mystery. There was no evidence of infection on the post-mortem examination.

Summary of Clinical Issues Identified.

Kirsty was seriously ill from the moment of her admission due to an unexplained illness, pulmonary oedema that she had suffered from repeatedly in the past but from which she had always managed to recover.

In the hospital records there are some clinical concerns that I would raise.

1. *Shortly after admission it should have been apparent that she fulfilled the criterion for admission to a High Dependency Unit, or in the absence of that an Intensive Care environment. This would not necessarily be to initiate ventilation but to ensure that there was proper assessment and monitoring of her condition. Continuous monitoring*

with charting observations every 20-30 minutes would be typical in this setting.

2. *Kirsty's monitoring was inadequate both in terms of frequency and range of parameters checked. Throughout her admission, her observations steadily deteriorated with frequent periods of worrying instability.*

3. *Despite Kirsty's previous admissions, her observations and response to treatment on her final admission were worse than on the previous admissions. Her heart rate and respiratory rate were higher, and her oxygen levels did not stabilise when given additional oxygen. There was no recognition of this. Her respiratory rate was in excess of 50 breaths per minute (the last five admissions with pulmonary oedema recorded values of between 20 and 40). Her pulse oximetry dropped below 92% in high flow oxygen compared to previous normalisation to high 90s or 100% in between 2 and 5 l/min of oxygen. Her heart rate was constantly in excess of 120-140/min, increasing as the night progressed, compared to rates of 85 to 130/min on previous admissions. Her capillary refill time, blood pressure, and fluid balance were not assessed or monitored properly, and investigations to support the clinical assessment were not requested, such as blood gas analysis (which had been done in the past).*

4. *The medical assessments through the night were not comprehensive in terms of the basic standards for recognising illness in children. In particular, staff did not document Kirsty's conscious level, the adequacy of her circulation, or the level of her hydration. Nursing records on admission referred to her feeling cold, and the anaesthetic review twelve hours after admission reported dehydration and prolonged capillary refill, indicating circulatory insufficiency that may have been present for much of her illness. A fluid balance chart requested on admission appeared to document an inadequate urine output consistent with this (less than 1 ml per Kg per hour overall), which is especially low considering the doses of Frusemide given. There is no input record despite the plan at 6 PM for Kirsty to be on a fluid balance chart. There were no measures or investigations*

to assess this in more detail, such as by measuring a blood gas to identify acidosis or a repeat of her electrolyte (salt) levels.

5. Nursing notes were scanty and infrequent and did not record the clinical progress between admission and her transfer to Intensive Care.

6. Medical notes were incomplete and did not record all of the clinical reviews; monitoring requirements were not clearly specified, and there was no check that earlier management plans had been implemented.

7. There appears to have been considerable delay in instituting some prescribed treatments. For example, intravenous antibiotics were requested at 6 PM by the SHO, but the drug chart indicated that antibiotics were not administered until 1.10 AM the following day (a delay of seven hours and ten minutes). It is not clear whether the third dose of IV Frusemide was given, as it was crossed off and "error" written over the prescription on the drug chart.

A more thorough and timely assessment and investigation of Kirsty's illness would have added information to the clinical picture. I believe that such information would have emphasised the seriousness of her condition and expedited her transfer to Intensive Care.

Commentary.

Kirsty's bouts of pulmonary oedema were long-standing, unpredictable, and unexplained. The condition over many years had responded to the interventions that were repeated during her final admission, and hence it was very reasonable to reinstitute the same.

Treatment of pulmonary oedema is usually directed at the underlying cause, which had never been identified in Kirsty. However, once the diagnosis of pulmonary oedema has been made, oxygen and diuretics are the first step in its management. The dose of Frusemide was appropriate, and the oxygen was delivered at a high rate to try and correct Kirsty's low oxygen *level. Without improvement, there are other interventions that require intensive care. These include ventilation to push fluid out of the spaces and tubes in the lungs back into the circulation. At 5 AM on 29 August 2003 this next step was put into action, but Kirsty died in the process. When managing pulmonary oedema, maintaining metabolic circulatory stability is important. Acidosis and circulatory insufficiency would impede recovery.*

Kirsty did not have these assessed, and so potentially treatable abnormalities in her perfusion, blood pressure, electrolytes, acid base balance, and urine output were not identified.

Kirsty died very soon after her admission to the Intensive Care Unit and in fact shortly after she was intubated, ready to place her on a life support machine. We will never know if full resuscitation implemented earlier could have influenced the outcome and prevented her death. However, certain aspects of her assessment and monitoring may have prompted earlier intervention if done differently. There was a slow and steady decline in her condition determined by heart and respiratory rates, and maintaining Kirsty's oxygenation was progressively more difficult through the night. Her conscious level and circulatory adequacy were not comprehensively assessed, and she was not investigated to determine whether there was any metabolic disturbance, such as acidosis. Additional information from these may have prompted an earlier referral to the Intensive Care Unit.

Many hospitals use early warning guidelines, which serve as a prompt, and help identify critically ill patients. From the time of Kirsty's admission, she would have met the usual criteria for being monitored in a High Dependency Unit or, in the absence of such a facility, a General Intensive Care Unit.

The medical staff did review Kirsty fairly frequently through the night and documented their attendance in the notes. The registrar did not document his review and findings until approximately seven hours following her admission, and his statement reported that he had conflicting commitments during the evening, especially on the neonatal Intensive Care Unit. The statement of the paediatric bank nurse provided a recollection of continuing concern during the evening following

Kirsty's admission. She also detailed some difficulty of obtaining a medical review after a poor response of Kirsty's condition to interventions. She or her line manager ought to have been able to contact the Consultant on call directly.

It is usual practice for the consultant to provide backup for both opinion and direct clinical support when there are high service demands. It is not clear whether the consultant knew of Kirsty's admission when she was first transferred to the ward. There is also confusion about whether the Consultant was spoken to at 3 AM on 29 August 2003, which was written in the registrar's plan. The Consultant was contacted at 5 AM and, according to his own statement, advised that further diuretics should be given rather than transferring her to the Intensive Care Unit. It is not clear how he was provided with the comprehensive clinical information about her condition, given that the recorded assessments and monitoring were inadequate. The discussion did not prompt further evaluation or investigation. Kirsty was transferred to the Intensive Care Unit very shortly after her review by the ITU anaesthetist registrar. The Consultant attended the hospital while her resuscitation was in progress just prior to her death.

I believe that the senior medical reviews of Kirsty during her final illness were neither comprehensive nor within a reasonable time frame. The Consultant's decision to attend would have been dependant on his being contacted and being provided with accurate clinical information. The information from junior doctor assessments and from monitoring was inadequate, and the Consultant was contacted very late in the clinical course. This constituted a failure of the system at several steps, including inadequate recognition, assessment, and investigation and monitoring of serious illness, confounded by poor documentation and communication.

The Trust's Response to the Clinical Aspects of the Complaint.

After the receipt of the original letter of complaint on 5 January 2004, the Trust obtained statements from all key professionals involved in the case that night with Kirsty (Paediatric Registrar, SHO, Consultant, and the Bank Nurse).

As the process progressed, there were three letters from the Chief Executive (9 February 2004, 22 April, 4 August) and two meetings with the parents (16 March, 12 July). The process was hampered by the lack of documentation, inadequate assessments, and poor monitoring in the medical records, combined with conflicting and inconsistent accounts that undermined the investigation of clinical aspects of the case.

The Trust's response acknowledged that Kirsty had shown a poor response to treatments but identified mitigating factors, such as the heavy clinical work load faced by the staff that was only appreciated in hindsight. There was not a clear apology until the end of the third letter. The response described measures to create individualised illness management plans for older children with complex medical conditions. If implemented these would now help to improve the care and communication between professionals about children with serious and complex illnesses, such as Kirsty. Other actions drawn from the lessons learnt from the review of Kirsty's care included a system of flagging children with special needs on the hospital's patient administration system and developing summary history sheets at the front of the patient's notes in order to avoid delays and repetition in the clinical process. More recently, staffing levels are reported to have improved, and it is now accepted that anyone caring for an ill child can contact the Consultant with concerns that they feel need to be addressed at a more senior level. These are all reassuring developments.

However, several key issues in the original letter of complaint and which are identifiable in the clinical records were not properly acknowledged or apologised for, and so the complaint remained unresolved. The case was referred to the HC, whose report was finalised on 16 February 2006. This concluded that there was no scope for the HC to take the complaint further and that measures put in place by the Trust would have reduced the risk of similar problems in the future. The conclusions about clinical aspects of the case in the report are questionable. The HC's report concluded that the delay in senior medical reviews did not influence her management because the SHO had undertaken an assessment and discussed this with the Registrar. However the SHO's assessment was incomplete and his management plan was not implemented until much later. In addition, although some blood tests may not have needed repeating, some, especially electrolytes, ought to have been repeated, and additional tests such as blood gas analysis might have guided management. In this situation, a senior and ideally Consultant review could have provided a more comprehensive appraisal of Kirsty's illness.

The Trust should have acknowledged these shortcomings early in the course of the complaints process.

Recommendations.

In addition to the action already implemented, there are several further recommendations that may be useful to consider in relation to the current care practices and guidelines at the hospital.

1. *Critically ill children need to be identified. There is a widespread use of Early Warning prompts that help identify which children require high dependency or intensive care. This would help encourage the comprehensive assessment of sick children.*
2. *All medical staff above SHO providing emergency out-of-hours paediatric care require accreditation in advanced paediatric life support (APLS), and patients should be allocated to appropriately trained nurses (APLS or NPLS). These skills benefit from being reinforced by departmental teaching activities and should be summarised and encouraged during departmental induction.*
3. *There needs to be an appropriate facility equipped with monitoring equipment and suitable observation charts to care for critically ill children, and if not, there needs to be accepted thresholds, based on the Early Warning Criteria, for children to be transferred to a more appropriate setting.*

4. *Clinical Notes Audit should be part of junior medical staff induction and departmental audit activity in line with CNST requirements. This can help avert the consequences of poor documentation and facilitate the investigation of clinical incidents, improving the safety of the clinical process.*

5. *Combined medical and nursing notes are used in many hospitals to improve the communication between medical and nursing staff. Communication and documentation was problematic in this case.*

6. *Observation charts need to be appropriate for the complexity and seriousness of the patient's condition. The monitoring chart used in this case was not appropriate and was too basic for the purpose required. The type of monitoring chart used for critically ill children should be reviewed.*

Findings.

7. *The clinical advice I have received is very clear. There were significant failings in the care provided to Kirsty during her last illness in 2003. Monitoring of her condition was inadequate; there was a failure to recognise the seriousness of her condition; and there were delays in seeking and obtaining reviews by senior doctors. While a plan to contact the consultant was written in the notes at 3 AM, telephone records indicated this did not happen until 5 PM. There were clear indications that Kirsty needed care more intensive than that available on the paediatric ward, either in a High Dependency Unit or in Intensive Care, but she was not transferred until her condition had already deteriorated too far for recovery.*

8. *I therefore uphold Mr. Pearce's complaint that the care provided to his daughter fell below a reasonable standard.*

Conclusion.

9. *This is a desperately sad case. While it will never be possible to say for certain whether Kirsty would have survived her*

illness had she been transferred to the ICU at an earlier stage, there seems little doubt that her chances would have been improved.

10. *I recommend that the Trust write to Mr. and Mrs. Pearce to apologise for the shortcomings identified in this report.*

11. *Kirsty was a unique person, and her individual medical needs and illness were very unusual. Nevertheless, I believe that lessons can be learnt from the circumstances of this complaint, and I recommend that the Trust give careful consideration to the comments and recommendations of the independent adviser, identify what action should be taken to address his concerns, and draw up an action plan with appropriate time scales and with people named to take responsibility for its implementation, so that the failings identified in this report may be avoided in future.*

12. *The Trust has accepted my recommendations and will write to Mr. and Mrs. Pearce within one month of the final report. It will provide the Ombudsman with a copy of its action plan within three months of the date of the issue of the final report.*

Senior Investigating Officer
Duly authorised in accordance with Paragraph 12 of schedule 1 to the Health Service Commissioners Act 1993, 7th September 2006.

Every time I read the ombudsman's report, I find myself getting angrier than ever as I realise the level of incompetence in the care given to Kirsty the night she died. Most of the problems were associated with basic medical and nursing care, but nobody appears to be that concerned over this. It is as though those responsible are saying, "Ignore it, and it will go away." Usually it does, and so many very poor medical practitioners get away with their misdemeanours, as in Kirsty's case.

One of the most frustrating things about this type of investigation is the lengths those concerned will go to to cover up their mistakes and how quickly their colleagues stand shoulder to shoulder with them even though they are well aware of their dishonesty. It is very hard fighting against the system in this area, and I find myself struggling alone with just the support of the immediate family. I have found the struggle very hard but also quite exhilarating. After all, it is all for Kirsty.

I will never give up, and if these people want a fight, then they can have one with me. They will never beat me.

CHAPTER 13

WHEN KIRSTY WAS SUFFERING FROM HER LAST ILLNESS, PEGGY was with her the whole time. She watched our beloved daughter slowly die before her eyes, the most awful thing that could be thrust upon any mother. Peggy had carried Kirsty for full term and with my support had remained with her for seventeen and a half years. We loved her, nurtured her, and protected her for all those years. But when it came to the expected medical support, we and Kirsty were let down.

We can never forgive the very poor medical care given to Kirsty. The doctors that were supposed to care for her on her last night did not know what to do, and instead of using common sense and calling for the consultant, they allowed Kirsty to leave this world when it was nowhere near her time to go.

Peggy and I were appalled at the standard of care on the ward that night. For starters, to allow a patient to fully dehydrate is medically criminal, and to not call on the expertise of the on-call paediatric consultant is unbelievable. The registrar and the SHO were very busy with a heavy workload and did not have the time to deal with Kirsty, which is why they should have called for help.

Kirsty was a wonderful, loving, and funny young lady. She loved life and gave many people who came into contact with her, especially other sick children, a wonderful feeling of happiness. She came into contact with very many of these children over the years at the various hospitals she attended, and they would never forget her.

The many doctors who met Kirsty were nonplussed when this lovely girl they saw each month would present them with a new medical problem for which they had no answers.

The registrar that night was responsible for two paediatric wards, gynaecology, triage, and accident and emergency, and apparently he was tied up for a number of hours assisting with a difficult birth. This does not excuse him for failing to give Kirsty the help she needed and calling for assistance from somebody more qualified. He knew he needed help but did not seek it, and so Kirsty died.

As nurses, Peggy and I know that doctors will avoid calling a consultant out in the night for two reasons: first, the doctor must not give the impression that he can't cope, and second, he probably feels it would not be a good move careerwise. After all, a registrar hopes to become a consultant one day, and he needs to show he can handle all situations with skill and confidence.

In hospitals in the United Kingdom, there is a big problem with staffing levels because there is never enough money to hire enough personnel. Chief executives are given insufficient budgets, and I have yet to see a hospital that can run within its budget. That is solely the reason why situations like Kirsty's arise, and they will continue to happen until hospitals are given the appropriate funds to run a good service.

One of the worst expressions that arise when something disastrous happens, as it did with Kirsty, is, "We must ensure that this never happens again." If the people uttering these words were to stop and think, they would realise that this is no comfort to parents sitting in front of them, as we were, who have just lost their child. This is an utterance that stems from society in general. When it was said to us, it just sounded so insincere and matter-of-fact.

The ombudsman stated that all doctors above SHO status should be qualified according to the acute paediatric life support standard, and all paediatric nurses should gain this qualification or neonatal paediatric life support if they are providing emergency paediatric care for the newborn. I am shocked if this is not the case, though not surprised after what happened to Kirsty. This should be a routine part of their paediatric training. If people are not appropriately trained but working in this area, then this is a recipe for disaster. This may well have been the case with Kirsty on the night she died.

It took three years for the Trust to do the decent thing and apologise for the failings in Kirsty's care, and that was only because the ombudsman suggested in the report that they do so; otherwise, I am sure they would have continued to ignore us. We did not accept the first apology because, as I told the chief executive of the Trust, it was not spontaneous and was only given at the behest of the ombudsman. We did accept the second apology because it appeared sincere.

The big problem with the National Health Service thinking, as I have already said, is that they believe everybody will sue them for mistakes made. This is far from the truth. All some people require is an apology and to be sure that the organisations concerned are truly sorry for the mistakes made. The worst thing is to make money from the death of a loved one, and sadly this is what some relatives do when neglect is proven in the death of a child. If Peggy and I had done this, what would we have felt after the money had gone? Certainly not that this had been compensation for our daughter's death, but guilty at the thought that Kirsty had gone and we had lined our pockets. We could never have lived with that.

Chapter 14

Each April Peggy and I have, like so many other people, a standing invitation to attend a memorial service at the church in the square next to Great Ormond Street Hospital so that we may remember all the children who have passed away that were the patients of that wonderful place. Hundreds of parents attend, and we all carry a picture of the child or children we've lost. Each child's name is read out, and then the parents light a candle for them. It is an amazing and wonderful afternoon. The tears that are shed are real, and readings by some of the parents are from the heart.

To see the pictures of these children around the church is heartbreaking. We all understand that they have gone home to God and remain safe within his arms, and that when the time comes, we shall all be together again.

I am sure that many people have arranged private memorials to remember and pay respects to the children they have lost. For Kirsty, we were pleased to have this honour for both her eighteenth and twenty-first birthdays; we arranged private memorials to remember our lovely daughter. Both days were unforgettable, as we were both sad and happy, sad because she is here no more, and happy to have beautiful memories that we shall cherish forever.

We go to her resting place every day to cut her lawn and tend to the flowers. Sadly this is all we are able to do for Kirsty now. It gives us such great pleasure, but, my God, how we miss her.

At the cemetery, Peggy and I have formed firm and lasting friendships with a number of people, including Diane and Jim, the parents of Christopher, and Elaine, the mother of Zoë. I feel sure that our children arranged for us to meet in this way, and we are grateful for that. We are a great comfort to each other, for when one says to the other, "I know how you feel," we know that is true. Peggy and I have a lot of love for these very special friends.

It is very noticeable how someone who has lost a mother of ninety years has the same feelings of loss as we do being the parents of a seventeen-year-old. Sometimes we can be quite selfish and claim that no one has had to suffer the way we have, though in our hearts we know this is not so.

Another special friend is Brenda, the sweet and gentle minister who was able to conduct the funeral and the two lovely memorial services for Kirsty. She is a lovely lady who chose her vocation wisely.

The things that I miss about Kirsty are numerous, but the following are the ones that come immediately to mind.

> The courage she showed to get through each day.
> Empathy for others, especially children.
> The smile that was always on her face, even in bad times.
> Her determination to get herself mobile once more.
> Her beautiful singing of songs that she loved.
> Her lack of complaint, no matter how much pain she suffered.
> Her trust in the doctors looking after her.
> Her trust in me, her dad, who looked after her in Mum's absence.

And the thing I miss most of all is my wonderful, irreplaceable daughter.

When a child dies, so many emotions rise up within you, and all at the same time. I felt anguish, horror, fear, disbelief, desolation, grief, and last but not least, anger.

When your child dies in a hospital setting, you start to question how, and why, and who was at fault, if anyone at all. This is when your faith is sorely tested, and because I am not a very religious person, it was easy for me to blame God for allowing this to happen. I repeated to Peggy over and over again, "How could he allow this to happen to Kirsty? After all, she has never committed a sin, and she believed in and loved him." Perhaps the expression "Suffer the little children to come unto me" is literal. The only explanation possible is that God may have taken Kirsty to save her from further suffering. If so, then I must accept this, as there is no other choice.

We all place our trust in the medical profession when it involves the care of our loved ones, but sometimes that trust is misplaced, and horrifying events destroy that trust.

We knew immediately when Kirsty died that something had tragically gone wrong and stated this then. Nobody believed that what we were saying could possibly be true; but then the parliamentary health service ombudsman became involved, and after a three-year battle, the Trust accepted our complaint and apologised for the substandard care given to Kirsty. Because of this case, many changes in procedures and an increase in staff have been implemented at the hospital where she died. It always seems to me, however, that these things are never thought necessary until a disaster occurs. This echoes the well-known saying about "closing the door after the horse has bolted."

As a direct result of Kirsty's case and the intervention by the parliamentary health service ombudsman, a number of changes have been made to procedures and training criteria within the Trust and regular reviews are made to ensure that the things that happened to Kirsty never occur again in the future. Still, all of that is not very comforting to somebody that has lost his or her child. Of course, being a pessimist with regard to promises made by the medical fraternity in this country concerning better care for patients, I will not hold my breath for things to improve.

One notable change at the hospital where Kirsty passed away is that doctors and nurses must be qualified in the care of critically ill children and they must keep their qualifications up-to-date. I hope this lasts, though of course why this was not part of paediatric nurses' basic training I shall never understand. It is wrong to let people who do not have the correct qualifications treat seriously ill children, or any other sick person. I know that the University Hospitals National Health Service Foundation Trust is dealing with these issues at this time, but this should have been routinely dealt with in the past. In Kirsty's case, it was too little, too late.

One of the most stressful things to suffer is the National Health Service complaints procedure, which seems to go on forever. The first step is to send a letter of complaint to the hospital concerned. The hospital responds by promising to hold an internal investigation, which is carried out by their own staff, of course. This should never be the case, as nobody can seriously believe that an investigation of that type could possibly be independent and neutral. After this, if the explanations as to what happened are rejected by the complainers, a meeting is held with senior staff, including the chief executive officer, to attempt to get the Trust to understand how it was at fault, as in our case for the death of our daughter. In our meeting with the Trust, nothing was resolved, and we left bitterer than ever.

One week later, we received a letter informing us that the Trust would investigate further our complaints, one of which was that the medical staff lied in their statements. We only made these accusations because we knew them to be true; no way would we have done so otherwise.

After many weeks, we received another letter, informing us that our complaint could not be taken any further and that the hospital could not hold their staff responsible for anything that happened that fateful night, even though Kirsty had died as a result of poor medical and nursing care. Peggy and I were astounded at the blatant disregard for what had happened to our precious daughter.

Our concerns were even greater when we were informed that the body we appealed to, which is specifically set up to monitor the performances in the hospitals and ensure correct procedures and treatment, namely the Healthcare Commission, had reviewed the complaint at our request and after fourteen months made their decision to support the hospital. To us, it was a devastating result. The Healthcare Commission informed us in writing of their decision to support the Trust and rejected our claims of negligence by them out of hand.

It was at that point that we realised that the only other option left open to us was to appeal to the parliamentary health service ombudsman; we knew this would be our last throw of the dice because if they also threw out our complaint, then there was no one else that we could approach. I am happy to say that the ombudsman's department went totally against the grain and supported us fully by upholding our serious complaint against the Trust and its staff; both medical and nursing factions were found to be in the wrong. The ombudsman's department made very important stipulations to the Trust. These were to improve things all round with the care of seriously sick children and to ensure staffing and equipment were upgraded; this included, of course, correctly trained staff in this area. What the ombudsman was actually saying was, "Get your act together and try behaving as carers should." The ombudsman also made it clear to the Healthcare Commission that they should also get their act together. Things did improve over the next two years, and not long after that, the

Healthcare Commission became nonexistent. I should like to think that was partly because of cases such as Kirsty's. Because of the changes being made, many children will be safer in that particular hospital environment, though that will not help Kirsty.

Perhaps when reading this, you will think that I am very bitter, and of course, you would be right. My forgiving the perpetrators of my daughter's demise will never happen.

I am hoping that if I make enough waves, then many children in our hospitals in the future will be kept safe.

We received our long-overdue apology from the Trust after three years and three months from the date of the original letter of complaint. To my way of thinking, it was quite insincere and had been foisted on the Trust by the ombudsman. I believe that the whole complaints procedure is deliberately designed to last more than three years in order that guilty parties are protected by the statute of limitations legislation, which prevents a lawsuit being processed after a three-year period. This law can be overruled by a judge in the High Court, but this rarely happens.

This kind of law is ludicrous and illustrates why the statute is one of the many antiquated laws in this country. By comparison, if a murder is committed, then the law will ensure that the perpetrator is hunted until found, even if it takes a lifetime. As far as we are concerned, Kirsty's death was as much a crime as any other.

The three-year law would not have affected us personally anyway, as we had stated to the Trust at the beginning of the complaints procedure that this was not about money. We only wanted justice for Kirsty; no amount of money can bring her back or replace her.

Peggy and I have complained to the General Medical Council regarding the two doctors responsible for Kirsty's care the night she died. We want an apology from them; they owe us that much. There was most certainly reluctance on their part to hold their hands up and admit their failures in the care of Kirsty. The worst thing in medicine is for doctors not to take responsibility for their actions. In failing to render all possible treatment to a patient such as Kirsty, they broke their sacred promise of the Hippocratic Oath that doctors take upon qualifying. The oath in general is swearing that they will treat to the best of their ability the patients in their care. Sadly, this did not happen with Kirsty.

Paragraph five of the modern Hippocratic Oath states, "I will not be ashamed to say, I know not, nor will I fail to call in my colleagues when the skills of another are needed for a patient's recovery."

Clearly the oath was not honoured in Kirsty's case; she was forgotten and left to die in front of her mother, distressed, in pain, and frightened. It was not until there was no hope of recovery for her that action was taken; this was an obvious breaking of their duty of care. I believe that no other doctor would have acted in the same manner as those who were supposed to take care of my daughter. The doctors caring for Kirsty during her final illness would have failed the well-documented Bolam test by virtue of the fact that they failed to offer all possible treatment that was available to her until it was too late and her situation was already terminal.

The Bolam test was named after the relatives of a patient who were trying to establish clear-cut duty-of-care guidelines. In 1957 in the High Court of the United Kingdom, it was decided that in cases of alleged medical negligence, a test should be used to determine the standard of care owed to patients by medical practitioners. It was established that there can be no breach in the duty of care so long as the doctor acted in accordance with a responsible body of medical opinion. In Kirsty's case, however, there was a clear breach of care; this was decided by the ombudsman and her independent expert in their report.

One of the biggest problems with complaining about the care of loved ones against the health service, apart from the obvious denials that follow, is to successfully complain about the individuals who are directly involved in the negligent care. In Kirsty's case, this was the registrar and his junior, the SHO.

The ombudsman upheld our complaint, but we felt that the hands-on individuals who had walked away unscathed should also be investigated. I wrote a letter to the General Medical Council and complained of the poor care by these doctors, informing them that Peggy and I wanted these doctors to face up to and be rapped over the knuckles for providing care that was below a reasonable standard for our daughter.

Peggy and I are not vindictive people, and we informed the General Medical Council that we were not demanding the doctors be struck or even suspended, though we did expect them to be disciplined by their peers in some way.

I received a reply to my letter from the General Medical Council in which they agreed to an investigation of their own to determine whether or not the two doctors would face a hearing in front of their Fitness to Practice panel.

Though almost four years had passed since Kirsty's death, Peggy and I remained committed to ensuring that justice is done on her behalf. A number of people have suggested to me that I would be wasting my time in trying to find satisfaction in Kirsty's case and that the system cannot be beaten. I disagree with them because I have great faith in British justice and know that we will be vindicated in our efforts. The people who make these negative statements have never been confronted with the trauma of losing a child; if they had been, then their attitudes would be in the reverse. At the end of the day, I know I will not be beaten and justice will be mine.

CHAPTER 15

THE THIRTEEN HOURS PEGGY SPENT AT THE BEDSIDE THE NIGHT Kirsty died was the worst night of her life. She felt so helpless because there was nothing she could do other than comfort her, and things were made even worse when the doctor was too busy to see Kirsty but did not have the sense to call the duty paediatric consultant. If he had done that, Kirsty most likely would be here today; we are adamant about that.

I feel so guilty for not being at my daughter's side when she died, but in no way did I think that would happen on that particular night. I was sure that Kirsty would have a rough night but return home within thirty-six hours, as she usually did. Kirsty endured many bad times because of her various medical problems, but she always came through smiling, and I thought this would be the end result again. I believe that I let her down by not being there; if I had been there, as a nurse I would have chased the medical staff until they had done the right thing. I am so sorry, Kirsty, please forgive me.

Peggy feels guilty because I was not called to the hospital sooner, but she firmly believed that everything was under control. She must not blame herself. Peggy most certainly has nothing to reproach herself for, since like me, she did not believe that Kirsty would not make it through the night. She often talks about it and wonders whether she did the right thing by Kirsty. Peggy, you had no idea what would happen, so stop beating yourself up about it.

I conducted a study of the time that Peggy spent in caring for Kirsty and came up with some interesting statistics. In one week, Peggy would spend one hundred hours with Kirsty dealing with her needs. I would take care of her for the remaining sixty-eight hours, but even then, Peggy would be with me for at least ten of those hours. In seventeen years, that was 88,400 hours or over ten years for Peggy, and 60,112 hours or almost seven years for me. We wish we could have another seventeen years.

We were offered respite on many occasions, but we preferred to take care of Kirsty ourselves. It's not that we had a mistrust of other people, but we would rather have that responsibility ourselves—plus Kirsty was used to the way we cared for her. She was our daughter, and nobody could care for her the way we did. I am so glad that we made this choice.

Nobody should get the idea that we think we were the only ones in this situation. Thousands of parents have been in the same boat that we were, and they show great love and care for their children. Like us, they ensure their children get as much out of life as possible in the time that is left to them. They deserve a lot of respect for all their efforts.

When somebody would say to Peggy or myself, "You spoil Kirsty by giving her too much," this would anger me because thousands of children such as Kirsty were all living on borrowed time and nobody knew when this time would run out. Most of these children were given financial benefits from the government. In Kirsty's case, she received the disability living allowance, a benefit to help with daily living, and she also received income support, which she was entitled to once she became sixteen years old. We made sure Kirsty used that money as she saw fit.

The people making silly remarks about how children such as Kirsty are spoilt would be more to the point if they had said she spoilt herself. Of course, she was entitled to do that; after all, it was her own money that she was spoiling herself with. This was her entitlement, and we were pleased for her. Children are a special and most precious part of our lives, and nobody has the right to take them away from us. They are supposed to be our future, but quite often there is no future for them, all because of incompetence and complacency. Neither of these failings have a place in medicine.

Sometimes I believe doctors feel they are a law unto themselves. I can remember the neurosurgeon saying to me after I had queried the use of Cyclosporine with Kirsty, "Doctors can try any drug they wish if they think it will do the job." I was annoyed and said to her, "Fine, as long as you take responsibility when something goes wrong, as it did with Kirsty." I do not like hit-and-miss medicine, and neither do I like patients being given medicines because a doctor *thinks* it could be useful. This hit-and-miss type of treatment was often used in the care of my daughter, and it went wrong every time. This is what happened with Kirsty and Cyclosporine. This drug is not meant to be used for arthritic conditions, and clearly it had an adverse reaction on Kirsty. She suffered badly and needlessly by being prescribed this drug, as she did with others.

In UK common law, acceptable standards of clinical care are reached by using responsible customary practices, not guidelines, simply because no two patients are the same. Much thought must be given to each case individually. Kirsty suffered a number of adverse reactions to drugs. Under regulations covering this area, the reactions should have been reported to the Committee on Safety of Medicines, but I doubt if this was the case with Kirsty. The British National Formulary, which is a drug guide that all doctors use, has a yellow card at the back of the book that makes reporting problems a simple procedure to follow.

I do not believe that Kirsty's problems with drugs were ever reported, and as they were so serious, they most certainly should have been.

I heard on a news channel that soldiers fighting in Iraq had to wait for seven hours after being wounded before receiving medical treatment. In a different setting but on the same theme, Kirsty had to wait for thirteen hours before she was admitted to the intensive care unit, where she urgently needed to be, and because of that she died. That is a terribly scandalous situation for any patient to be in. She was also not given antibiotics that had been ordered seven hours previously, even though she was in desperate need. Her treatment was shameful, which is why the ombudsman upheld our complaints. The Trust apologised, but we know that was only because the ombudsman suggested they do so. Hospitals can be very devious when dealing with complaints from the general public, and they are experts at twisting and turning to keep themselves out of trouble; they will usually support each other no matter what.

Kirsty had a most interesting hospital history. In all, she had 101 admissions to different hospitals around the world. The countries involved were England, the United States, France, and Mauritius, so she was well-known internationally, though none of the clinicians from these countries could figure her out.

Countless seminars in many countries have discussed Kirsty's case, and none have been able to give answers to her problems. Every time she had an appointment with her specialists and they could give us no answers, Peggy and I became more and more frustrated. So were the experts. As one of them said to me, "We are the people that are supposed to know, and when we don't, we tend to get pretty angry as well." Kirsty's specialist paediatrician at Great Ormond Street Hospital made the point that "One of the problems with Kirsty is that when we think we are getting somewhere, she presents us with another new problem, and then we are back to square one."

As an example of how baffling Kirsty could be, it was not until seven years after her death that she was given her final diagnosis. The name of this extra syndrome is mentioned later in the book.

Kirsty presented doctors with a new problem on fourteen separate occasions, and when she died, they were no nearer to an answer than they had been.

There must be many children around the world who have problems without any obvious answers, and Peggy and I understand. We sympathise with their plight.

One of the most heartbreaking and sobering sights is to see disabled and terminally ill children interacting and joining in play together. There are no complaints but much laughter. This is where real empathy for others' misfortunes can be found; these children can teach adults how to care about and love each other more.

One of our frustrations with Kirsty is that she grew up with children around her of the same age, but because of her problems lingered behind them in her advancement. As a consequence, those children lost interest in playing with her because she couldn't do the things that they could.

Kirsty's answer was to involve herself with children younger than her. They loved having this older girl interested enough to play with them, and Kirsty could not have been happier.

CHAPTER 16

Peggy and I thought it would be nice to go away together for a break, and so on 12 September 2006, we went to San Diego. This was three years after we buried Kirsty. The main reason for going was because we managed to get tickets to see the internationally acclaimed psychic medium John Edward, a man we had seen many times on television after Kirsty's passing.

We do believe in the afterlife and that people like John are able to connect the bereaved with their departed loved ones, though of course, we have respect for others that do not have these beliefs. I always say to these people if they confront me over this issue, "Only time will tell." When it came time to leave for our trip, we realised that we would not be able to visit Kirsty's grave for two weeks. We knew we would feel guilty about this, but Peggy helped me to get through this by saying, "Don't be upset, because wherever we are, you know that Kirsty will be with us." We went to the cemetery to say good-bye to Kirsty, and then left for Gatwick Airport for the start of our trip.

The flight lasted for fifteen hours overall because we had to make a connection in Dallas to continue our flight to San Diego. The flight was quite enjoyable, though a little tiring. We arrived at San Diego Airport late evening and landed at 9.30 p.m. By the time we cleared customs and immigration and then arrived in a taxi at the resort, it was eleven o'clock, and we were pretty tired.

In San Diego, we stayed at a resort called the Bahia, which was very comfortable and pleasantly staffed by people who could not do enough to make our stay as pleasant as possible. The evening of the day after arriving, we went to the John Edward presentation at the Westin Horton Plaza Hotel, a very old but plush building. John was giving his presentation in the ballroom. We were ushered in and sat in our seats surrounded by four hundred other people, who had also lost loved ones and were praying that they would be brought through for them. When John made his entry into the ballroom, there was silence for a moment, followed by thunderous cheering and clapping; it was obvious how popular he is.

John Edward is a very gentle but rapidly speaking man, and quite the comedian. Within moments, he had everybody engrossed and fully relaxed—well, at least that was how Peggy and I felt. For three hours, John worked extremely hard trying to bring people through, with some success. Unfortunately for us, Kirsty was not one of those that came through, though Peggy agreed with me when I said I felt her presence. We were very happy for those who made contact through John with their departed loved ones.

There were many tears shed that night, ours included, but there were also some radiant faces that belonged to the people that had success.

People we spoke to after the presentation agreed with us that, though we may not have had a reading, it was still a wonderful experience to be part of that presentation.

Before going to San Diego and one year after Kirsty's death, we went for a reading with Carol Bohmer, a well-known medium, and she managed to bring Kirsty through to us. The things she relayed to us from Kirsty were things that only we knew, so we were content to accept her as being a very sincere medium.

One of the messages from Kirsty was to stop feeling guilty for not being with her when she passed away, because there was nothing I could have done that would have changed the outcome. I realise this is so now, but at that time, nothing could have changed my thinking. Even though we were happy with Carol's reading, we felt compelled to be part of the John Edward evening. We are glad we did attend that evening.

We spent the remaining ten days of our trip visiting places of interest in and around San Diego. We visited Old Town, one of the places where western legend Wyatt Earp imposed his will. We often went downtown, where we had many meals and shopped in the open-air mall, a five-story building with escalators to each floor. It would be easy to wander around for hours there.

We visited the zoo, but most of the animals either had their backs to us or would not come out into the open. It was still nice wandering around there and seeing so many tropical birds.

We went to Sea World, one place Kirsty would have loved, since she had seen the original in Florida. She especially would have liked the dolphins and the orca whale.

We also took an excursion into Mexico and visited Tijuana. I have never come across so many beggars on the streets before, including one who was begging at the side of his limousine. We left there in haste and went on to Rosario and Ensenada, and overall we had a very nice day.

The place that made the most impression upon us was Fort Rosecrans Military Reservation, located on a peninsula of San Diego overlooking the bay. It was so sad and yet so peaceful. This place, which had 91,467 internments, is without doubt the largest cemetery I have seen. We were overawed. The cemetery also contains the families of the military personnel interned there, which is such a wonderful gesture by the authorities.

We spent a couple of hours looking and marvelling at this place of tribute to the young men and women who had given their lives for their country.

We missed Tim whilst we were away and also the visiting of Kirsty's grave. This is such an important part of our daily lives now and being unable to do so is quite depressing, so we were looking forward to going home and settling into our routines once more, Peggy going back to work and me trying to find things to do, as I had now been retired for some time.

Eventually we reached the day when it was time to leave San Diego, and then we just wanted to get home. We'd had a really relaxing holiday, but we also knew that there is no place like home.

The flight back to London went smoothly, and it was a relief when we arrived back at Gatwick. We seemed to get through the customs check very quickly and jumped into our car for the final part of the journey home.

Once we arrived home, we went straight to the cemetery to visit Kirsty's garden. Christopher's parents, Diane and Jim, had taken good care of the plot whilst we were away. It was so very neat and tidy, and we felt very grateful to them.

The understanding in the cemetery between friends is that if one family is away, then another will take care of their loved one's plot. This ensures that these areas are tended at all times. With this kind of relationship, you do not have to worry if not at home at any time, but nonetheless we are always grateful.

Every day that Peggy and I tend to Kirsty's garden, we find it hard to believe that we have only that to be able to do for her. It is hard for us because we know that just a little care and common sense could have avoided this.

CHAPTER 17

I BELIEVE THAT THE WORST THINGS IN MEDICINE ARE FOR DOCTORS not to take responsibility for their actions and to fail to render all possible treatment to a patient in need. In the situation they found themselves in with Kirsty, I feel that they broke their sacred promise from the Hippocratic Oath that doctors take upon qualifying. The oath in general is swearing that you will treat to the best of your ability the patients in your care. Sadly this did not happen with Kirsty. I am sure that the doctors responsible for Kirsty's care either did not know the Hippocratic Oath or did not take it; my understanding is that if doctors do not wish to take it, they are not compelled to do so. If it is not compulsory to take the oath, why does it even exist? One of the biggest problems with complaining about the care of loved ones against the health service, apart from the obvious denials that follow, is to successfully complain about the individuals that are directly involved in the care that was so obviously lacking. In Kirsty's case, this was the registrar and his junior, the SHO.

We had successfully had our complaint upheld by the ombudsman but felt that the hands-on individuals that had walked away unscathed should also be investigated for their incompetent and complacent care towards Kirsty. I wrote a letter to the General Medical Council and complained of the poor care by these doctors. In my letter, I informed them that Peggy and I wanted these doctors to face up to their peers and be rapped over the knuckles for providing care that was below a reasonable standard for our daughter. I did not think that was too much to ask.

Peggy and I are not vindictive people and so informed the GMC that we were not demanding the doctors be struck or even suspended, though we did expect them to be disciplined by their peers in one way or another.

I received a reply to my letter from the GMC, in which they agreed to an investigation of their own to determine whether or not the two doctors would face a hearing in front of their Fitness to Practice panel.

Though almost four years had passed since Kirsty's death and the inevitable stress that came with it, Peggy and I remained committed to ensuring that justice is done on her behalf. A number of people have approached me and suggested that I am just wasting my time in trying to find satisfaction in Kirsty's case; they also have said that the system cannot be beaten. This I totally disagree with, because I have great faith in British justice and know that we will be vindicated in our efforts. The people that make such negative statements are those that have never been confronted with the trauma of losing a child.

One of the most notable dates in our memories is 25 June 2007. This is when the hospital paid homage to Kirsty with the honour of having a special room named after her. I believe one of the reasons for this was that there was some guilt over the way that Kirsty was treated on the night that she had died, but the gesture in itself was quite sincere.

The name of the room, inscribed on a nice plaque attached to the door, is "The Kirsty Jayne Pearce Paediatric High Dependency Room". All the doctors and nursing staff attended the room-naming ceremony, as well as the CEO of the hospital, who made a nice dedication to Kirsty. The ceremony was very dignified, and we are grateful that our daughter's name will live on in the place in which she spent such a large part of her life.

After the ceremony, we all went off for tea and biscuits, and this gave us the opportunity to meet up once again with the many doctors and nurses who had cared for Kirsty. There were many tears on that occasion.

That afternoon was very difficult for Peggy because that was the first time that she had returned to the ward since Kirsty's passing. It took an awful lot of courage for Peggy to be there, and I love her deeply for the determination she showed and the dignified manner in which she held herself.

The memories brought back to us were both good and bad. On the one hand, we thought of the fifty-one times that Kirsty needed to be admitted for crisis intervention and was then discharged home on fifty of these occasions. We also thought of the sad fact that she did not come home after the fifty-first admission.

Peggy was very controlled that afternoon, but I knew she was hurting inside.

I was also very sad that day and shed tears that nobody could see, not that it would have mattered to me as I know that Peggy and I had every right to do so.

I don't think that there is any worse feeling than when parents lose a child. You just cannot accept it or indeed get over it; the pain is there every day of your life.

How awful it must be for the mother that loses this beautiful child that she carried for nine months, brought into the world, nurtured for so many years, and then lost her in what appears to be the flicker of an eyelid. No man knows this feeling.

Since Kirsty's passing, Peggy and I have visited her grave twice every day. In the morning, we spend time with her alone, and then in the evening we meet other people there that we have met over the recent years who have also lost their loved ones. We have all become friends simply because of grief.

It is very noticeable how someone who has lost a mother of ninety years and those like us who have lost a daughter of seventeen years have the same feelings of loss over our personal tragedies. Sometimes we can be quite selfish and claim that no one has had to suffer the way we have, though in our hearts we know this is not so.

When losing a loved one, the first inclination is to find out who was to blame, if anybody. In Kirsty's case, everybody was in the firing line because anger overtakes reality and reasoning to a certain degree. After all, we had lost a most precious gift, and so somebody had to be blamed.

Over the following months and years, Peggy and I blamed everybody we could think of. First in the firing line was God. After all, he was supposed to protect our children and not let them suffer for so many years and then cruelly snatch them away from us. What had Kirsty done in her short life that warranted this kind of nastiness? What little faith we had was sorely put to the test.

Next was the Trust, whose procedures we felt were very amateurish. It had no defined caring plan and lacked any form of urgency in caring for sick children.

And then there were the doctors, a registrar that had no idea of the basic skills for leading a team, and a SHO that blindly followed, because he did not know how else to behave.

Junior doctors are notorious for not calling for assistance from senior colleagues when necessary. The reason for this hesitancy is very simple and frightening: in some instances they like to impress their consultants and consequently try to cope in situations that only their seniors can manage. They do not call for help until it is too late, as in the case of Kirsty, who had almost left us—only then did they do the obvious. The ombudsman in his report agreed with this.

It is human nature to place the blame for a tragedy on anyone and everyone, and so all are fair game during the initial period following the death of a loved one. This especially applies to children. When Kirsty passed away, our whole lives were totally disrupted. For me, it meant that I would never again prepare her medicines, take her for appointments, watch soaps with her, go to the shops when she needed something, or have her sitting in the front of the car with me and watch her fiddling the dials for the radio.

Peggy misses doing all the things that mothers do for their daughters, and for Kirsty, this was the normal things, such as bathing and feeding. Most of all, Peggy misses the fun times they had together. The house would be full of their laughter at these times, and it was lovely to hear mother and daughter having such a great time together. How we both wish these times could return.

Sadly there's mostly silence in the house now.

When Peggy is at work, I spend considerable time talking to Kirsty. I know within my heart that she can hear me; she replies in her own inimitable way.

One evening Peggy and I were feeling pretty low, and as usual we asked Kirsty to let us know that she could hear us. We went to bed, and at 2.00 a.m. we were both woken when the television in the lounge came on at full volume. The only reason we could find for this and accept was that Kirsty was telling us she was around. After marvelling at this, we both slept for the rest of the night and felt quite refreshed upon awakening.

After Kirsty left us, many strange things happened with the electronics around the house that could not be explained even by qualified electricians. We now accept that Kirsty is just reminding us that she is still around.

Many people would question our belief that Kirsty is still having such an impact on our lives and suggest that we are imagining things. Most of the people who think this way have yet to lose someone close and so have no idea of what can be. Once this unfortunate occurrence happens to them, I am sure their views will change pretty quickly.

My feeling about death is that when we die, our soul leaves the body and goes on to a better existence. I believe the soul is a type of electrical element and that there is no way this can be destroyed; this may partly explain the electrical phenomena in the house.

I am sure that there are people around that would mock my views, and I would welcome their explanations. I don't believe that I would disregard or disrespect their views.

Since Kirsty's passing, we have read many books by internationally acclaimed psychic mediums, such as John Edward, James Van Praagh, Dr. Jane Greer, and Gordon Smith. Peggy and I agree that no author is any better than the other for relieving the anguish we feel. They are all excellent. After reading the books of these particular authors, I believe it is clear that there is life after death. To acknowledge this is a definitive moment and one that will remain with you forever.

I would recommend the following four books: *Crossing Over* by John Edward; *The Afterlife Connection* by Dr. Jane Greer; *Through My Eyes* by Gordon Smith; and *Reaching to Heaven* by James Van Praagh. They have given me much insight and a better understanding of the afterlife. The books must be read with an open mind, with no preconceived ideas that everything is straightforward in life or death. After reading them, the fears that I had regarding death were much diminished.

All these mediums bring healing to people who can be destroyed by the grief they feel as a result of losing someone special, especially when they realise and accept that their loved ones still exist and have not departed at the point of death. The one thing that these authors have in common is the very powerful belief in life after death and a reconnection to the loved ones at the appropriate time for each person. Peggy and I believe in this very strongly and think that we will all be together again in a far better world than we are at this time.

Peggy and I went to San Diego to see John Edward in the company of many other people, and although we did not get a personal reading felt uplifted and fulfilled by just being part of that gathering. It was a very nice experience.

We did have a personal reading from Carol Bohmer, a respected medium in England, and were amazed at the way she brought Kirsty through to us.

We had not met Carol previously, and she knew nothing about us. We gave her no information about us or Kirsty, but she knew that Kirsty was confined to a wheelchair and that she had a particular problem with her right hip. She also knew about my guilt, which I still cannot lose even though Kirsty tells me that I must do so.

Having the reading with Carol was a wonderful experience, and we went home with a less heavy heart.

The reading was recorded, and so we always have that to listen to if we are feeling low.

We also gained a lot of comfort from the books written by the experts, and the one thing Peggy and I agreed with each other about was that not one was any better than the other for relieving the anguish we felt. They were all excellent.

I would recommend that people read the four books that I have mentioned above; they have given me much insight and a better understanding of the afterlife. The books must be read with an open mind and no preconceived ideas that everything is straightforward in life or indeed death; but after reading them, the fears that I had regarding death were much diminished. All the above books I found to be extremely interesting and most importantly very comforting. I would recommend them to anyone who has an open mind, and indeed those who do not, as I am sure that a few more people would then be very much less skeptical in their thoughts.

The one thing that people must be very careful about is that when searching for a good psychic medium; do not take the first one that comes along. Grief can make you very vulnerable, and many unscrupulous cranks and fakes are ready to take advantage of you. However, there are many honest mediums who will give a reading.

Before going for a reading, allow an appropriate length of time to elapse after the passing of the loved one. Peggy and I found that six months was the right time for us; we were then ready. The six months following the death of a loved one are the most traumatic months of anyone's life. Trying to come to terms with what has happened is extremely difficult. My feelings are that searching for answers from a psychic medium right away at the deepest time of grieving may be too soon after the traumas that have only just passed.

Peggy and I made a mistake with our first foray into psychic medium help. We were looking for comfort, but ended up with a psychotherapist who had advertised herself as a psychic medium and proceeded to instruct us on how to deal with our grief. That was not what we needed at that time.

I remember how one day we were watching John Edward on television. At the end of the program, he was giving words of comfort to his viewing audience and warned his audience about being taken for a ride and given false hopes by people not qualified in the skills of psychic medium interaction. For us, that warning came too late, though since that episode we only go to acclaimed psychic mediums of international fame.

We now listen very carefully to advice given by experts such as John and do not rush into anything to do with his field without thinking. We should have waited for more time to elapse after Kirsty's passing before looking for the answers to all the things we were seeking.

We met Carol Bohmer by sheer luck when trying to book a reading with a very well-known psychic medium by the name of Tony Stockwell. We had seen him on television many times and felt we could be comfortable talking to him. Tony is the complete opposite of John, who is a very rapid narrator. Tony speaks slowly and is precise in his speech.

Though obviously both men take their professions very seriously, they have one thing in common; they both have a certain amount of comedy in their repertoire. This is the method they use to get close to their audience and help them to relax; it certainly worked for Peggy and me.

When we tried to make a booking with Tony, we were informed that there was a waiting time of at least one year, which is not unusual when trying to get a one-to-one reading with somebody of his standing. We were also informed that we could trace our position on the waiting list if we contacted his booking staff monthly.

I did phone a few times to check how things were going and on one occasion was offered the phone number of a psychic medium, Carol Bohmer, who had trained and worked with both Tony Stockwell and Colin Fry, another internationally acclaimed medium we had seen many times on television.

I called Carol, who had been recommended by a member of Tony Stockwell's staff, and was able to get a reading arranged for two weeks ahead. We were a little apprehensive but also excited that there was a chance that Carol could bring Kirsty through for us.

When Peggy and I went for our reading with Carol, about a year had passed since Kirsty's death. We were prepared and had all the questions that we wished answered stored away in our minds.

We went to Carol's house, and she led us into a very nice, neat, and pleasantly lit room. Peggy and I sat facing Carol. I saw a very pleasant and motherly type of lady, with a gentle voice. Peggy and I both felt very much at ease in her company.

For about five minutes, we sat and spoke about things in general, not mentioning the expectations we had of hearing from Kirsty. We spoke mainly about the weather, as one usually does in England.

Eventually Carol said she was ready to start. She almost immediately made contact with my mother. This lasted for about ten minutes, and then I asked Mother to leave us because we really were hoping to hear from Kirsty. My mother did as I asked, and then Carol told us that a young girl was there. She was standing and playing with her long hair, and she said to Carol, "I am very pretty, you know." Peggy and I agreed that she was indeed a very pretty girl; we knew that Kirsty was making contact with us.

Kirsty then told Carol that she was not very happy for not completing her studies here; now she had to return to school where she was. It was true what Kirsty said about her schooling; because of illness, she had missed most of her studies.

Carol then went on to describe Kirsty's funeral, which was attended by about three hundred people. Kirsty told Carol that she was there waving to us but we did not see her. She also described the huge picture of herself and Tim that was placed on her casket. Actually the picture was not that big, but Kirsty being so small herself, it would appear that way to her.

Kirsty told Carol to thank us for everything we had done for her during her time here. I asked her to tell Kirsty that it was a pleasure and we wished we could have cared for her another seventeen years.

Kirsty then gave the number thirteen to Carol, who leaned forward to write it down. As she did so, she said she felt a wheelchair being slid under her and asked if Kirsty had been in this type of chair. We explained to her that Kirsty had been confined to a wheelchair from the age of thirteen. Carol asked if Kirsty had a problem with her right hip, as Kirsty was telling her this was the case. We validated this and explained that Kirsty was due for a right hip replacement at any time but then passed away before it could be carried out.

After about an hour, Kirsty started to pull back, and so we had no choice but to say good-bye to our angel once more. How that hurt! Both Peggy and I had tears running down our faces.

The reading from Carol was very exhilarating for Peggy and me, and the time we spent with her was one of the most beautiful episodes of our lives. What we had hoped for happened, and it made us feel so good to know that Kirsty is in a safer and happier place and nobody can ever hurt her again.

It must be understood that Peggy and I had given Carol no information whatsoever about any member of our family, past or present, and we had not made her acquaintance prior to the reading. She knew nothing about us, so what she told us about Kirsty was truly amazing. The decision to ask for help from a medium is obviously not one to be taken lightly. In our case, it worked very well and gave us much hope for the future. We know that what happened on the night of the reading was meant to be, and we know that Kirsty was the one who guided us down the right path.

People might mock my beliefs about mediums being able to make contact with loved ones that have passed over. That is their choice, and I would never argue with their reasoning. However, it has been about two and a half years since we had that reading from Carol, and we are able to cope much better with Kirsty's passing because of it. Of course, we miss her as much as ever and still cry for her. If we didn't, then that would make us very insensitive.

It is much easier for me to communicate with Kirsty now because I know she can hear me. Even though I cannot see her, I know she is at home with us; this makes our loss easier to deal with.

CHAPTER 18

WHEN DEALING WITH COMPLAINTS ABOUT AN OFFICIAL BODY SUCH as the National Health Service, it is not uncommon to feel that you have hit a brick wall in an effort to find justice. It takes a lot of patience to persevere and not let the official bodies get you down. This can take its toll if you allow it to.

Very few people complain unless there is a reason to do so, but getting this across to the bodies that are being complained about can be time-consuming and tiring. The National Health Service and similar organisations are under the impression that anybody who makes a complaint must be after monetary compensation. This is a misconception.

Many people who have a complaint against a hospital, medical or nursing staff, or a general practitioner, are looking for answers as to why a loved one passed away whilst in their care. In many of these cases, all they are looking for is an explanation and an apology as to what may have gone wrong.

Every week without fail, there is a disaster in a hospital that cannot be accounted for initially, though at the end of the day, it is found to be a breaking of the duty of care by a nurse or doctor.

If you have little understanding of medicine or its practices, most likely you will accept the first explanation you are given regarding the death of someone close. Doing so may help enable a total miscarriage of justice for your loved one.

When Kirsty passed away under such suspicious circumstances, we sat and talked it through to find out what we should do. We decided that we would not sue, as this would not bring our daughter back to us. However, we knew that we had to find out what had gone wrong. We were determined to find the answers, even though it has taken more than seven years to date trying to do so.

When people complain to an official body about its failures or conduct in the treatment of a loved one, especially a child, defence mechanisms of those complained against go into overdrive. Then denials come thick and fast, followed by a total rejection of the complaint as the hospital tries to convince you there never should have been a complaint in the first place. This is when you must dig in your heels and complain even more. For myself, Peggy tells me that I am like a big dog with a bone and don't give up easily.

Peggy and I got tough with the Trust and dug our heels in; there was no way we were going to be treated like idiots. We were determined not to let this one get away, and in the end, it paid dividends; from the point of view of the ombudsman's report, we had somebody on our side at last. Though the ombudsman had supported us in our fight, we knew that there was still a very steep hill to climb ahead in our battle for justice.

It is very important to find the correct way of complaining and the right department to complain to; otherwise, it can end up being a very daunting process and can take many months—and then after all that, perhaps getting nowhere because you did it the wrong way. With complaints against the health service, there is a complaints procedure that you must follow; otherwise, the complaint could be thrown out if their procedures are not followed correctly, and that most certainly would be very traumatic for the bereaved. Fortunately for us, I understood their procedures very well and understood fully where I had to go.

We made our initial complaint to the Trust responsible for Kirsty's care on the night that she died. After getting nowhere fast, we had two meetings with the Trust management. These meetings were a waste of time and got us nowhere. This is fully what I expected, as I quickly realised that the Trust would defend themselves and admit to nothing.

Peggy was very upset and I was very angry, though I did tell her that we had other options and we should expect a long battle with officialdom.

After exhausting our options with the Trust, we decided to complain of our dissatisfaction to the Healthcare Commission. This also turned out to be a waste of our time. By its own admission, the Healthcare Commission's function is to "promote continuous improvements in the quality of the NHS and independent healthcare," but sometimes it does not live up to this function. The Healthcare Commission's stance was to support the Trust and its staff fully; they informed us that they were rejecting our complaint.

We had to find some other organisation that could help us, not because the Healthcare Commission rebuffed our complaint, but because we were adamant that we had a very good reason to disagree with its findings. So we kept going. After all, we had lost a daughter to what can only be described as very poor medical care, and we were determined to get justice on her behalf.

We decided to complain to the health service parliamentary ombudsman about both the Trust for denying our complaint and the Healthcare Commission for supporting the Trust in this denial. The ombudsman's function is to carry out independent investigations into complaints about unfair or improper actions or poor service by government departments and their agencies; this includes the National Health Service.

The ombudsman supported us fully and upheld the serious complaints we had against the hospital, stating that Kirsty's care was below reasonable standard. We knew that standard could not have been much poorer. The process to that point had taken three years, but it had been very worthwhile to persevere the way Peggy and I had done over that time. We will be forever grateful to the ombudsman for providing us with an extremely positive report, though the reality was that we were very far from obtaining the justice for Kirsty that she was entitled to.

Peggy and I were very happy with the ombudsman's finding because, apart from anything else, we knew that changes to training and procedures recommended by him would be an aid to better care for children in the future. Of course, whatever happened, this would not bring Kirsty back to us; that was a thing we could never forget.

The case against the hospital was resolved, or so we thought, but very much later they found themselves back in the firing line. We duly received the apologies over the death of Kirsty three years later than we should have. These apologies were issued only because the ombudsman recommended they should be.

I still remained dissatisfied, though, because as much as the hospital had eventually recognised their failings and apologised for those failings, the main instigators walked away without a stain on their characters.

I decided that the doctors concerned with Kirsty's care on the night she passed away should be brought to task. I was not happy with regard to the way things were left dangling; they still had to answer for their failings. I wrote to the General Medical Council, the regulator of the medical profession.

The purpose of the General Medical Council is to protect, promote, and maintain the health and safety of the community by ensuring proper standards in the practice of medicine. I felt certain that I would get a fair hearing from the Council and would then be in the position of reaching the final closure that we had been seeking for so long. How mistaken can you be?

On 30 November 2006, I wrote to the General Medical Council and made a formal complaint against the two doctors responsible for the care of Kirsty on her final admission. I presented my concerns about the very poor treatment given to Kirsty and the lack of interest shown by the registrar responsible for her care. In my opinion, and that of our family's general practitioner, the registrar had done nothing for Kirsty; he was complacent in the extreme and seemed to give the impression that if he did not look at the problem, it would eventually go away. That is why Mencap called her passing a death by indifference.

I received a reply to my letter within two weeks, in which the Council informed me of the procedures that had to be carried out in order to go forward with my complaint. Before it could consider my complaint, I had to send the Council any documents I had regarding Kirsty's stay and the treatment that she received in the hospital the night she died. Fortunately I had copies of all the medical records for that night. The Council also asked for a copy of the ombudsman's report.

I made copies of all the documents I had and sent them to the General Medical Council, who acknowledged their receipt promptly. The Council sent me forms to sign giving them permission to ask for copies of Kirsty's medical records from the hospital.

Eventually the Council obtained all the necessary documents. I was informed that the two doctors in question would receive a copy of my complaint and be given a chance to comment on the issues I had raised. My understanding is that they did not respond, so the Council then proceeded with its enquiries to see whether there was any basis for my complaints.

I knew that the correct procedure would be adhered to, as this is the only way that fairness could be achieved, not only for Peggy and me but also for the doctors being complained against. Many complaints are filed against doctors every year in England, somewhere in the region of five thousand. Some complaints have substance and others do not, so the General Medical Council has to ensure fairness to both the doctors and the complainants—or so we thought.

The investigations carried out on behalf of the General Medical Council are very thorough and do not favour either side, according to their doctrine. Expert witnesses are used, and special reports are prepared many weeks in advance of any hearing that may take place.

The General Medical Council also alerts the employers of the doctors concerned that they are under investigation. This gives the employers the opportunity of informing the General Medical Council as to whether they have any concerns regarding the doctors' performances.

I received a couple of letters over the next several months informing me that the Council was looking at my complaint, which they claimed they took very seriously.

Then on 17 April 2007, I received another letter from the General Medical Council, informing me that a case examiner would need to instruct an expert to consider the concerns that I had raised. I fully understood this and knew that this would ensure there are no miscarriages of justice on either side.

Later that year, on 17 December, I received another letter from the General Medical Council, informing me that the investigations into Kirsty's death were complete and the case was being prepared for consideration by the Fitness to Practice panel at the General Medical Council offices in Manchester sometime in the future. The Fitness to Practice panel is the body designated to hear all cases against doctors accused of some wrongdoing. There are a number of possible outcomes if a case is decided against a doctor, such as warnings, suspensions, retraining in weak areas, or in severe cases, being struck off the medical register. Both sides in this type of case are given four months to prepare, and so we knew we had some time to wait before a hearing would take place.

We received a further letter in February 2008 from the General Medical Council's investigations officer, informing us that she was responsible for the administrative running of the case against the doctors concerned. She also told us that the General Medical Council had instructed solicitors Field Fisher Waterhouse LLP to act on the Council's behalf. The solicitors that the General Medical Council had instructed are rated the fifth top law firm out of Europe's top fifty, so this was indicative of how seriously this case was being taken—or so we thought.

We were visited at home by Kate Emerson, a very pleasant young assistant from the law firm, and asked to give statements as part of the preparation for the case. This took about three hours, and it was very thorough. I felt so sorry for Peggy, who had to once again go over the events of the terrible night that we lost Kirsty. It was very distressing for her to relive the thirteen hours that she stood by Kirsty's bed watching her life ebb away. We wanted the general public to be aware of Kirsty's story, so that they could be aware of how things can go so drastically wrong when putting their trust in the medical profession; people have the right to know what they are up against when going against officialdom. I do not attempt to tar all doctors by the same brush, but those who do go wrong should be named and shamed. We are obviously extremely happy with the report compiled by the ombudsman, which was placed on her official website. The fact that the report is now in the public domain is a great achievement for Peggy and me.

The publication of such reports also helps people in all walks of life to understand a little more of what the ombudsman can do when needed.

Like a lot of people, Peggy and I knew nothing of the ombudsman's work. We discovered the ombudsman's department as we investigated who might help us. We are so glad we did, because without them we would have been at a loss to know where to turn.

From the time we made our initial complaint to obtaining the ombudsman's investigation report, three years had passed, though it didn't seem that long. By the time the General Medical Council had completed its case, it would be just over five years since Kirsty had passed away.

The case presentation team investigating officer informed me that the press would attend the hearing because it was a high-profile case. Peggy and I would be happy if the press did attend, as long as they printed only the facts of the case. We wanted Kirsty's case to be highlighted to ensure that what happened to her will not happen to another child. We also wanted doctors to be fully aware of the treatments that are open to them when dealing with children and to ensure these recognized treatments are given routinely to the children who need them.

Our intention never has been to destroy anybody's career, but we did expect some gesture and apology from the doctors. We wanted the doctors to be tried by the Fitness to Practice panel; whatever punishment they received would have been justified. Instead, they continue their lives as before; they were never made to answer for their mistakes.

CHAPTER 19

THE DOCTORS RESPONSIBLE FOR KIRSTY'S CARE WERE NOT OPEN to suggestion from Peggy that fateful night that would turn out to be Kirsty's last night alive, even though they were aware that she was a trained nurse and was in a position to perhaps advise on how Kirsty was usually treated when admitted during a crisis. We had seen this many times over seventeen years and were in the position of being able to help.

Doctors do not like to be advised by parents because they always feel under threat, especially more so because we are both trained nurses. Peggy had cared for Kirsty for over seventeen years as her mother and main carer, and so perhaps it would have been wise to have listened to her.

Many doctors find relatives irritating if they try to help in acute situations. They don't like to be put under pressure and hear suggestions made to them that perhaps were obviously sensible and should have been implemented earlier. When Peggy suggested to one doctor that perhaps the introduction of fluids might be appropriate, he was not interested, and so Kirsty became dehydrated. This led to exhaustion and finally to cardiac arrest. The reason she wanted this done was because she felt, quite rightly, that there was a real danger of dehydration, which is what did happen to Kirsty eventually that night. If the doctor had just listened to Peggy, I am sure in my own mind that Kirsty would not have become exhausted and then gone into cardiac arrest. Of course, if he had arranged with the anaesthetist to admit her to the intensive care unit at least twelve hours sooner than he did, then perhaps Kirsty would have been here today; she was a definite candidate for intensive care nursing. I have always claimed that Peggy and I cared for Kirsty over seventeen years and kept her safe; it only took the medical profession thirteen hours of substandard care to lose her.

When anybody is suffering from pulmonary oedema, it is critically important to monitor the fluid balance of the body to ensure that dehydration or overhydration does not occur. This is a tricky balancing act and must be treated very seriously, as both are life-threatening situations.

A good doctor will not allow this to happen, though in Kirsty's case it did.

You often hear the statement, "Trust me, I'm a doctor." After what happened to Kirsty, that is the one thing we will never do again. After all, how can you trust incompetence?

The medical profession does not give enough respect to parents' views regarding their sick children. They must listen more to what is said to them and work as a team with the parents. If they had done that with Kirsty, we are sure she would be here today.

During Kirsty's life, I introduced and maintained what I described as a fact sheet. The idea behind this was that her problems were so complicated and the overall picture so unique that doing this would assist any new doctors meeting her for the first time and make it easier for them to understand what she was all about. Over the years, many people found it a very useful tool for doctors new to Kirsty to use the fact sheet as an aid to help with their own diagnosis when first meeting her. Doctors that used the fact sheet saved a lot of time in treating Kirsty, which in turn helped her to recover more quickly.

The doctor who initially dealt with Kirsty the night she died was advised of the fact sheet in the notes, but did not seem very interested and made no effort to read it. Thus, the normal interaction between parent and doctor did not happen.

It was very clear to Peggy within a short time that the doctor had no idea what he was dealing with when it came to Kirsty's problems. He had never met her before and did not understand the seriousness of her condition. Even at that point, the alarm bells were ringing, but as Peggy was told that the paediatric registrar would come to see Kirsty shortly, she felt that things could only get better. What a mistake that was, because Kirsty's condition from that point onward continued in a downward spiral that could only be described as nothing short of disaster, culminating in the death of our lovely daughter.

It was five hours after Kirsty's admission that the registrar first met her, and by that time she was very poorly indeed.

When a medical profession takes responsibility for a loved one who is very sick, certain feelings automatically emerge. First is the feeling of confidence that things will improve. Then there is the awful thought that things could go wrong and in fact get worse. It is a very thin line between the two.

I have known a few people, including myself, who start praying and ask God to help. Like me, some may not be that religious, but that does not seem to matter when you need help. He could, of course, perform a miracle.

Peggy and I were asking for God's help that night for Kirsty. When it did not happen, then I directed my anger initially at him. God had failed in his duty to protect our daughter. I told him that it was his responsibility, and nothing would sway me from this thought at that time. Much later, and that was at least nine months in the future, I realised that God was not the one who was responsible, but rather the medical team that had forgotten their basic medical skills. When I think back, I realise how lacking I was in my religious beliefs; but since Kirsty's passing, I have come to understand that there is a God and he is all-powerful. I do call him when I need his help, as just about everybody in the world does when needing to, but I also feel guilty when I realise how I have neglected him in the past.

Peggy and I both pray for Kirsty, and in our hearts we know that God hears our prayers and is looking after our daughter as only he can. We feel comfortable with these beliefs; we know she is now safe from harm.

As I have stated previously, when a disaster occurs, those who feel wronged immediately look for the responsible parties and set out to confront them as soon as possible, though in the case of doctors employed by the National Health Service, this is very difficult. The closing of ranks is very obvious, and it happens immediately when a doctor is accused of any wrongdoing; they don't hang around waiting to be hung.

We were unable to talk to the doctors treating Kirsty after she died, and they were not at any of the meetings we attended, another example of closing ranks.

Peggy and I have been battling for seven years in our search for the justice Kirsty is entitled to, and we know this may take much longer for completion; we will never give up in our quest.

CHAPTER 20

BEFORE KIRSTY'S DEATH, I HAD HEARD OF THE DREAMS AND visitations that some people claimed to have had from loved ones who had passed over. At that time, I found these claims difficult to accept. But after my daughter passed over, I gradually found my views changing, and my skepticism waned.

One person who had a big influence on me was the man I consider to be one of the top two psychic mediums in the world, John Edward; the other is Gordon Smith, known throughout the world as "The Psychic Barber". Peggy and I gained great comfort from John and his writings and the many television presentations he starred in. Of course, there was also the trip to San Diego that we embarked on to see him in person, a great and fulfilling experience that we will never forget.

There were three points that John made, three points that I found to be so relevant when dealing with the loss of Kirsty. He suggested we "appreciate, communicate, and validate" (in his book *Crossing Over*) when dealing with loved ones who have passed on. I found this to be the most rewarding and comforting experience of my life. It helped me so much during the many low periods that I had, especially in the early years after losing Kirsty. I am able to cope better now with these feelings when they return, as they sometimes do.

I'd always believed that when people died, they would go on and continue their lifetime experiences on another plain; to me, life continuance after death was a reality, and I will never accept that there is no better place than here on earth. It was not until I read John's book that I began to realise what I really believed in. I know there is a God and that someday we will all meet him; this will be in a better place than where we are at this time.

To me, a dream is where you are talking about your loved one, but only see him from a distance and do not actually speak to that person. A visitation is different; you can actually see your loved one, speak to her, and touch her. The examples below will show what I mean.

Two dreams I've had stand out in my mind. In one, I received a phone call from a hospital telling me that Kirsty had been admitted, but I was not told where the hospital was. When I asked for information, the line went dead. In the second dream, I saw Kirsty in a car, but when I chased after the car and tried to get in with her, the dream ended. On both of these occasions, when waking, I felt upset and robbed; on both occasions, I had tears running down my face.

The visitation situations were totally different, though I was asleep. In the first one, I heard a noise in the kitchen, so I went to investigate. Over by the sink, I could see Kirsty, who appeared happy to see me. As I spoke to her, we started to wander out into the hall; I asked her to come into the lounge. When we reached the staircase adjacent to the lounge, Kirsty said she could not stay but would have to return from where she came. I watched her go up the stairs, and at that point, I awoke with tears streaming down my face.

In the second visitation, I heard a noise in the small bedroom. This is the room that Kirsty told us she wanted to move into once both of her hip replacements were completed. I went into the bedroom and saw Kirsty with another little girl, whom I did not recognise, though I do believe that it was a little girl called Zoë, who had passed away three years prior to Kirsty and was laid to rest near Kirsty. This little girl did not speak, but watched as Kirsty came to me and I put my arms around her. She felt so solid! It was the most beautiful cuddle I have ever felt. After I let Kirsty go, she looked at me, smiled, and told me as before that she had to go. That was when I awoke, again with tears running down my face.

I have dreamt of Kirsty many times since, but these dreams cannot compare with what I call my visitations. They were so special. Peggy has had a number of what she says are visitations from Kirsty and has had a few conversations with her, but they are private to her.

There are many skeptics that would mock what I have written, but of course, that is their right, though eventually I am certain that these experiences will come to them sometime during their lives and then they may find their attitudes changing overnight.

I firmly believe that everyone has the right to their own ideas regarding life continuances after death and I would never try to change these, but by the same token, I would like to think that people respect mine.

It is believed that if you find a white feather in the house, you have been visited by an angel. So it can be understood how happy Peggy was when she found one on the kitchen unit next to the taps. Where the feather came from was a mystery, but as she said, "That is our angel."

Two days ago, Peggy and I were in the local town, and a small white feather floated across my body and landed at her feet. We knew what this signified, as we were talking about Kirsty at the time. That made our day.

There have been so many occurrences that we are unable to account for since Kirsty has passed. We tend to put our own interpretations on these events.

One of the strangest things to happen was at two o'clock one morning when Peggy and I were just about blasted out of our beds when the television in the lounge suddenly came on at full volume. We think that Kirsty was just reminding us that she is around, and that is fine by us.

Many things have happened around the home since Kirsty's passing, but none of them have caused us any concern whatsoever. We believe there is a reason for everything, and we are certain that things will continue to be this way in the future.

There are many photographs of Kirsty around the house, and I always talk to her through these because I know she can hear me. I could never believe otherwise. This is one way I have handled my longing for her since the day she passed.

On occasions, I have been certain of hearing her voice calling me, and each time I have responded. I hope these episodes will continue, for they are comforting and real. Peggy has not had these same experiences, so I believe that her contacts with Kirsty are made in a way that is special to her. Usually if Peggy sees a white feather, she will tell me that Kirsty is sending her a message, and usually it is to tell her not to worry about her now because she is fine. When I hear this, I feel very pleased for her.

We have all shed many tears for Kirsty since her passing, because grieving is never ending and losing her was the most painful experience of our lives. We feel nothing but genuine, deep sympathy for other parents who have had to go through the same situation as ourselves, and although we don't personally know many of them, we feel for them; we understand how they are hurting.

When we lost Kirsty, her death brought home to us just how vulnerable and fragile we really are. We cannot take anything for granted in our world, and common sense tells us that we can only take things as they come, whether they are God's will or not.

As stated previously, I blamed God for what happened to Kirsty, and it was only much later that I realised with hindsight that in her case, it was all because of human failings. We all make mistakes, but sometimes those mistakes can be avoided with care and common-sense thinking.

I think that everybody is aware of the term "guardian angels", and I would guess that most people believe that they are protected by their own. Some people claim to have more than one; if so, then they are very fortunate.

Peggy and I have our own guardian angel in our beloved daughter, Kirsty.

A guardian angel always ensures that you are aware of his or her presence at a pivotal time in your life. This can turn out to be a lifesaving situation. As an example, I would like to share with you what we experienced with our special guardian angel.

A year after Kirsty's passing, Peggy and I were on our way to the cemetery one afternoon. We were in our car, and I was driving. We were on the main road and reached a roundabout that we had to go around to get to the cemetery. We had the right-of-way, so we indicated our intention and commenced the turn. Suddenly a large BMW Saloon shot straight through the roundabout and hit us on the front passenger side. The force was so severe that the front of our car was ripped off in seconds, and we ended up facing the way from which we had come. The amazing result of this was that Peggy, who was sitting as usual in the passenger seat, and I suffered no physical harm whatsoever, though we were badly shaken.

The BMW was driven by a young woman who had her two-year-old daughter sitting on the back seat without any form of restraint. Though she was thrown off the seat by the severity of the crash, she suffered no injury.

Four lives could have been lost in this incident, but Peggy and I believe our guardian angels kept all of us safe.

There have been other, less serious occurrences that we have been protected against. We do know that everyone has their own guardian angel, and they should treasure them; we do.

The people I call the unbelievers would never accept that a guardian angel was looking down upon us the day of our accident. They would call it pure luck that we came out of it unscathed. I would like to believe that our beliefs have been vindicated, and these people with doubts I am sure will meet their guardian angels at the appropriate time. When this happens, I am sure they will thank God for their good fortune. I do not believe that people can go through life without becoming aware that these protective angels exist.

Even though I have belief in the guardian angels, I would never try and indoctrinate others to accept their existence. I do not need to. My understanding of guardian angels is that there is one for each day of the week. They all have specific names and responsibilities. Guardian angels are responsible to archangels; I would call the archangels their managers. The names of the guardian angels, and the duties they perform, are as follows:

> St. Gabriel (Monday), the Special Messenger of God
> St. Raphael (Tuesday), Healer and Guide for the Christian Pilgrim
> St. Uriel (Wednesday), Archangel of Justice
> St. Sealtiel (Thursday), Archangel of Worship and Contemplation
> St. Judiel (Friday), Archangel of Devine Mercy
> St. Barachiel (Saturday), Archangel of Divine Providence
> St. Michael (Sunday), Prince of Heavenly Hosts

I was born on a Monday, Tim was born on a Tuesday, Peggy was born on a Friday, and Kirsty was born on a Saturday, so we are aware of who our official guardian angel is. However, we are a family with a second guardian angel, and that is Kirsty. Of this we are absolutely certain.

As I attempt to put Kirsty's story into print, I see her looking at me from the many photographs around the room I call my study. Every time I look at her, it seems that a further sentence suddenly pops into my head and I am compelled to put it into print. Kirsty seems to give me so much encouragement and appears to give me the push I need when I start to get a little lethargic. It is as though she is the one writing this story, and I do know that I need her help.

CHAPTER 21

MAKING COMPLAINTS AGAINST THE MEDICAL PROFESSION CAN be a very long, drawn-out affair, and as the time passes, you find yourself going over and over again the reasons for the complaints in the first place. At the same time, you are questioning whether you are right in taking actions of this type, and you are trying to figure out what the consequences will be for those being complained about if and when a hearing takes place.

If I were to be honest, I could not care less about what happens to those that failed Kirsty because they continue their lives as before; the main thing is that they answer for their mistakes.

The General Medical Council takes pride in the manner with which they deal with complaints, and they are supposed to make sure they are seen to be fair to both parties. It is not unusual for doctors that have been found guilty of some form of misdemeanour to appeal against the findings in the high court in London.

On 17 December 2007, I received a letter from the General Medical Council informing me that the investigations into Kirsty's death were now complete and the case was being prepared for consideration by the Fitness to Practice panel. This is the body designated to hear all cases against doctors accused of some wrongdoing. There are a number of possible outcomes if things go against the doctor, such as warnings, suspensions, retraining in weak areas, or in severe cases being struck off the medical register.

It is now four years and four months since Kirsty died, and I feel no more forgiving now than when it happened; my contempt for the medical profession is as it was on that awful night. I just cannot forgive the doctors for their errors. Kirsty's death and the way she died cannot be forgotten or forgiven, and I still shed tears every day for my little princess.

Peggy and I comfort each other as necessary and spend a lot of our time with the memories we share of Kirsty. There are so many, lots of them funny and some sad; she is always in our thoughts and prayers.

When I think back, I realise how lacking I was in my religious beliefs; but since Kirsty's passing, I have come to understand that there is a God and he is all powerful. I do call for God's help when I need it, as does everybody else. I also feel guilty when I realise how I have neglected him in the past.

Peggy and I both pray for Kirsty, and in our hearts we know that God hears our prayers, and is looking after our daughter as only he can. We now feel comfortable with our beliefs. We know, as I have said previously, that Kirsty is now safe from harm.

I have explained how many concerns I had over the death of Kirsty and how the health service ombudsman supported us with our fight for justice into the poor service afforded to Kirsty on the night she died. Many changes were made in the hospital procedures pertaining to care for seriously ill children. It was agreed that these procedures should have been in place well before Kirsty's last illness. The expression that comes to mind often is "closing the door after the horse has bolted". I think this is very appropriate in Kirsty's case. The worst thing, of course, was for the Trust not to understand where they went wrong until three years after Kirsty's death—and then it was only after the ombudsman had put pressure on the Trust to do the right thing by Kirsty.

Now that the Trust has set new guidelines for the care of seriously ill children, there are the hope and expectations that these children in the future will be much safer when being cared for in the hospital where our daughter died.

Three years after Kirsty's passing, I was urged by a number of people to stand as a public member of the governing board of the Trust. After a lot of hesitation and soul-searching, I did stand and am happy to say that I was elected. Governors are not responsible for the day-to-day running of the hospital, but they are very influential in policymaking and can make things quite uncomfortable for directors that are responsible for the day-to-day management if they fall short of their responsibilities. After all, these policies relate directly to the quality of patient care.

After receiving the ombudsman's report, I was still not satisfied that my complaint over Kirsty's care had been fully resolved. After all, it is all very well to blame the hospital management when thing go wrong, but what about the people that were responsible for the hands-on care at any given time?

It struck me that the real people responsible for Kirsty's dilemma were not the management, but the doctors and nurses on duty that night. I knew that I had to go on and ensure that all areas of the complaint were dealt with. I am so glad that I did carry on fighting because if I hadn't, at some stage in the future, I would have known I had let Kirsty down.

I knew that the governing body for doctors in the United Kingdom was the General Medical Council, and so I decided to write to them and complain about the poor medical care given to my daughter by one of their own.

When making complaints about the medical care in my country, there is always the worry that a cover-up will be attempted to safeguard the interests (as in this case) of the people charged with the responsibilities and ultimately the safety of a very sick child. I had this worry about the complaint I made to the ombudsman after the Trust, followed by the Healthcare Commission, had ruled against my complaint to them. At one stage, I felt that I was just wasting my time, but this was ultimately proven to be an unnecessary concern as the ombudsman ruled in our favour against them both.

I contacted the General Medical Council by letter on 30 November 2006, presenting them with my concerns about the very poor treatment given to Kirsty the night she died and the lack of interest shown by the registrar responsible for her care. I felt that he was complacent in the extreme and thought that if he did not look at the problem, it would eventually go away, which of course it did not; quite the opposite happened, because it got worse as the night wore on.

The General Medical Council, who are there to regulate doctors and also to ensure good medical practice, are a very proud body, whose intentions are to ensure first-class care throughout any illness their doctors are confronted with. They do not look very kindly on poor medical practices, and any doctor that disregards this doctrine does so at his or her peril. Unfortunately for us, the General Medical Council failed to live up to its promises or reputation; they let us down badly.

The General Medical Council replied one week later and explained that before they could consider my complaint, they needed me to send them any documents I had regarding Kirsty's stay and treatment that she received in the hospital the night she died. They also asked for a copy of the ombudsman's report to be sent.

I made copies of all the documents I had and sent them to the General Medical Council's investigation department, who acknowledged their receipt promptly and at the same time sent me forms to sign giving them permission to ask for copies of Kirsty's medical records from the hospital.

Eventually all the documents were obtained by the General Medical Council, and they informed me that they would be providing the two doctors concerned with a copy of my complaint and giving them a chance to comment on the issues I had raised. The doctors thus were given the chance to respond if they so wished. My understanding was that they did not respond, and so the General Medical Council then proceeded with their enquiries to see whether or not there was any basis for my complaints.

There are many complaints against doctors every year, and some have substance and others do not, so the General Medical Council has to ensure fairness to the doctors and the complainant.

The investigations carried out on behalf of the General Medical Council are very thorough and do not favour either side. Expert witnesses are used, and special reports are prepared many weeks in advance of any hearing that may take place. No chances are taken on a miscarriage of justice occurring—or so they say.

The General Medical Council also has the policy of alerting the employers of the doctors concerned that they are under investigation. This gives the employers the opportunity of informing the General Medical Council's investigators as to whether they have any concerns regarding the doctors' performances. The whole business is very open and fair to all parties—sometimes.

In August the General Medical Council wrote to inform me that the investigation was complete and the papers were to be passed to the case examiners for a decision whether to proceed with the case or not.

In January 2008 I was informed that the case examiners had made their decision regarding the doctor's hearing, and had decided to refer him to a public hearing by a "Fitness to Practice" panel at the General Medical Council's offices in Manchester sometime in the future.

Both sides in this type of case are given four months to prepare, so we knew we had some time to wait before a hearing would take place.

We received a further letter in February 2008 from the General Medical Council's investigations officer, informing us that she was responsible for the administrative running of the case against the doctor concerned. At the same time, she told us that the General Medical Council had instructed solicitors Field Fisher Waterhouse LLP to act on their behalf.

The solicitors that the General Medical Council instructed are rated the fifth top law firm out of Europe's top fifty, so this was indicative of how seriously this case was being taken—or so we thought.

We were visited at home by Kate, a very pleasant young assistant from the law firm, and asked to give statements as part of the preparation for the case. This took about three hours, and it was very thorough. At this time I felt so sorry for Peggy, who had to once again go over the events of the terrible night that we lost Kirsty. It was very distressing for her to relive the thirteen hours that she stood by Kirsty's bed watching her life ebb away; I had great sympathy and admiration for her as she coped in a very difficult and heartbreaking situation.

Over the years, I have shed many tears for Kirsty, but not being a mother, I had no real understanding of the anguish that Peggy was going through. I do know that she is still suffering as much now as she did that awful night. One thing we do share in common, however, is the feeling of utter contempt for the doctor that was supposed to care for Kirsty.

On 14 March 2008, I received a letter from the parliamentary and health service ombudsman's department in London, informing us that from time to time, the ombudsman publishes digests of anonymised case summaries and also includes such summaries in its annual report; those publications also appear on the ombudsman's website. Apparently the intention of such publications is to share learning from their casework and to generate a greater understanding about their work in general and its impact on individuals and public services.

The ombudsman asked whether or not Peggy or I would have any objections if they wished to include an anonymised summary of the investigation report that was sent to us on behalf of Kirsty on 7 September 2006 in one of their publications. We very quickly informed the ombudsman that we were more than happy for them to use Kirsty's report and would look forward to seeing it on the website.

Our feelings with regard to Kirsty's story being placed into the public domain were that the general public should be made aware of how things can go so drastically wrong when putting your trust in the medical profession. I do not attempt to tar all doctors by the same brush, but those who do go wrong should be named and shamed. That is all we can now do for Kirsty. Also, the publication of such reports helps all walks of life to understand a little more of what the ombudsman can do when needed.

Like a lot of people, Peggy and I knew nothing of their work and, like many others, only found out by investigating as to who might help us. We are so glad we did, because without them we would have been completely at a loss to know where to turn.

The only way to reach the ombudsman and seek their help is to go through the formal complaints procedures. Once you have exhausted those channels, such as we did with the National Health Service and the Healthcare Commission, you can then send your appeal to the ombudsman. As we discovered, this can be very time-consuming.

From the time we made our initial complaint until we obtained the ombudsman's investigation report took three years, a lot of patience, and certainly a lot of resilience. This entire process greatly increased the stress that we had already been under for such a long time.

By the time the General Medical Council completed their case, it would be just over five years since Kirsty passed away.

The case presentation team investigating officer eventually spoke to me by phone and informed me that the press was sure to be present at the hearing. I understood this because they attend high-profile cases, and Kirsty, if nothing else, most certainly was that. The officer also informed me that we would need to discuss the press situation on a date nearer the hearing.

As far as Peggy and I were concerned, we were quite happy if the press attended, so long as they only printed the facts of the case. We would have liked Kirsty's case to be highlighted, if only to ensure that what happened to her possibly may not happen again to another child. We wanted doctors to be fully aware of the treatments that are open to them and ensure these recognized treatments are given routinely to the children that need them.

One of the things that amazed us was to discover that a sick child like Kirsty could be cared for by doctors that provide emergency out-of-hours paediatric care and yet may not have the required accreditation in advanced paediatric life support (APLS) and also by nurses that did not have accreditation in APLS and NPLS (neonatal paediatric life support). Of course, that should not have been the case, and this problem should never have arisen. It is quite amazing how shoddy workmanship can encroach into such an important area as children's care, but of course it does happen.

My own feelings about the accreditation issues are that these skills should be part of doctors' and nurses' basic training, and then perhaps there would be fewer instances of mistakes being made in the care of very sick children like Kirsty.

The medical and nursing staff in paediatrics at the hospital where our daughter died are having to acquire their accreditation in APLS and NPLS. This was one of the vital areas that the ombudsman recommended should be tightened up quickly. It is hoped that now children will have the benefit of well-trained nursing and medical staff. Perhaps the children there will be much safer in the future. I know this is too late for Kirsty, but it will benefit all the other children that follow her. She will be happy about that.

As a governor of the Trust, I go to the hospital regularly to attend meetings and observe what is going on. If I see anything that needs addressing, then I do just that. The paediatric wards are my first ports of call, and I am always received pleasantly and professionally.

Hospitals are terribly daunting places for young children, especially when they need to be admitted, so it's important that the wards are made as pleasant and welcoming as possible. Pictures of Disney characters are hung in the hospital where Kirsty stayed on many occasions, and there are plenty of these to be seen on the ward that was Kirsty's home so many times. Parents are encouraged to stay with their children as long as they wish. Many of them stay overnight, and this helps in the settling-in process.

Whenever Kirsty was hospitalized, Peggy stayed with her overnight, and then I would take over during the day. This is what we did for over seventeen years, which amounted to a lot of time spent there. Kirsty had just over one hundred admissions between Great Ormond Street and Basildon hospitals. I also dispensed all medications for Kirsty, other than drips when she was in the hospital. Kirsty's drugs on the ward were in a locked cupboard, to which only I had the key. This special dispensation was given because I was a registered nurse. The nurses did not need to medicate Kirsty, as I ensured that she was medicated at the correct time. Kirsty had to take fourteen different medicines each day, so perhaps the nurses on the wards thought I was a godsend because they were saved quite of lot of pill-popping. I know that they were happy with that.

The nursing staff had very little to do with Kirsty, as Peggy and I handled all bathing, feeding, bed-changing, medicine dispensing, and toileting. Peggy also brought to the hospital food cooked at home, as Kirsty loved her mum's home cooking; she was never able to cope with hospital food. Kirsty's needs were catered for by her family, and this made it easy for the ward staff. The staff did not complain because they knew that Kirsty was in the best hands possible. We knew that too.

CHAPTER 22

Kirsty's family and friends all continue to suffer over her death, especially as we know this need not have happened; had a little more thought and care been given to her problems the night she died, then she may in all probability have survived. This has made us all very bitter.

One person Kirsty loved to see when in the hospital was her brother Tim, who worked as an IT analyst in the same hospital. It was very easy for him to visit her, as he was on site all day. When Kirsty died, Tim found it was impossible to continue working in the hospital where she had passed away; it caused him much pain, so he left and joined a company in London.

Tim is a very sensitive young man and remains very upset over what occurred on the night he lost his sister. He is twenty-five years old now and still sheds tears over Kirsty's death. At times he says to me, "Why, Dad, how come this happened to Kirsty?" He knew they should have saved her. I was unable to give Tim an answer because I didn't know myself.

Tim is beginning to get some order into his life. He was helped tremendously by his then-girlfriend Aimee. She was a great comfort to him, and fortunately Kirsty was able to get to know her for a short time prior to her death. Tim and Aimee have since split up, and he now has a new girlfriend, who presented him with a beautiful son. They named him Owen David Charles. Kirsty would have loved him.

Peggy and I believe that Kirsty knew that something would happen to her because of two remarks she passed prior to her death. She said to Peggy one day, "When I see my granny, I must thank her for giving me such a lovely mum." Peggy's mother had never met Kirsty, as she had died many years before her birth.

And when Kirsty first met Aimee, she was not too happy at the thought of Tim possibly marrying her. She said, "If it happens, it will be over my dead body." However, a few days before she died, Kirsty changed her mind, saying, "If Tim and Aimee do get married, they have my blessing."

These two thoughts of Kirsty's are very poignant and reinforce our belief that she was more in control of her own destiny than we could possibly imagine. It was a tough final journey for her, but she took it with courage and as much dignity as she could. We are extremely proud of her and will forever hold her close to our hearts.

Peggy misses her little girl as only a mother can and shows it every day in the tears she sheds. I miss her also, but obviously in a different way than her mum. After all, her little body was carried by her mother for nine months, and to lose her in such a cruel way was totally devastating and would leave a scar that could not possibly heal. I am heartbroken for her.

I had never given much thought to the possibility of there being an afterlife, and so consequently very rarely did I ever get drawn into discussions on this topic. I think I was almost a skeptic inasmuch as my view was that people had the right to believe in whatsoever and whomsoever they wished; nothing had been proven to me that would support the theory of an afterlife.

Things started to change for me when Peggy was reading a book entitled *Crossing Over* by a very well-known American psychic medium by the name of John Edward. I had heard of him but had read none of his books, nor had I seen any of his TV presentations that were on every night in England. When Peggy finished the book, she suggested that I try it because she thought I would find comfort in it.

At this time, we had actually just begun to start watching John's presentation on TV, and I found myself hooked on what was being shown and suggested by this very pleasant funny man. At that time I realized that the humour was what I would call his "settling tool" for relaxing his audience at the start of each show. It most certainly worked for us.

I started to read *Crossing Over* and became totally engrossed by its content. This, coupled with the TV presentations, started to give me the comfort that Peggy spoke of.

In September 2006 we found out that John would be appearing at a hotel in San Diego. We thought that as we had never had a break since Kirsty's death, we could kill two birds with one stone: see John and have a holiday at the same time.

I booked the holiday and purchased the tickets for the show in April. We impatiently waited for September to arrive, which it duly did though somewhat slowly. We left England, which was quite miserable weatherwise, and happily flew off to San Diego.

Because the flight was late, our journey became seventeen hours instead of fourteen, which meant that we arrived midevening. Dusk had fallen, but we soon forgot about the lateness when we saw San Diego so beautifully ablaze with thousands of lights. It really was a lovely sight.

We stayed at a resort called the Bahia, which was very comfortable and pleasantly staffed by people that just could not do enough to make our stay as pleasant as possible.

We went to the John Edward presentation at a hotel in downtown San Diego called the Westin Horton Plaza, which was a very plush, old, grand-looking building. Once there, we proceeded to the ballroom where the event was being held and were totally mesmerized by this charming, confident medium.

Although we did not get read by John that night, it was still a tremendous occasion that we felt had been very worthwhile attending.

After the presentation was finished, I remember saying to Peggy that any skepticism I'd had was now a distant memory and that I did accept there is an afterlife. As I said at Kirsty's funeral, "We will meet again." Of that I am certain.

After returning from our holiday, we were fortunate enough to win a private reading by the United Kingdom's best psychic medium, Gordon Smith. He is known throughout the world as "the psychic barber", though I am not sure that he cuts much hair these days.

The reading with Gordon was absolutely fantastic and just increased my belief in the afterlife. As I said previously, he did connect us with our beloved Kirsty; I will leave it at that. All I can say and Peggy agrees is that it was the most wonderful experience of our lives and we would love to go through the same thing once more.

When Peggy and I returned home, we talked about the meeting we'd had with Gordon and agreed that it was predetermined and most certainly by Kirsty herself. Our beliefs in the afterlife had really firmed, and we are now stronger converts than ever.

CHAPTER 23

O N 3 APRIL 2008, KATE FROM THE LAW FIRM CONTACTED ME TO say that all investigations were now complete by the General Medical Council and that a barrister named Christopher Kennedy of Manchester had been given instruction to handle the case against the doctors on our behalf. I was curious as to his skills and upon checking, found out he was a very tough and tenacious lawyer. This gave us a lot of comfort and confidence in his ability to represent us in this case. Of course, in the end, this came to absolutely nothing.

I was concerned that Kirsty's story be told accurately, so I contacted the General Medical Council and asked whether or not I would be allowed to see their experts' report about Kirsty's case and the transcripts of the actual hearing, once finished. I was informed that this would be allowed once the hearing had ended.

I was very pleased at the General Medical Council's attitude to my request, mainly because it is central to my story. Much later I was proven to be overoptimistic in believing that the council would be fair to us in any way. We misguidedly thought that the council was open in its dealings with complainants, which is not the case with most official bodies that I have fought against over the last four years.

Kate informed me that the registrar would be given all copies of evidence in the case and time to prepare his defence. The actual charges would then be set by counsel.

Peggy and I have found that the years since Kirsty's death have been the most stressful period of our lives, and the pain has never diminished; the telling of her story is very hard, though I know it has to be done.

The reason for our actions against the registrar was not a simple matter of revenge, though we are and always will be extremely angry. Our main purpose is our hope that the events that occurred with Kirsty on the night she died will never be repeated. Perhaps in a small way, this book will help to make a difference.

I believe that some doctors think that they are experts in their field, when in fact they are not; they are on a constant learning curve and quite often lack the experience required in dealing with very difficult and complex cases. Instead of seeking help when needed from a better qualified and more experienced colleague, they continue to go blindly ahead with very poor offerings of substandard medical care. That is exactly what happened in the case of Kirsty. It would only have taken one or two sensible decisions in her treatment to have saved her, and I am certain that if this had been done, she would be home in the care of her family today.

There is an expression probably known to all, and that is "Never count your chickens before they are hatched." This means, of course, that taking things for granted is bad policy, and we found this out to our cost. The following is a prime example. After having been informed that a nine-day hearing in front of the Fitness to Practice panel would be held at the General Medical Council's offices in Manchester on 22 September 2008, we were then hit with the bombshell on 20 May that the hearing was being considered for cancellation, because legal counsel for the General Medical Council did not believe there was a realistic chance of obtaining a conviction against the doctor responsible for Kirsty's care. Counsel stated that "although the doctor's conduct fell short of what was expected of him, and could be described as negligent, the investigating doctor was not prepared to characterize that negligence as sufficiently grave to justify a charge of misconduct."

It appeared to Peggy and me that the fact Kirsty had died because of this "negligence" was of no consequence to those who were there to protect her, those charged with the responsibility of ensuring that the medical profession honoured its obligations in providing the best care possible. We know that the registrar broke his duty of care toward our daughter, and we also knew that once the medical profession closed ranks over an issue such as this, we would have an almighty fight on our hands to obtain justice for Kirsty. I vowed that no matter what adversaries we confronted, the fight would go on. Nothing would deter me in my determination to obtain the justice to which Kirsty was entitled.

The case was then considered by a member of the investigation committee on appeal from Peggy and me in order to make a final decision on whether it should go forward. We knew this would be a lost cause because, since the investigating doctor was a member of the General Medical Council himself, it was hard to believe that he would come to any decision other than that requested by his fellow medical professionals. In addition, we figured the General Medical Council would not want the media involved. It can be very embarrassing for any official body, such as the General Medical Council, to be hounded by the press, but sometimes that is all those fighting for justice can do. If I have to look for media involvement, I would not hesitate.

Sure enough, on 29 July 2008, I received a letter from the council that the investigating committee member had decided that the case against the doctor should be abandoned. This to me and Peggy was nothing more than a blatant attempt to cover up the truth.

One statement the General Medical Council sent out was that Peggy and I would have been devastated had the case gone to a hearing and we had lost.

I do not believe for one instant that this would have been the case. This was a very poor assumption on the legal counsel's part and was nothing more than an attempt to put the General Medical Council in a better light and give the impression that it cared. After what we had gone through and the fights we'd already had with various different organizations and the obvious wheeling and dealing going on in the background, we had become tough, and we just wanted the doctor to face his accusers and take responsibility for his actions on the night Kirsty died. I believe that we will persevere longer than those against us.

Originally the General Medical Council had informed us that the press would be at the proposed hearing and nearer the date originally booked, they would discuss this with us. This may still happen in the future, but then I will deal with the press on my terms.

As can be imagined, we could not believe that the General Medical Council would be so callous as to dangle a carrot in front of us and then cruelly snatch it away. Once again, I have come to realise that governmental and other departments within the so-called system only work for themselves; it is up to the individuals involved with them to fight like hell to obtain any form of fairness and justice. Peggy and I had an advantage over other private citizens because, as trained nurses for many years, we knew where the doctors had failed and were able to challenge them at the clinical level. Something that most doctors do not like is being proven wrong by a nurse—it is a very hard pill for them to swallow.

Once the decision had been made to abandon the hearing, we had to decide where to go from there. The one thing I was sure of was that

I would not give up the fight, no matter how long it took, and I was determined to explore every avenue open to me. My next step was to write to the professor who made the decision to cancel the hearing, to tell him why he had done the wrong thing and why he should change his decision. I also sent letters to the president and chief executive of the General Medical Council and asked them to intervene, but there was no response; obviously they were not interested in allowing this problem to linger any longer than necessary.

When I called the General Medical Council to try and find out what the situation was, I was informed that it was inappropriate for the president or the chief executive to respond to me in person. This was the same response I received when I wrote to the minister of health and the prime minister. Nobody was prepared to get involved in a situation that was not of any benefit to them.

So I called the General Medical Council again and asked to speak to someone about my daughter. This time I was able to get the assistant director of investigations to call me back. I told her that I wanted a meeting at the General Medical Council's offices in London to discuss my daughter's death. She was not keen on this until I told her that failure to grant me this request meant that I would tell my story to the press and on national television.

Once I had made my threat, she totally capitulated and said we could meet in London at a date suitable to both parties. Two days later, we arranged the meeting for 22 September 2008, the same date as the promised hearing that should have taken place in Manchester.

When I spoke to the assistant director, she stressed that she would not be visiting the decision made for the cancelling of the original hearing with the Fitness to Practice panel. I made every effort I could to make her change her mind. I asked whether she had a medical background, and she confirmed that she did not. I then suggested that she should have a doctor sit in at the meeting so at least someone on their side would have an understanding of the medical procedures that Kirsty should have received but failed to get.

I knew that all my suggestions were going to be ignored. She replied that it was not necessary, and that she was sure the meeting would be useful. I could not believe that she would attempt to be any fairer than her colleagues in Manchester, and I felt this might turn out to be a pointless exercise. We would just have to wait and see.

My concern was trying to figure out how one day there are grounds for a hearing scheduled to last for nine days in front of the Fitness to Practice panel because of our concerns and those of the General Medical Council, but then out of the blue the hearing was to be abandoned. To us it really did not make sense that any doctor could be classed as "negligent" over the death of a child, but "not negligent enough" to face his peers. This was totally beyond the belief of Peggy and myself.

When we went to the meeting in London, Peggy and I would be fighting as hard as we could in Kirsty's honour, equally as hard as we had done over the past four and a half years, because until we get justice, we shall be unable to find closure. We need Kirsty to know that we fought as hard as possible for her, and we know she would approve of all our efforts on her behalf. I can hear her saying now, as she used to, "Kick butt, Dad," and so I must try to do so for her.

CHAPTER 24

As I have mentioned, we were able to meet the family of Christopher, the young man who died six months prior to Kirsty's passing. He was aged twenty when he was killed in a road accident. We have remained firm friends with his family. Diane, his mother, composed the following, which she has agreed should be in my book. I am very happy to do this.

Life After the Loss of a Child

What is it like to lose a son, a daughter, a child? Well, I'll tell you, my friend, because there but for the grace of God go I, go you, go us. Your life changes beyond recognition. No longer is there fun, laughter, hope, and ambition. You go through each day, just to get over another day of pain, longing, sadness, anger, and frustration.

Why me? Why my child? Is it something I've done? Am I being punished? This keeps going round and round in your head. You're haunted; you're a shell of the person you were before. And yet, people see you out and about, they see you smile, they see you acting so-called normal (whatever *normal* is supposed to mean). "How are you?" they ask, and you reply, "I'm fine, thanks." You can actually see the relief on their faces when they realise you are not going to get too heavy. In fact, what you want to say is, "Do you really want to know how I feel? Do you really? Well, I feel like crap, I feel my life is over, I feel that I am just biding my time here on earth waiting for my death so that I can be with my child again, so I can finally be at peace." Of course, you cannot say any of that, but that is what is in your heart.

Another emotion you feel is guilt. "Guilt?" you ask. Well, the guilt is the feeling you get for the rest of your family, because you can no longer give them 100 per cent. This part of you, this overwhelming part of you, is just not there anymore. You know deep down they understand this, but at the same time they must think, *Mum, what about me? I'm still here. You still have me.* And this is where it's hard, because it's like you have a leg in both camps, earth and heaven. Half of you wants to die and be with your child, but the other half does not want to leave the others. (Don't forget that they have lost their sibling and are also grieving.) In your head, the thought comes, *Haven't they been through enough too?* To lose you as well would devastate them, so hence the guilt.

I always say now that everything in life will be bittersweet. Sweet because there will be weddings, births, holidays, and many other occasions when all should be happy and excited, and yes, you will feel some of these emotions. But always and forever will be this feeling and knowledge that your child is not there. You look around for that one face, and it is missing. You see all your family with their children, and you no longer have yours. How do you ever get over this? Well, you won't. Never, never, never, and that is as good as it can ever get.

When people say to me that time is a healer, they really have no idea how useless those words are. They offer no comfort whatsoever, because time does not heal, not when you have lost your child. You should never outlive that child.

I have been told many times that I should move on. What exactly that means I will never understand. How can you move on when you have lost such a very special person in your life? My son/daughter are my past, my present, and definitely my future.

I know that Diane was in deep mourning when she composed the above, and she shed many tears when she was actually writing her piece. It was certainly worth the effort. I found it to be poignant and realistic in its message to those who have not lost their dear children. None of us will ever get over losing a child, and the only thing that keeps us going is the certainty that that day will come when we are all together again. But before that happens, we have to get on with our lives in the best manner possible. We will not forget those we have lost, but will cherish those memories.

My way of coping is to talk to Kirsty every day. I know she can hear me, and this gives me great comfort.

The number of sick children I have met during my nursing career runs into the thousands, and every one of them is full of courage and bravery; this of course includes my own daughter, Kirsty. Another thing I admire about these children is the empathy they have for each other; they are truly wonderful examples of what the world should be all about. God bless them all.

CHAPTER 25

T HE TWENTY-SECOND OF SEPTEMBER ARRIVED, AND PEGGY AND
I set off for our meeting with the General Medical Council, who
were being represented by an assistant director of investigations and the
manager of case presentations.

When we arrived at the offices of the Council, we were ushered into
the lift, taken two floors up to the administrative floor, and guided into an
office, where we were introduced to the people who were there to conduct
the meeting.

The first thing we were told after the usual introductions was that tea
and food were on their way. We informed them that we were not there
to attend a tea party but to seek justice for the mismanagement of our
daughter's medical care at the hands of a negligent doctor, who appeared
to be getting away with what I called "blue murder."

Blue murder is an expression that is widely used in the English language;
it can refer to a number of different interpretations. The meaning in this
instance was to escape punishment for, or detection of, a blameworthy
act. The expression is considered to be slang and is widely used in the true
cockney (London) language. Being a cockney myself, that is, someone
born within the sound of Bow bells, meant that I could quite casually use
that term in everyday life when necessary.

It was obvious from the onset of the meeting that they felt this was just
a blip in their daily routine. I don't believe that I have ever met two more
insignificant people in my life. They had brought no records with them
of Kirsty's case, made no notes, and seemed disinterested in what we had
to say. When I suggested that a recording be made of the meeting, they
said it was not necessary, and then they asked why I thought this should
be. I explained that this meeting should be on record as part of the official
and very serious investigation into Kirsty's death. When I requested that
a doctor be present for the meeting, they again refused but asked my
reasons. Slowly, and through gritted teeth, I reminded them that they by
their own admission knew nothing of medical matters, so somebody was

needed who could understand and discuss my complaints regarding the clinical failures in the care of Kirsty.

My patience with these people was quickly vanishing. I felt like banging their heads together, because Peggy and I were becoming very frustrated over their obvious disinterest with what was going on.

On at least two occasions whilst I was trying to talk to these people, the door to the office we were in flew open, and a flunky bearing more food, fruit, and drink strolled in, even though we had not touched the previous offerings. This was more like attending a garden party than an investigative meeting. Once again we declined.

The whole situation was becoming nothing more than a farce. I was extremely angry at this point.

We had been there for about twenty minutes and felt we were not getting through to these people. I informed them that the official report following the investigation into my daughter's death stated that the registrar was negligent and broke his duty of care to Kirsty. However, they informed us that his negligence was not serious enough to warrant a hearing in front of the Fitness to Practice panel and did not make him a threat when practicing in the future.

When I officially complained to the General Medical Council about the substandard care given to Kirsty on the night she died and included the full support of the ombudsman in his lengthy report, I assumed that these doctors would have to face their peers. I was totally shocked when the General Medical Council refused us the hearing; I just could not believe that they could be so immoral and unjust.

I could not believe that both doctors involved in Kirsty's care would not be held accountable for their actions (or rather, lack of them) the night Kirsty died. The attitude of the people we were meeting with brought Peggy to tears and made me all the more angry over what I felt was an attempt to close ranks in the medical profession, which is normal and routine in England. These two people were very cold fish and most certainly did not share our concerns over the poor care Kirsty received the night she passed away.

The General Medical Council appears to be a law unto itself. At that meeting, we were told that they were not there to punish doctors but to ensure that they did not pose a threat in the future. When I asked them to expand upon this, I was told that criteria for their rules were set in parliament and there was nothing they could do in cases such as Kirsty's unless those criteria were amended. It is appalling to think that many other cases like Kirsty's are dealt with in this manner. There must be thousands of parents like Peggy and me who cannot move on if they lose a child, do not understand the very complex systems in this country, or hit a brick wall at their every turn. We at least are able to fight this corrupt situation because of our knowledge of medical matters. It does not mean that it is any easier for us than other people that may be unfortunate enough to find themselves in our situation.

There were more than five thousand complaints in 2007 that the General Medical Council received about failures by the medical profession. I cannot believe that many of these ended successfully for those who lost a dear family member to negligence.

The meeting dragged on for fifty minutes, and it was obvious that we were not making any progress. Peggy was still very upset at the stubborn refusal of these people to accept the wrongdoing done by a member of the medical profession. We decided to leave, because it was pointless to continue talking to people who had no insight or concern into Kirsty's demise.

I was so upset by the procedures that morning. The people with whom we met were unprofessional in the manner with which they had conducted the meeting. I told them that, like the general public, we considered the General Medical Council to be a joke. Instead of having patients' interests at heart, they made it abundantly clear by their actions that they looked after themselves and their members first, and the general public came nowhere for any kind of consideration.

Before we left, I handed over a letter of complaint against the professor and consultant responsible for the drawing up of the report on Kirsty, which I knew contained obvious flaws. Getting the General Medical Council to acknowledge these would probably be a waste of time, though I had to try. Like a drowning man, I was just clutching at straws.

I told them on leaving their office that I was born in London and that I thought I had met all the artful dodgers as in *Oliver Twist* who had ever existed, but then I met the General Medical Council and they were by far the most artful of the lot.

We left the building. The air outside was so much sweeter, and the sun was out. To say that we were glad to be outside is an understatement, and even the general public appeared more pleasant than those we had just left.

On reflection, Peggy and I felt that the most infuriating thing about the meeting was the sheer fact that they did not understand a thing we were saying, but in the main, just sat nodding their heads. This reminded me of the little model dogs that people have in the back windows of their cars, which are about as useful.

Peggy and I went to catch our train home. We were quite subdued because we had expected something positive from the meeting; we were both deep in our own thoughts.

When we arrived home, we sat and had a good chat about the events of the day. Once we'd had a cup of tea, which is a cure for almost anything in England, we decided on our next move.

I knew that since I had submitted a written complaint about the investigators of the General Medical Council and their flawed report, somebody else would have to review the whole case. There was a chance that person could agree with us.

We were not complaining for the sake of being pests or just trying to cause trouble. We knew things went badly wrong the night Kirsty died, and we were determined to make somebody listen.

A week passed, and then we received a letter from the General Medical Council informing us the complaint about the report had been received and would be dealt with as soon as possible. Since the complaint was against two people, they would deal with them individually. That was fine with us as long as it was a correct and proper review.

I would have been very surprised if anything came of my latest complaint because I could not see officers of the Council going against each other, though I would have loved to be proven wrong. We knew it would be a hell of a battle to change things that are so set in stone, as had been proven by the stubbornness of the General Medical Council, but we would not cede the battle easily.

I often wonder if other people are as dogmatic as myself. Was I being unreasonable in my demands of the General Medical Council? Somehow, I don't think so. Fortunately for Peggy and me, our determination to reap justice for Kirsty is rock solid. If we have to go on for a further five years, we shall do so.

I have mentioned John Baron, the member of parliament serving the Conservative party. John knew Kirsty very well and had made visits to her in the hospital on a number of occasions when she was very sick. Kirsty was proud to call John her friend. He is a sincere and honest man who constantly fights for the underdog and often succeeds.

At my suggestion, John invited Peggy and me to visit him in his office in parliament to discuss the situation as it stood at this time. Unfortunately we were unable to have this meeting because of the many commitments that John had. We understood and accepted this. Our main concerns were the apparent guidelines of parliament to the General Medical Council on how to make decisions in the Fitness to Practice cases they deal with. We do not know how many of the cases get thrown out each year because of poor investigating and unfair decision making by the people who are there to protect the public and who fail miserably on all fronts, though I suspect that there must be very many.

The people who make the reports on Fitness to Practice cases are medically knowledgeable. They are professors and consultants, as in Kirsty's case. This makes it all the more unbelievable when the reports they provide show a doctor was negligent but recommend that a person should not face a panel and answer to his misdemeanours after a child has died. It's as though they pat him on the back and say, as they did in Kirsty's case, "This was a one-off and we know this will not be repeated, so you may carry on with your career. Your fitness to practice is not impaired." How sick their decision making is.

Two paragraphs of the letter sent to me after our meeting with the General Medical Council give an indication of how the Council hides behind the rules and allows doctors to escape punishment for the mistakes they make, and in this country they make many. The letter states, "The General Medical Council's fitness to practice procedures are intended by Parliament to investigate whether a doctor's fitness to practice is impaired. Under the Medical Act, the sanctions available are not intended to be punitive but to protect patients and the public interest, although they may have a punitive effect."

I would call that totally misleading and very confusing. How allowing a doctor to escape punishment for his wrongdoing, particularly as in the death of Kirsty, can be a protection for patients and in the public interest baffles me, especially if a patient like Kirsty dies because of substandard care.

The next paragraph states, "It is entirely legitimate, and fully understandable given your personal experience, to engage a public debate about whether the GMC or an equivalent body should in fact be granted powers that allow doctors to be punished as an end in itself in response to complaints such as yours. However, unless Parliament gives the GMC powers to act in this way, we cannot regard punishment in itself as a reason to act against a doctor."

Finally, the letter summarizes, "I fully acknowledge that you remain resolute in your disagreement with our decision; as I explained when we met, I am satisfied that the decision was properly taken, in line with the powers and procedures currently available to us."

Actually, all the above really means is that the doctors are protected much more than the patients and the public interest is not considered at all.

Public debate is never an option, because the public is less important than those who break the rules and give inferior care. The mechanism will always be there to protect the medical profession.

I was hoping that the meeting with John Baron in Parliament would have set off a chain of events that possibly might change the unfair situation with regard to deaths by negligence of the medical professionals. I know there will be powerful resistance to any changes within the General Medical Council regarding their doctors being made more accountable, but it must be done.

The General Medical Council appears to be happy with what they would call a fair and professional approach to the patients requiring medical care, and at the same time complacency with what is going on within the profession. However, there must be something wrong if there are thousands of complaints each year; they cannot all be unfounded. The reason many complaints are not dealt with properly is because many of the complainers are not sure of how to set the ball rolling. They eventually decide that the procedure is too complicated and long and will lead nowhere anyway, so they just give up.

Many complaints that receive a resolution end up with the same result, suspension for six months. This is ludicrous, because some cases are much more serious than others.

As an example of unbelievable leniency by the GMC, I will pass on a short item found in the *Sun* newspaper on 25 November 2008:

NHS PERVS

> Ten medics are free to work in the NHS despite being probed over sex crimes, General Medical Council figures show. The watchdog took no further action against seven doctors accused of offences including indecent assault, attempted rape, and indecent behaviour. Three were given warnings for allegedly soliciting sex from prostitutes.

It is no wonder the public in general sees the GMC as a joke, as sick as sickness itself. Of course, the Council very quickly informed Peggy and me that the Fitness to Practice panel was not there to punish their members but to ensure they would be fit to practice in the future. This fits in quite nicely with the example above. The question that needs answering is, "Are those medics fit to practice if found guilty?" I think not.

In my opinion, it is quite wrong for Parliament to allow this unjust situation to go on. It appears that the General Medical Council are a law unto themselves. This is a terrible situation. If things in their present state are allowed to continue, those that should be listened to will be ignored, and because of this nobody is guaranteed justice.

As stated earlier in this book, one of the most annoying and unsatisfactory things about dealing with the General Medical Council is how they act like politicians and tell you that it is inappropriate for their senior officers to talk to you when a request is made. This happens all the time, and my example of this is when I tried to get answers from the prime minister, the health minister, and the lord chancellor over the mismanagement in Kirsty's case. I am sure that none of these people even had a view of my correspondence. It is so very difficult to get answers from anybody that really counts, so consequently like myself, you end up talking to a nondescript person and get no real help whatsoever. I must say that if other people are like me, then they just do not give up and fight all the harder for what they know is right. I believe that when you know you are right, you should dig your heels in and become such a nuisance to the authorities that they are forced to take action on your behalf. There is no other path to take when looking for closure. If this upsets many people on the way when seeking this closure, it just does not matter. Like the General Medical Council, they are supposed to support the public, though in the real world this just does not happen.

The General Medical Council sent a response to my letter of complaint about the two doctors that engineered the report that allowed the registrar in Kirsty's case to walk away from his responsibilities regarding the death of my precious daughter. The very same people that stated that he was negligent and broke his duty of care towards her now stated that, as this was a one-off, he was not likely to offend in this way against another child; therefore, no further action would be taken. I would have thought that he should not be given the chance to slip the net, because one death is too many and the opportunity of that ever happening again should never be given to a man that fails once.

I fully expected the General Medical Council would not uphold my complaint against the two doctors that their report was flawed and that they had acted unreasonably and improperly—there was absolutely no surprise at that decision. Again we had the situation where Parliament pulled the strings. I felt it suited the GMC that their members were in the position where they could break the rules and get off without a stain on their character, plus the stigma of failure could not be attached to the General Medical Council because of these same rules. I suppose the General Medical Council would be quite happy that not one of the five thousand-plus complaints they receive each year resulted in doctors being deregistered.

Though this latest setback was disappointing, I was determined that I would not be deterred in seeking justice for Kirsty. Over the past seven years, many departments tried to claim no responsibility for Kirsty's death, but each time I would not allow this to end there. At the end of the day, some of the departments I complained to acknowledged their errors and offered their apologies. The two people who have not done this are the doctors who were not committed enough to keep my daughter alive when it was in their power to do so. They scuttled away like scared rabbits, with me always hovering behind them. I will chase them to the end of my days so that Kirsty will be avenged and other children will not succumb to poor medical care.

In this country, almost daily one hears of poor medical care of sick children or others, and it is disgusting to think that the General Medical Council hide behind Parliamentary legislation to escape their responsibilities. Even worse, they allow this type of legislation to be used as a means of allowing doctors to escape their wrongdoing. The whole system needs changing and brought into the twenty-first century. The medical profession is the greatest exponent of "closing the door after the horse has bolted," and this will never change.

Of the many emotions that the human body is able to call upon, it seems to me that the one that comes into play more often than any other is anger. As the years passed, this anger would come to the fore many times for Peggy and myself. We knew that nobody really cared about Kirsty's plight; everybody other than the parliamentary ombudsman had failed in their duty to our daughter. This became a bitter pill to swallow as the years passed, and so we had to take other steps in order to get justice for Kirsty. One of the thoughts I had that went constantly through my mind was the possibility that a crime had been committed in the failure to give Kirsty the treatment to which she was entitled. The senior doctor responsible for Kirsty's care on the night she died was the registrar; he was seen as being guilty of negligent behaviour and breaking his duty of care to Kirsty, according to the General Medical Council investigators. They were the body that found him guilty in these areas, plus they found that he was responsible for many clinical errors. In this situation, I am sure Peggy and I had every right to be angry when that doctor was allowed to walk away without a stain on his character. I was determined that this would never happen again.

I contacted the local police and explained the situation regarding Kirsty to them. They gave me a contact number for the criminal investigation department in my area, and also the name of a detective sergeant, whom I eventually called and gave my story to. He asked if he could come and visit Peggy and me at home. We were grateful for this and agreed to him visiting the same day.

The detective sergeant visited as promised, and we were able to go over the whole situation with him. He said that our complaint, if proven, could lead to a charge of manslaughter, and he hoped we were aware of this. I explained that we were aware of this but felt that we had no choice other than to fight as hard as we could to make the doctor face up to his responsibilities. This really was an indication of how deeply my anger went. If people would accuse me of being vindictive, then so be it, because I know I had a perfectly legitimate reason to be this way, and I firmly believe that no other parent would act any differently than I. My feelings were that there was no course that I could take other than to involve the police, as I knew that the situation would be investigated thoroughly and if there was an offence committed, then justice would take its course.

The detective sergeant said that he would contact the coroner and let us know the outcome. He told us that the investigation would take some time, which we were well aware of. We had already been in this battle for five years at that time and had nothing but time to use. We were grateful to anybody who tried to help in our fight.

John Baron was informed of the decision by the General Medical Council to abandon the case. He promised to contact the chief executive officer at the General Medical Council and suggest that their decision to cancel the hearing regarding Kirsty's medical neglect should be thought through very carefully and all attempts should be made to ensure that the incompetent doctor in Kirsty's case should be made to face his peers at a full hearing of the Fitness to Practice panel. He pledged to take the case to the minister for health if the Council refused. John stated that it was an appalling decision to cancel the hearing and said he would pull out all the stops to get this reversed. Like Peggy and me, he is very angry and will fight very hard to see justice is done. We are so grateful to John, and we know that he will fight as hard as possible to seek justice for Kirsty.

I informed John that I would give Kirsty's story to the media eventually, because Kirsty's story is in the public interest. I suspected media coverage would be necessary before we reached a satisfactory result, but we would hold off until every other avenue open to us had been exhausted.

The one thing I would like to reiterate is that our fight has nothing to do with money, as some people that I know have suggested. No amount of money will bring our lovely daughter back, and apart from that, the statute of limitations had run out three years previously. As will be realized, the statute of limitations, the act that covers compensation claims, which are allowed in law up to three years after realizing a problem occurred, came into force for Kirsty's case four years ago, and so we are well outside the limitations. The only things we want are that the doctor that made such a mockery of the medical profession's claims of "patients first and foremost" should be brought to task, and at the very least, retrained in the treatment of seriously ill children, in order that he does not repeat his errors for the children he may deal with in the future. All children must be protected, so perhaps my story about Kirsty will be a tool that helps to ensure this happens. We do owe it to our lovely daughter Kirsty's memory to fight for her past and other children's futures. As stated previously, there are over five thousand complaints made against the medical profession each year; many of the complaints are about children, and others are about adults. Many of these complaints are not dealt with in front of the Fitness to Practice panel, and so there are many miscarriages of justice when the accused doctors get off with their misdemeanours without a stain on their characters. This is totally unacceptable and leaves many complainers in a state of limbo, unable to find any kind of closure. In Kirsty's case, we are still seeking that closure, because at the moment Peggy and I are just unable to move on.

Most of the complaints that result in *any* punishment, other than a very few, end up with the same result, that is, suspension for six months. This is ludicrous because some cases are very much more serious than others; this just does not make sense.

If this kind of behaviour, when proven, is not seen to be dealt with correctly and in a manner that indicates to the general public that the General Medical Council is prepared to root out and punish those found guilty of these criminal acts, it is no wonder the public in general see them as one big joke. But, of course, as the Council told Peggy and myself, the Fitness to Practice panel is not there to punish their members but rather to ensure they are fit to practice in the future. The question that needs answering is, "Are those practicing medics fit to practice, if guilty?" I think not.

I am hoping that my constant snapping at the heels of the General Medical Council and the possible further input by John Baron in the House of Commons will perhaps be an aid to changing the archaic and totally unfair attitude of the medical fraternity. I will not hold my breath for any significant changes to come from the cobwebbed, hallowed halls of the General Medical Council's rule makers, or indeed Parliament itself, because they will tell you that changes to their policies are unnecessary; they will tell you that the General Medical Council have everything under control.

True to his word, John Baron involved himself in Kirsty's case and sent me a copy of the letter he wrote to the General Medical Council's chief executive. I reprint that letter below:

House of Commons

22nd December 2008

Dear Mr. Scott,

I have been contacted by my above-named constituent regarding the tragic death of his daughter Kirsty. I am familiar with his exchange of letters with the General Medical Council on the subject of calling the Registrar before a Fitness to Practice hearing. Frankly, I am very concerned that this case is not considered suitable for such a hearing. The actions of the Registrar have been widely criticised. Mr. Pearce does not wish the Registrar to be punished without a fair hearing, but proper evaluation of this doctor's fitness to practice cannot surely take place unless he is brought before his Peers.

I therefore request that the General Medical Council reconsiders its position on this issue and instigate a hearing.

I look forward to hearing from you.

Yours Sincerely,
John Baron MP

The response to John's letter from the General Medical Council was to say thanks but no thanks; there was just no way they would accept that the doctor caring for Kirsty on the night she died had broken his duty of care, even though everybody else other than the doctor himself knew that he was guilty of neglect.

Peggy and I are so pleased and grateful that we have somebody of John's stature helping us in this fight for Kirsty. If anyone can bring the General Medical Council to its senses and obtain the justice that Kirsty deserves, it is John.

I reiterate that our fight has nothing to do with money, as no amount will bring our lovely daughter back. All we want is to see the registrar taken to task in front of his peers and at the very least retrained in the treatment of seriously ill children so that he does not repeat his errors.

Kirsty

The situation with the police fizzled out and seemed to die a natural death. The detective sergeant who met with us initially called us back once to let us know he was chasing things up, whatever that means, and that he would get back to us in due course as soon as possible. That message was two years ago. We have heard nothing from him since, so I assume that the police have bigger fish to fry.

CHAPTER 26

Today is 25 December 2008, the sixth Christmas we have spent without Kirsty. It is heartbreaking, and we know there is nothing we can do to change what has happened.

Peggy, Tim, Kirsty, and I still buy each other Christmas presents, as we have always done since Kirsty left us. This year Kirsty bought me a new electric razor, Peggy an electric toothbrush, and Tim his favourite Calvin Klein toiletries, which can be smelt throughout the house.

Kirsty always liked the special DVDs that were released just prior to Christmas, and this year was no different. This year's big release was *Mama Mia*, a fantasy film that incorporated all the songs of ABBA, a favourite group that Kirsty had followed over the years. Peggy sat with Kirsty and watched the DVD with her.

Peggy and I also gave Kirsty an "angel of hope" figurine, and Tim gave her a beautiful Royal Doulton Disney Princess Cinderella figurine. This takes pride of place in her room.

As usual, when we sat down to eat our Christmas meal, a special place was prepared for Kirsty, with her food on her plate and a can of Coke at the side of her plate. We have done this ever since Kirsty left us, and though some people may think this odd, it gives us comfort to still include Kirsty in our routine.

Peggy and I feel so sorry for parents who have lost their children and find difficulty in coming to terms with what has happened. Like us, they must be brought to tears on special occasions, such as Christmas and birthdays. We send our love to them all. We know that there is no getting over the loss of a child; you just have to learn to live with it.

My own way of getting through each day is to acknowledge Kirsty. Every morning I get out of bed and talk to her. I also talk about her whenever the opportunity arises, and I think of her constantly.

As Peggy watches all the DVDs with Kirsty, I sit and watch all the soaps with her. This was our usual routine, and I see no reason to stop this. It makes me very happy.

John Baron's efforts to make the GMC understand the gravity of Kirsty's plight came to nothing, as I previously stated, though he did his utmost to help. I have asked him to ask questions in the House of Commons regarding why the General Medical Council is allowed to function in the manner it does. Justice for children in Kirsty's situation must be achieved, and I will continue the fight to ensure this happens no matter how long it may take.

It was a privilege to be Kirsty's dad, and through her, I feel I have become a better person, with much more understanding of others' needs. I am brokenhearted over what happened to Kirsty, as are Peggy and Tim, but we feel fortunate to have had the time we had with her. We often talk about her, and to her, and feel her presence around us at all times.

No parent expects a child to die before them, but so often the reality is that it does happen. There are no rules carved in stone that say opposite to this.

Kirsty weighed in at three pounds twelve ounces, and this was considered a very light birth weight, but we were not too concerned, as her general health appeared to be very good. Once she reached five pounds, it was felt she could be allowed home.

For the first two weeks of Kirsty's homecoming, everything went well, and we all enjoyed playing with her and making a fuss of her. By that time, Tim had gotten used to having her around and understood that she was a permanent fixture at home. Or so we thought. We became complacent and comfortable with what was going on. Not for one moment did we envisage what could possibly happen to Kirsty over the seventeen years that would follow.

When Kirsty was a month old, she suddenly became unwell, not eating; she was vomiting and appeared to be in respiratory distress. This was to be the beginning of regular admissions to hospitals, numbering 101. Kirsty's admissions were shared by Great Ormond Street and Basildon, our local hospital. There were other hospitals that were privileged to share Kirsty's care, in America, France, and Mauritius. She had the services of many internationally renowned doctors, both here and abroad, who all tried to figure out what Kirsty was all about with the problems she suffered, but they all failed to diagnose her.

The problem for doctors was that Kirsty suffered from fourteen different problems and was unique in the medical world. Though each one of her problems had a diagnosis in themselves, they could not be grouped together and given one name. In an effort to resolve this, a paper is being written by Professor Patricia Woo and Doctor Karen Davies, who are both consultant paediatricians in rheumatology. When the paper is completed, it will be published in medical journals.

Though Kirsty only lived for seventeen years—and we know that we were luckier than many other parents that lost their young children at a much earlier age, we still wanted more time with her. Unfortunately this was denied us.

Like other disabled children, Kirsty had so much empathy for others she met and said on more than one occasion that she felt so sorry for them. She knew that many other children suffered as much as, and sometimes much more than, she, and we found that the many other children we met at various hospitals had this natural empathy for each other. We felt privileged to be able to observe this natural behaviour between, in the main, very unfortunate sick children. I often wonder why adults cannot be as grown-up as their children.

Kirsty had her own views on the way children were referred to, and she hated the expression "kids". As she always said, "Goats have kids, and people have children." She also did not like being called "mate" and would inform anyone who addressed her in that manner that "mates" worked on ships. Of course, she was right.

Apart from the obvious problems that children suffer from when ill, there were always those associated with general living and socializing. We found that other children (termed as normal) were not willing to interact naturally with Kirsty because she was unable to keep up with their demands in the play area. Consequently much of Kirsty's time was spent with adults. She did have a couple of friends, but they were not always available because of their school demands.

Because of illness, Kirsty's education was a problem for her. In a year she usually spent only two to three weeks in school. Though she lost so much schooling, she was a very clever young lady, who literally taught herself with the aid of Mum and learnt from her own experiences in life.

The major problem in learning for Kirsty was that she had severe eye problems, being blind in her right eye and having serious problems in her left. This caused bad coordination problems for her, though she made every effort to counteract this by working hard on her writing and reading. We are so proud of her efforts.

Kirsty enjoyed going on holidays with Peg, Tim, and myself, especially to Florida, where she gleefully made contact with as many Disney characters as she could. Her pleasure was in telling them all how much she loved them, and they responded by giving her many hugs. Cinderella was the character that spent time talking, and she gave Kirsty lots of her time. Kirsty had two trips to Florida and many to Paris, where she again met her Disney friends. She was so happy she also visited her mum's birthplace in Mauritius.

Kirsty was one young girl who totally believed that all Disney characters were real. I know this would appear to be unbelievable to some people, but that was her belief. Who are we to contradict the way she felt? She also believed in Father Christmas, and why not? Anyway, we loved her for who she was.

There are times when unfortunately those that are meant to treat you make mistakes and try treatments that strictly are not meant for the condition the patient is suffering from. This happened to Kirsty, who amongst her complaints was suffering from polyarticular junior chronic arthritis, which affects more than one joint. In Kirsty's case, it affected every joint of the body.

One of the drugs tried on Kirsty was Cyclosporine, which is used to counteract organ rejection after transplants. When I queried why she was prescribed this drug, I was informed that it had been found to be useful in the treatment of some patients suffering from arthritis.

Kirsty suffered severe side effects from the Cyclosporine. She suffered severe tremors, which led to an epileptiform type of seizures (grand mal). These were occurring every fifteen minutes, and so Kirsty was unconscious for quite a while and eventually had to be transferred to intensive care. This was no help, and she then had to be transferred to Great Ormond Street for specialist care. Unfortunately for Kirsty, her body had taken such a pounding from the effects of the seizures that she suffered a left ischemic transient attack. This was even more traumatic for her, and it took five weeks to get her back to what would be called her normal self.

It is very hard to get hospitals to accept that they have gone wrong, and so when I suggested that the prescribed drug had caused Kirsty's seizures, this was initially rejected. To prove to me that they were right, the hospital carried out a lumber puncture, which showed that there were four possibilities that may have caused the problem. They conceded that Cyclosporine was one of the four. It was six weeks later that the consultant neurologist, under much pressure from me, agreed that I was right to blame the drug.

The other drug that caused distress for Kirsty was Indomethacin, which is a recognized treatment for rheumatoid arthritis but unfortunately, like the majority of drugs, has some nasty side effects. One such side effect is the inducement of depression, and Kirsty suffered from this.

I called Great Ormond Street to tell them that I would bring Kirsty to see them and explained why. They were not too happy, because she had no appointment. This did not concern me, though, and as far as I was concerned, protocol could go out of the window. I was only concerned about Kirsty's welfare and not the feelings of the medical profession.

We saw the registrar that had prescribed the drug, and she realised that I was right to take Kirsty to see her because she was so obviously depressed. I was amazed, though, when she informed me that she was unaware of this side effect. Nonetheless, she agreed to stop the Indomethacin, and Kirsty returned to her normal happy self within two days, much to our relief.

Kirsty was never without a smile on her face, and like all children, took whatever was thrown at her without complaint. All these young children should be cherished, as I am sure they are. Our daughter certainly was.

It angers me tremendously when the medical profession refuses to admit to their mistakes. This was the case in the death of our beautiful daughter. Of course, nobody would admit to blame, even though the parliamentary ombudsman who investigated the case found many problems associated with seriously poor care.

As stated previously, the General Medical Council, who are there to monitor their doctors to ensure the safety of all in their care, informed me that though the doctor's behaviour could be termed as negligent, it was not negligent enough to warrant a hearing in front of the Fitness to Practice panel. This was after initially promising us a nine-day hearing in Manchester. It really does beggar belief. After all, our daughter died partly because of this negligence. Always remember to think twice when you are told, "Trust me, I am a doctor", because though they are there to protect your loved ones, this does not always turn out to be the case.

There is so much more to Kirsty's story that will be published later in the year. In this book, I am writing about her life and death. She died a very frightened young lady, in pain and without dignity. As she lay dying, she still believed that the people that had let her down would save her and ensure that she was back home where she belonged as soon as possible. This did not happen.

CHAPTER 27

THE GENERAL MEDICAL COUNCIL SHOULD BE ASHAMED OF THE PART they played in compounding the errors of their doctors and blocking our efforts to gain justice for Kirsty. Parliament should be ashamed for allowing the General Medical Council to operate in accordance with the rules they set, according to what I have been told by the General Medical Council themselves.

It is an awful indictment of a system that allows disabled children to be treated as second-class citizens; they have rights that should be respected, not forgotten.

On Saturday, 29 April 2009, Peggy and I attended a service of thanksgiving and remembrance at the Church of St. George the Martyr, Queens Square, London. This is a service that takes place at the same time every year to honour those children that were treated in Great Ormond Street Hospital and very sadly passed over. We have attended this service every year since Kirsty passed away, and it is such a beautiful event, especially as the name of each child that has passed is read out by the Reverend Jim Linthicum, who is the senior chaplain at Great Ormond Street Hospital. There was not a dry eye amongst the hundreds of parents that were there paying their respects to those they love and have lost, and it is the most moving, wonderful, and sad event.

Another nice thing about that day was the meeting of other parents that we knew in previous years. Talking about our children was a great pleasure, one we knew we would repeat again and again over the coming years.

We miss and love our beautiful young daughter and cherish the memories that she left with us. She is forever in our thoughts and will continue to be so every day.

Peggy and I would love to communicate with other parents that have had situations such as ours, and contact can be made through Mencap. Mencap is a voluntary organisation concerned with disabled children that have learning difficulties, such as Kirsty.

Mencap have been a great support to me and Peggy over the past two years and are fighting in our corner. In partnership with John Baron, the MP, they have called Kirsty's passing "death by indifference". Death by indifference is basically where a doctor is indifferent to a sick patient's needs and the patient does not receive treatment that is very obviously needed, even though the doctor may be aware of what treatment is required.

We still have interaction with Kirsty. Peggy watches all the new Disney films with her in her room; and I, as I always did, watch all the soaps with her. I know that she looks on approvingly.

We visit Kirsty's grave every day and lay new turfs every year. This does not stop the grieving, but it certainly helps us to cope with her loss to a certain extent.

We are advised by some people that we will get over what has happened, but these, of course, are people that have never lost a child. I can confirm to them that parents who have lost a child never heal; the void that loss creates remains with you always.

The following I found to be interesting: It takes forty-seven muscles to frown and it takes seventeen to smile, but it doesn't take any to just stand there with a dumb look on your face.

I feel that this little factoid fits in well with the medics dealing with Kirsty the night she died.

The night that Kirsty was admitted to the hospital for what turned out to be the final illness of her short life was most horrendous for Peggy and me because this was nothing more than a routine admission for her—or should have been. We thought that within thirty-six hours, she would return home well, as was the norm. If the doctors had done their best, then this would have happened—but they did not.

Kirsty presented with pulmonary oedema (fluid on the lung), a respiratory rate of seventy per minute, a pulse rate of 140 per minute, and an oxygen level (pulse oximetry) of 96 per cent, and there were crackling noises in her chest.

The parliamentary ombudsman's investigations found that Kirsty was a candidate for ITU on admission, but she was not transferred until thirteen hours later; by then, she was in a terminal state, and it was too late to save her. We will never forgive the medical fraternity for what happened to Kirsty, because they know, as we do, that if they had done their job, she would have survived.

I found the General Medical Council immoral in their attitude and approach in decision making, saying that the doctor dealing with Kirsty could be considered negligent in his behaviour, but not negligent enough to face a hearing, even though that negligence has to be part of the reason why Kirsty died. Such a decision is totally unbelievable.

According to the General Medical Council, they are governed by the rules as laid down by Parliament. If that be so, then Parliament is as guilty as the General Medical Council themselves and needs to take a long hard look at itself, and for once in a term, use some common sense, if that is at all possible. I would not expect that to happen, though.

There are many interpretations of justice, but the one I think is most appropriate for Kirsty is as follows.

Justice is generally understood to mean what is right, fair, appropriate, and deserved.

Justice is achieved when an unjust act is redressed and the victim feels whole again.

Justice also means that the offender is held accountable for his behaviour.

It is believed that, in general, justice is meant more for the society as a whole than for the individual victims, because it is designed to prove repeatedly that people are safe within their society.

Injustice is surely dishonest, as every such act is a crime against society in general and merely an attempt to escape retribution for proven committed offences, as that against Kirsty. In my opinion, bodies like the General Medical Council that ignore cases such as that of Kirsty can only be considered as guilty as the perpetrators in this case, and they too should stand up and bow their heads in shame. The cover-up in this case simply shows that they did not want the facts in her case to be brought out into the open. It is a most immoral way to act, and this will continue to be the case so long as Parliament uses the antiquated laws that allow the General Medical Council to create these injustices. The laws that the General Medical Council work by need to be totally reviewed in fairness to society generally, but especially for those like Kirsty, who is the victim of one of the worst injustices there could be.

The problem is that Parliament will do nothing, because it is not in their interests, and the injustices will continue because they stem from the laws that the General Medical Council work by. According to them, these are governed by Parliament, and would anybody believe that Parliament would listen to anyone such as me?

I have tried extremely hard over the past six years, as have John Baron, our local MP, and Mencap, but they too have succeeded in getting nowhere, because of the stubbornness and refusal of the General Medical Council to act in a fair and impartial manner. I do believe that the GMC need to be looked at very closely and changes made, and I would hope that John could possibly ask questions in the House of Commons regarding the changes that need to be made.

Our message to Kirsty is one that I know she hears because she is with us always; she has become our guardian angel, and we will continue to fight for justice on her behalf no matter how long the road may be.

Peggy, Tim, and I will never forget the lovely smiling face that would greet us each morning of her life, the wonderful giggle that she had, the thanks she gave for any little thing we would do for her—things that gave us as much pleasure doing as she receiving. Kirsty had many friends, though unfortunately or not, most of them were the young people she met in hospitals. They were so great together, always helping each other as much as possible and never complaining, no matter how difficult or hard things were for them. One of the most pleasing things, and it often happened, would be to be in London or back home in Basildon, when we were out shopping and we would hear a voice calling out, "Hello, Kirsty." You could bet your life that it would be one of the special little friends she had met in one hospital or another. Kirsty loved it when spontaneous things such as that happened, and you would see that the happy, smiling faces of the other children showed that they were as happy to see her as she them. The children from the hospitals that Kirsty knew belonged to what she described as their "special club". They were very beautiful, special beings. Each one of these children that passed on, and there were many of them, deserves their place in heaven, and of course, my beautiful daughter was one of them. Thank you for just being you, Kirsty. We are all very proud of you, a very special young lady. God bless you.

CHAPTER 28

THIS STORY HAS BEEN ABOUT MY DAUGHTER, KIRSTY, WHO WAS taken ill and died as a result of poor medical care in a period of only thirteen hours; writing it was the hardest thing that I have ever had to do in my lifetime.

I am certain that the procedures needed to keep Kirsty alive were not implemented. The fact is that the doctors were complacent and indifferent to my daughter's needs.

The General Medical Council, which lays great claim in being fair and impartial to the general public in the United Kingdom, quite proudly boasting, "Our purpose is to protect and maintain the health and safety of the community by ensuring proper standards in the practice of medicine," failed to honour their pledge and give Kirsty the justice owed her. When I first made a complaint to the GMC, I firmly believed that their boasts about fairness in dealing with the general public would hold true; but after three years of fighting, I know that the fairness talked about is only their interpretation and only goes one way. I would call it biased, on behalf of its own members.

The GMC were as complacent and indifferent as the doctors treating Kirsty. Even though they themselves agreed that the doctor concerned with Kirsty had shown negligent behaviour, and the parliamentary ombudsman had found him severely guilty in administering poor care to my daughter, he was never punished. As the GMC put it, "Though the doctor's behaviour could be considered negligent, it was not negligent enough to warrant him facing a Fitness to Practice panel", even taking into account that Kirsty died as a result of that negligence. For as long as I live, I shall never understand the inane and pathetic body that calls itself the General Medical Council. To me they appear totally immoral in their dealings with such cases as Kirsty's.

It is impossible to have meetings with the people who count in England because you are informed that it is inappropriate for ministers or their officers responsible for public departments to get involved. I am sure that people such as the minister of health do not have sight of the letters I sent; they are screened from such annoyances.

I really worked hard in seeking justice for Kirsty, but to no avail so far. I would hope that anyone having read this book would understand my anger. To gain respect, you must first give it; but unfortunately the GMC respects no one.

Injustices will continue to flourish under the present system in operation in the United Kingdom. This will continue to be the case until a government of the future ensures that fairness in all walks of life is put into practice as an emergency. I do not believe that this implementation will be smooth sailing.

The blame for injustices such as Kirsty's must be laid firmly at the door of Parliament, as the General Medical Council work in accordance with legislation laid down by that body.

John Baron, member of parliament, is still working very hard on behalf of Kirsty, as he has done ever since her death, Fairly recently he has had the support of Lesley Campbell from Mencap, an organization that concerns itself with equal rights for all people with learning disabilities. They are in the process of arranging a debate in Westminster Hall over the issue of "death by indifference"; this is hopefully to be attended by members of parliament from all parties, though I should imagine it would be boycotted by the medical fraternity. Peggy and I will attend the debate, if it happens, and we are sure it will be a lively affair, which will be widely reported by the national press. I am not sure whether I shall be allowed to speak, though I will make all effort to do so.

CHAPTER 29

WHEN TRYING TO WRITE A STORY BASED ON FACT, THERE IS always the possibility that new information suddenly materialises, totally unexpectedly and completely out of the blue. This is exactly what happened in the story of Kirsty. In the fall of the year, 16 December 2009 arrived without any indication that things would be any different than any other day; we had no inkling of what was about to unfold. As usual when we got out of bed, we had our showers, visited Kirsty, and then finally had breakfast. I was surprised to receive a message later that morning from Professor Patricia Woo, at Great Ormond Street Hospital, London. She told me that Kirsty's DNA had been stored in the pathology department for the previous seven years.

I was then surprised even more when she asked if it would be all right if she sent the sample to St. James's Hospital in Leeds for testing, in the hope that even though Kirsty had passed, something conclusive might be revealed. Kirsty's DNA had been tested in the past, but without confirmation of anything that could explain her problems. I was happy to help in any way possible and told her to go for it. This she did, and then it was just the little matter of waiting for the results. I knew that it would take some time for the results to come back, so I was not expecting news before Christmas.

Peggy and I prepared ourselves for another Christmas without Kirsty; we knew we would be shedding more tears.

This would also be the first Christmas that Tim was not at home. He was now living with his partner Rebecca in Camberly, Surrey, a lovely area and ideal for bringing up children. They had moved into their own apartment in August 2009. What really pleased Peggy and me was that they were expecting the birth of their first child on December 16, and they knew that it would be a boy.

Peggy and I were so pleased for Tim and Rebecca, and just as pleased to know that we were going to be grandparents to our son's child. The baby was born 21 December 2009; he thought he would keep his parents waiting a few days longer than expected. After much struggling, he had to be brought into this world by Caesarean section, which was traumatic for Rebecca. Not that it was that easy for Tim, because he was a total wreck for a couple of days; it was a worrying time for us all.

Owen David Charles arrived with a birth weight of eight pounds ten ounces, a large bundle of joy for us all. The important thing was that he and Mum were perfectly well, thank God.

After Owen's birth, Peggy and I were discussing how pleased we were that Mum and baby were safe. God knows how we, and particularly Tim, would have coped had anything gone wrong, especially after losing Kirsty the way we did.

I was also thinking how, in one breath, I was initially blaming God for not saving Kirsty and then thanking him for protecting Owen. The point I make is that, when it suits us, we recognise God, but when it doesn't, we don't. I suppose that is the fickleness of man.

On 20 January 2010, Professor Patricia Woo, paediatric consultant at Great Ormond Street hospital, contacted me to inform me that the results from the testing of Kirsty's DNA were back. The results showed that Kirsty had been suffering from a disease called Aicardi-Goutieres syndrome. This was unbelievable information, especially when it was realised that it had taken twenty-four years to find this diagnosis, which was after Kirsty had been dead for six and a half years. This disease is very rare, and even though tests were repeated over the years, all had returned as negative. Apparently the syndrome is caused by a gene mutation, and it is very difficult to confirm, as most tests do return results of negative.

The disease was first described by Jean Aicardi and Francoise Goutieres as an early onset of genetic brain disorder, mimicking the features of viral infections affecting a child in the womb.

There is no cure for the disease, only supportive therapy for the problems associated with it. Those affected tend to die fairly young, so perhaps we were very fortunate to have had Kirsty for as long as we did.

We were very lucky in one respect with Kirsty, inasmuch as she did not suffer from mental retardation, as so many of those affected did.

The fact that we, and the many doctors that Kirsty was treated by, were not aware that she had this awful syndrome for the whole of her life is unbelievable.

With hindsight, perhaps it was better for Peggy and me not to know about this problem; otherwise, we would have feared the worst for Kirsty each and every day that passed.

It must be a living hell for parents that know they have children suffering from Aicardi-Goutieres syndrome; being made aware of the prognosis of this disease must make them totally distraught.

The amazing thing about Kirsty's illness was that, though she had so many different problems, not all of them were associated with this awful disease. Those that were not are retinal vasculitis, rheumatoid factor positive destructive arthritis, renal vasculitis leading to reduced filtration rate, and periodic pulmonary oedema. Of course this still left many other problems that were directly involved in this disease.

The answer to the many episodes of pulmonary oedema that Kirsty suffered from was still not discovered.

This latest revelation regarding Kirsty's health was totally unexpected; to try and comprehend what exactly this meant was very hard and somewhat unbelievable.

I contacted Professor Woo at Great Ormond Street hospital in London and asked her how it was that this disease had not been discovered at birth.

Professor Woo explained that when Kirsty was a month old, many of her problems began to surface. Because of this, many repetitive blood tests were carried out, but unfortunately though she had been tested for Aicardi-Goutieres syndrome a number of times as she got older, nothing came up positive.

The disease is very rare, and to think that it took twenty-four years to diagnose does nothing more than make me realise how mysterious and complex the world of medicine is.

CHAPTER 30

IT WAS IN 2004 THAT I FELT THERE SHOULD BE AN INQUEST WITH regard to the causes of Kirsty's death; I knew that something had gone badly wrong with the care, or lack of it, that she was given on the night she died.

I wrote a letter to the Essex coroner about my concerns over Kirsty's death and suggested to her that an inquest would be the only way that the truth could be revealed as to why she died. Six weeks later, the coroner contacted me to say that she understood that I had appealed to the Healthcare Commission and asked them to investigate Kirsty's death.

The coroner informed me that she was willing to grant the inquest providing that the Healthcare Commission supported my complaint.

I had no reason to believe that the result would be that we would not get this support; after all, the watchdog, as they were known, was sure to recognise the poor medical care given to Kirsty on the night that she died.

It took fourteen months to furnish the report to the coroner. Unbelievably the Healthcare Commission stated that as far as they were concerned, the hospital's treatment of Kirsty was fair and just and there could be no blame attached to the doctors or nursing staff that could remotely be considered as a contributing factor in her passing.

We were then informed by the coroner that there would be no inquest.

To say that Peggy and I were deflated over the coroner's decision would be an understatement. We were totally distressed; we knew that the decision that the coroner had made was wrong.

Over the years whilst fighting in Kirsty's corner, I found that I have become more resilient to what we call "knock backs". I actually found that my determination was stronger than ever in seeking the justice Kirsty was owed.

I was determined that someone would listen to me, so much so that I wrote to three people that I felt just had to help. That was a big mistake because unless you help yourself, those in the position to do so just don't want to know.

The first person I wrote to was the lord chancellor, to complain about the refusal to give an inquest on Kirsty's death; my understanding was that he could overrule the coroner, being that he was her boss.

The second person I hoped would help was the minister for health, who I felt could look into my charge of a breakdown in the system generally.

The final person I wrote to was the prime minister because, I thought, he ran the country, so he was in prime position to intervene on our behalf.

Each of the departments overseen by these people have multitudes of minions in place to ensure that they are not bothered by the little people in my country; and so each of these, one for each department, sent me the same message: that it was inappropriate for them or their officers to deal directly with me. Not one of these government departments would give me any advice on what steps I could take or where I could possibly get the help I needed; obviously we were of no significance to them. It seemed that if we were to win this battle, we would have to go it alone. After these letdowns, I was determined to go on. I would let nothing sway me from my path; I was determined to get justice for Kirsty eventually.

At the end of the day, I realised that if I were to get anywhere, then I would have to rely upon myself, because unless you are in the public eye in England, nobody is interested in any problem you may have.

There is a certain amount of satisfaction in tearing down the barriers the official bodies put in place to thwart the attempts of people like myself to get justice for wrongdoings in the public sector. In fact, in my situation, I could imagine the audible sighs of frustration on their part when they realised they were unable to keep me quiet.

It does take an awful lot of determination and resilience to beat them, when all the aces appear to be in their hands, but beating them is possible if you don't give up.

CHAPTER 31

FROM 2004 TO 2010, THE CONSTANT LETTERS TO AUTHORITIES AND government departments seemed never ending, but the end result was always the same: nobody was interested in what had happened to Kirsty.

I firmly believe that unless you are somebody in the public eye in England, you have an uphill battle in your fight for justice; people that are supposed to care just do not care.

After years of constantly fighting authority, I decided to have another try with the coroner. This was the same lady that I had complained about to the lord chancellor after she refused an inquest on Kirsty in 2005. I was wondering what her reaction would be and whether or not she would remember me.

On 20 February 2010, I wrote to the Essex coroner requesting that she reconsider her decision of 26 March 2005 refusing an inquest into the death of Kirsty.

In my letter to the coroner, I explained to her that as she had made her previous decision not to hold an inquest on Kirsty based on the findings of the Healthcare Commission's report, a report that was later described as "seriously flawed" by the parliamentary health service ombudsman, would it not now be appropriate to look at Kirsty's case anew and perhaps change her original decision?

I did not take it for granted that the coroner would be interested in looking at the case of Kirsty after so many years. I just hoped that this would turn out to be her decision.

On 18 March 2010, I received a letter from the coroner and was surprised and delighted when her response was as follows:

Kirsty

Dear Mr. Pearce,

Inquest touching upon the death of Kirsty Jayne Pearce.

I am in receipt of your letter dated 20ᵗʰ February 2010.

Firstly, I again would like to express my condolences to you and your family upon the tragic loss of your daughter Kirsty at such a young age, on 29 August 2003.

When you wrote to me some time ago, I told you that I would be willing to consider matters after the Healthcare Commission and other proceedings were completed.

I have reviewed the information you have now provided and I have decided that I will open an inquest touching upon the death of Kirsty.

I have passed all the information on to my Coroner's Officer who will contact you directly.

Yours Sincerely,

Caroline Beasley-Murray
HM Coroner for Essex and Thurrock

To think that the granting of an inquest in Kirsty's case had taken over six and a half years was scandalous, though I firmly believe that the coroner had previously been misled by the Healthcare Commission as a result of their very poor summarising of Kirsty's case. The coroner had been left with egg on her face simply because she had trusted the Healthcare Commission to present an unbiased report regarding Kirsty's death. She must have been very angry that her department had been abused in this manner; it must also have been very difficult for her to eat humble pie in her dealings with me after having refused the inquest upon Kirsty previously in 2005 based upon the Healthcare Commission's findings.

After I received the letter from the coroner and had digested the contents and implications, I am not ashamed to say it brought me to tears, simply because I had been fighting so long for Kirsty and seemingly getting nowhere. I had found myself getting more frustrated as time went by, and now having read the coroner's letter, it seemed to me to be a whole new ball game, one I was determined to win.

The coroner's letter lifted such a heavy load from my shoulders; I could see a glimmer of hope in gaining the justice that Kirsty was entitled to.

Once I had come down to earth after this decision by the coroner, I realised that there still was much more to do. I was determined not to get carried away thinking that this was the end of the battle—far from it.

I received a phone call from the coroner's officer on 25 March 2010 asking Peggy and me to go to his office in order to talk over the preparations for Kirsty's inquest. He also requested we go through the documents he had and provide him with others that he had been unable to locate.

We went to Chelmsford, which is the county town of Essex, on Thursday, 1 April 2010.

The coroner's officer was an ex-policeman, which is usually the case with people doing that particular job.

He was a very pleasant man, and after the usual introductions and pleasantries, he proceeded to go through all the information he had obtained regarding Kirsty's death. We were able to furnish him with one or two items that were relevant to the issues surrounding her death.

We were with the coroner's officer for about two hours, and he told us that it would be some time before the inquest as he needed to get all Kirsty's notes from her date of birth.

This I found strange because my feelings were that what happened on 22 February 1986 could hardly be relevant to what occurred on 28 to 29 August 2003 over the thirteen hours leading up to her death.

When we left the coroner's officer, Peggy and I talked over the meeting we'd had with him and felt that we needed to keep in close contact with what was happening, simply because we did not want any errors now that we had reached a very important stage in Kirsty's story.

Prior to meeting the coroner's officer, I spoke to the coroner by phone. She told me that she did remember me and more particularly Kirsty. She told me that she was pleased that she was speaking to me and was glad that she could now offer an inquest for Kirsty after such a long time.

I suppose the one thing that was beginning to emerge after all the years of rebuff from numerous official bodies was that, if you are firm in your beliefs, know that a wrong needs to be addressed, and persevere in righting those wrongs, then the chances are pretty good that success will come your way. As previously stated, there was no way I would be beaten.

I firmly believe that the General Medical Council did not wish for Kirsty's case to be released into the public domain, because it would have highlighted how shallow and immoral their dealings with the general public are; that is my view, and there is no way that view will ever change.

After the decision had been made to abandon Kirsty's case, I believe that the General Medical Council considered that the case was now dead and buried.

The General Medical Council even suggested that the only course open to me would be a judicial review at the High Court in London. This would not have been possible, though, simply because of the enormous expense in funding that kind of action at the highest court in the land.

To have taken this step would have meant that we would have had to take a second mortgage out on our home.

I was now putting all of my trust in the coroner's court to give her the chance of ruling on Kirsty's death, hoping that the years of fighting had all been worthwhile.

Four weeks passed after Peggy and I visited the coroner's officer, though in fact it felt more like four months. It appears to me that unless you are someone of note in our society, nothing moves very quickly; consequently a lot of time is wasted twiddling thumbs.

I have come to realise that officialdom in my country have two speeds, that is, slow and stop; there is no hurry on their part if you are trying to right a wrong. The requirements in my situation are patience, patience, and more patience, not that you are likely to get very far very fast even then.

On 11 May 2010, I sent a letter to the coroner asking if they could give me a date for the inquest. I also asked why they needed all of Kirsty's medical notes from her date of birth.

The coroner replied on 14 May and explained that, although the most relevant time in this case was the thirteen hours that Kirsty spent in the hospital prior to her death, it was important to gain an overall picture of the happenings during her life, particularly those of a similar nature that she had survived previously.

I understood the need to be correct in the way Kirsty's case was presented, but this did not stop me feeling concerns over the time it appeared to be taking to complete the case.

Though I was quite frustrated over the delay, it was obviously a stupid thing to antagonise the coroner with constant requests for inquest dates, so I decided to pull in my horns and leave her to finish her enquiries in peace.

Over the past almost seven years, the one person that has been my rock and supported me throughout has been Peggy, a wonderful wife and mother. She always encouraged me during the harder times and was at my side constantly. Without her support, this story could never have been told.

The next contact with the coroner's officer was on 17 June 2010; it was by e-mail and confirmed that there would be an inquest for Kirsty. It pointed out that, bearing in mind the ombudsman and other investigative parties had taken almost seven years to complete investigations, it should be accepted that the work being done by the coroner had so far only been for a period of two months. The coroner's officer also informed me that the coroner had the right to have her own expert report furnished as a comparison to those provided in the past. The coroner asked me to be patient with them as they needed things to be tied up in the correct manner; it could well take a few months yet to set up the inquest.

I think it is very easy to understand how frustrated I became at times over all the years of fighting for Kirsty; it just seemed to go on and on, though there is no way I will give up, even if it takes the rest of my life.

There were many times over the years that I felt unable to continue my writing, in the main because I felt everything was against us and that the justice I was seeking would never be found.

Though I had these down moments, it was Peggy who would constantly encourage me and tell me to never give up, probably because her faith was stronger than mine. Following Kirsty's death, she was and still is my rock; without her it would have much more difficult to carry on. To say I love her would be an understatement.

CHAPTER 32

IT SEEMED LIKE AN ETERNITY BEFORE WE HAD FURTHER CONTACT from the coroner, and I was beginning to fear that we never would.

I did contact the coroner's officer with the request that I be given a regular update with regard to the investigation by the coroner's department. This was agreed, and so I sat back in anticipation.

On 29 August 2010, Peggy and I, accompanied by various friends and family, commemorated the seventh year since Kirsty's passing by her graveside. This was no less painful than the day of her funeral, and I still cannot accept that things get easier as time passes; to us they appear to get harder and harder.

On 7 September 2010, the coroner's officer informed me that there was difficulty in finding a consultant paediatrician willing to carry out an expert independent report on Kirsty's case; it appeared that they did not wish to be involved in matters concerning the General Medical Council or the now-defunct Healthcare Commission.

I suggested to the coroner's officer that they should force these consultants to provide an independent specialist report by issuing a court order compelling them to do so.

On 9 September 2010, I received another letter from the coroner's officer to assure me that the inquest for Kirsty would definitely take place and that they would find a consultant to provide an independent report.

I felt pleased with the coroner's assurances, but not happy with the people being asked to help; to me, they were shallow and insignificant individuals.

It always amazes me how the medical profession manages to evade their responsibilities when asked to give an honest appraisal of any case that they are requested to view. The General Medical Council goes overboard to protect their own image and, in the process, protect those guilty of serious errors, such as in Kirsty's case. This really should not be allowed.

Things started to look up when I was informed by the coroner's officer on 30 September 2010 that a specialist consultant in paediatric medicine was prepared to take on Kirsty's case. All documentation and files had been handed over to him.

We were very pleased at this latest turn of events, and it was gratifying to know that there was at least one member of the medical profession who did not give a damn for the General Medical Council or its members.

I made a point of thanking the coroner's officer for all the hard work and effort that they were putting into Kirsty's case, for I know how difficult it was at times for them in trying to organise the inquest. I also knew that they were wrapped up in many other cases at the same time as Kirsty's.

At least we were now in the position of knowing things were on the move. Perhaps the whole episode could now speed up and be brought to a satisfactory conclusion.

The most difficult thing we found was that it was very painful not being able to bring Kirsty's case to a closure after seven years. Perhaps now that would change.

One very hard task was to go to the ward where Kirsty spent her last night and hand over sponsorship money that we had collected for taking part in the annual fun walk. We had done this for the past six years, and it is always to the benefit of the children's services.

Unlike me, Peggy just cannot go into Puffin ward again. After all, she watched Kirsty slowly pass away there over a long period of thirteen hours, and so I fully understand her reasoning. The bed she was in is still there.

I contacted the children's officer at Mencap, an organisation concerned with disabled children with learning difficulties, to give them the news regarding the forthcoming specialist's report. I felt obligated to do this, as they had tried very hard over the years to support me and Peggy.

Mencap informed me that they were still trying to obtain legal help on a pro bono contract. I was very grateful for this, as I felt I did not have the expertise to deal with legal representation from the medical side in the coroner's court, though if I had to, I would.

It was on 1 November 2010 that I received a message from the coroner's officer informing me that the specialist report being prepared for the coroner would be released to me. I thought this would be useful inasmuch as I would be able to compare that report with the ombudsman's and see whether or not they were in tandem with each other.

I realised that I could not remain on the governing body of the Trust and then oppose the Trust in the coroner's court. With great regret, I made the decision to stand down.

I agree that "time waits for no man" because suddenly I realised that we had come to another Christmas, the eighth one since Kirsty's passing and just as lonely for Peggy and me as the previous seven.

We still continued somewhat as though Kirsty was here, with decorations in her room and the special little gifts that we continued to buy her as we had always done.

One happy occurrence was on Christmas Eve, when Tim brought our grandson Owen to visit us. He had just celebrated his first birthday and was dressed in the Tottenham Hotspur football kit that we had bought him from the club.

Peggy took Owen in to see Kirsty's room. He could not fathom what this miniature Disney World was all about or, of course, the significance, but his face showed his delight.

We have promised Tim that when our grandson Owen reaches the age of four years, we will all go as a family to Disney World in Florida. This will be him following in the footsteps of his Aunty Kirsty. We are sure he will love it as much as she did on her two visits.

There are a number of significant events that have taken place since Kirsty's passing. They are special times that she would have been so happy to have seen and even been involved in, but unfortunately it was not to be.

When our niece Vanessa informed us in 2003 that she was to marry fiancé Ben on 5 September 2009, we, along with Kirsty, were very pleased for her, even though this was planned for six years ahead. Kirsty had often been reminded over those preceding years that she would be a bridesmaid when Vanessa married. To her it was something to look forward to. It was so sad that this did not happen.

Kirsty has also missed meeting her nephew Owen, son of her brother Tim, who was born on 21 December 2009, and also her great cousin Noah, the son of Vanessa and Ben, who was born on 4 November 2010. Had she met them, she would have loved them dearly.

I finally received the copy of the Specialist Medical report ordered by the Coroner on 6th June 2011, though this had taken eight months to prepare I think that it was well worth the wait.

The report clearly showed that we were correct in our beliefs that the lack of care given to our daughter Kirsty directly contributed to her death. We had been claiming this for almost eight years though nobody of note wanted to believe us, until now. We are now totally vindicated in what we had been claiming over those past years.

With the report came a message from the coroner's officer informing us that there would be a pre-inquest meeting at County Hall in the Coroner's office to finalise details for the inquest.

Dr Ian Maconochie FRCPCH FFAEM FRCPI PhD
Consultant in Paediatric/Emergency Medicine
St Mary's Hospital, Praed Street, London W2 1NY

Tele:: 020 3312 6139   Fax: 020 3312 6366

9th May 2011

Mr Paul Roberts
Coroner's Officer
H.M. Coroner Service
Essex & Thurrock
New Bridge House
60-68 New London Road
Chelmsford
Essex CM2 0PD

Dear Mr Roberts,

Re: Kirsty Jayne Pearce – Your Reference MS 1165/2010

Thank you for your letter of instruction dated 30th September 2010. I have had access to the following documents:

- Post Mortem results.
- Histopathology.
- General reports on Kirsty Jayne Pearce from Great Ormond Street, last dated 1st September 2003.
- Report from Directorate of Obstetrics, Paediatrics and Gynaecology on 24th July 2003.
- Great Ormond Street letter 6th February 2003.
- Middlesex Hospital letter dated 27th June 2003.
- Mixture of letters asking Kirsty to be involved in a clinical examinations project.
- Letter to the Clinical Psychologist on 12th June 2003.
- Great Ormond Street letter, May 2003 from Nephrologists.
- Great Ormond Street letter, 10th April 2003, from Rheumatology Department.

Haematological results from:

- 28th August 2003
- 25th July 2003
- 21st July 2003
- 23rd July 2003
- Consultant letter of apology from Dr Ware.
- Statement of Petchaye Pearce, headed on the General Medical Council. This letter has 28 paragraphs relating to Kirsty, as a statement, given by her mother, predominantly relating to the course of events surrounding Kirsty's death from 28th August 2003.
- Letter to the Health Service Ombudsman, dated 11th March 2006.
- Reply from the Ombudsman dated 13th June 2008.
- Letter from the Health Care Commission dated 21st November 2007. This letter includes the account given by the Independent Advisor, Consultant Paediatrician from the Royal Devon & Exeter Foundation NHS Trust, which I refer to subsequently as **Ref 1.**
- Letter from Charles Pearce to the Chief Executive of Basildon Hospital dated 5th January 2004.
- Reply from Basildon Chief Executive dated 9th February 2004.
- Letter of 24th March 2004 from Complaints Manager, Basildon Hospital, to Mr & Mrs Pearce, with ensuing complaints meeting minutes from a meeting held on 16th March 2004.
- Letter from Basildon & Thurrock on 22nd April 2004.
- Letter from the office of the Independent Convenor, Basildon Hospital, to Mr Pearce, dated 26th May 2004.
- Letter from Basildon & Thurrock University Hospitals, 16th July 2004, to Mr & Mrs Pearce.
- Notes of meeting held on 12th July 2004 between Mr & Mrs Pearce and representatives from the Hospital.
- Letter from Charles Pearce to Sir Graeme Catto, GMC.
- GMC replying to Mr Pearce on 8th January 2008.
- Letter from Field Fisher Waterhouse to Mr & Mrs Pearce about the General Medical Council, investigation re Dr Gangavati on 20th May 2008.

- The notes available from Basildon Thurrock Hospital relating to the admission to Penguin Unit on 28th August 2003 (which will be studied in detail).
- Statement by Dr Venkataranga Reddy, dated 20th January 2004
- Statement of Events, completed by Dr Gangavati on 21st January 2004.
- Statement from Alex Corthine dated 20th January 2004 (regular Bank nurse).
- Letter dated 15th January 2004 to Mrs Farebrother from Dr Stephen Ware.
- Conclusion of events.

You have asked me to consider the events that occurred on 28th & 29th August 2003 during the course of Kirsty Jane Pearce's management, up to the time of her death.
I will first refer to the clinical notes that are available, and comment up the relevant features of her management during the course of her admission.

Kirsty had direct access to Penguin Unit with the medical complaint of coughing and vomiting since that morning. At the time of her presentation to the ward she had a persistent cough. She had two nebulisers of salbutamol (ventolin), and Frusimide and Amiloride (these two latter medications are both types of diuretics, used to remove water from the body by increasing renal flow and subsequently increasing urine production).
Worrying from the outset of her attendance she was cyanosed (having the appearance of blue lips) and she had peripheral oxygen saturation of 66% in air. This is extremely low and of great concern, as the normal value for a healthy person of her age would be 98-100% in air. She was consequently given oxygen at high flow, at 10 litres per minute.

Blood tests which were abnormal showed the following results:
The white cell count was elevated at 29.2 (this is significantly high).
The C reactive protein was 4. This value is towards the low end of the normal range; note that this value may fall in the presence of serious infection.

The first clerking note is that she is a 17 year old female with multiple problems and she was well known to the department.
She had the following problems:

Prepared by: Dr Ian Maconochie FRCPCH FFAEM FRCPI PhD

Juvenile idiopathic arthritis, (polyarticular-rheumatoid factor positive)

Intracranial calcification

Recurrent pulmonary oedema (responds to Frusemide ordinarily)

Ophthalmology showed retinal detachments and cataracts.

Colitis (a problem with the bowel)

Asthma

Hypothyroidism.

The history of her complaint at this attendance to hospital was of persistent recurrent bouts of cough, with increased shortness of breath for 1 day which had not respond to Frusemide 5mls or to 2 salbutamol nebulisers. She had a cough, was not productive of sputum and she did not have fever. There was no chest pain, no urinary or bowel symptoms and her longstanding mobility problems were improving.

Her past medical history was as above.

Medications were:

Pain relieving drugs

Anti epileptic treatment

Drugs to deal with her bone problems

Preventive ulcer development tablets

Thyroxine and iron supplementation.

At 00.00am the clerking entry states – still breathless, respiratory rate 40 breaths per minute (*this is greatly elevated for a girl of her age*), pulse 130 beats per minutes (*elevated for a girl of her age*), peripheral oxygen saturations were at 98% in 12 litres of oxygen (*which is within the normal range but is produced by significant oxygen requirement, meaning that she is very ill*), and the chest examination showed bilateral creps (*less than before- these noises are associated with infection or pulmonary oedema*). The plan was to discuss with the registrar. Signed Dr Reddy.

At 00.10am tachypnoeic (*which means increased respiratory rate*) of 50 breaths per minute (*which is higher than before, so concerning*), heart rate 140 breaths per minute (*raised*), peripheral oxygen saturation 92-94% in 10 litres per minute (*these figures* are less than expected, given the high concentration and flow of oxygen), chest examination showed bilateral creps. The plan was to give another dose of Frusemide and monitor closely. The SHO then subsequently writes, (*I am unable to give the time owing to the absence of the margins*) still much the same, marginal improvement, peripheral oxygen saturation of 92-94% (*still abnormal*), pulse 140 (*raised*), chest bilateral creps.

The next entry is headed by

Paediatric registrar – still tachypnoeic, in distress, peripheral oxygen saturations decreased to 89-90%, bibasal creps still present, to discuss with Consultant on-call, Dr Ware. Also speak to anaesthetist, keep close monitoring. (*I agree with this management in that there is a worsening of her clinical condition and given the previous histories of pulmonary oedema and the failure of response to diuretics such as Frusemide, urgent intervention is required*).

On examination, breathless, unwell, lying in bed with 3 pillows, temperature 37.1° (*normal*), pulse 130 (*raised*), respiratory rate 40 (*raised*), peripheral oxygen saturation 96% in 10 litres of oxygen (*again at the very low end of acceptable figure for this amount of oxygen concentration*), chest bilateral creps mid zones, the JVP (*Jugular venous pressure – this may be elevated in heart failure and pulmonary oedema*) was level, and the heart sounds were also recorded as 1 & 2.. The abdomen was soft on examination at this time.

The impression was that she had pulmonary oedema +/- a lower respiratory tract infection. The chest X-ray showed pulmonary oedema, according to notes, ? infected on right side. The plan therefore was Kirsty to be given intravenous Frusemide, analgesia, Ceftriaxone (*an antibiotic*), fluid balance (*to measure the intake and output of her fluids*) and to discuss with registrar.

It is recorded that the registrar spoke with the Consultant at 05.00 in the notes.

The registrar writes "crash call to ITU at 06.31 hours" and further more writes -
On arrival, Kirsty was being resuscitated by the medical and anaesthetic team, about 15 minutes CPR carried out, intubated, bagged by anaesthetist, cardiac massage,

adrenaline x 3 doses given, no cardiac output, pulses not palpable, continue resuscitation, total of adrenaline x 7 doses, atropine 3 mgs given intravenous, still no pulses. Consultant, Dr Ware informed, declared dead at 07.00am.

There are additional retrospective clerking notes from the Specialist Registrar in Anaesthesia, detailing the events surrounding the admission at 05.10, which states that she was conscious, responding to commands, she was dyspnoeic (*breathing with difficulty*), breathing quickly, respiratory rate 50 breaths per minute (*elevated*), shallow, using accessory muscles of respiration (*abnormal breathing pattern*), tachycardia, increased heart rate of 140-150 beats per minute, poor capillary refill (*this is a marker of tissue perfusion*) which had been good, dehydrated, the saturations were 83-84% in 15 litres of oxygen (*this is a pre-terminal figure- i.e. a figure that would lead to cardiopulmonary arrest if sustained for a prolonged period of time*). She was being treated for pulmonary oedema by Frusemide x 3 doses and Salbutamol as she was wheezy. The Consultant on-call was contacted and said that she was in respiratory distress and therefore she was transferred to ITU with the intention for her to be ventilated.

She was intuabted and ventilated , but air entry became difficult because of stiff lungs and lots of blood tinged secretions coming from the ET tube (*endotracheal tube*) (? Pulmonary oedema). Patient went into bradycardia and asystole (*slow heart rate and then no heart rate*). Arrest call bleeped, CPR (*cardiopulmonary resuscitation*) continued, Adrenaline x 7 doses, Atropine 3mgs (*another resuscitation drug*). The Consultant on-call arrived and the ET tube was changed to a size 6 cuffed ET and CPR continued for a further 40 minutes.

The patient expired at 07.00.

There is also attached to the notes a short entry from the Medical registrar, which details much the same.

There is an observation chart also attached with the bundle of documents starting at 19.30 hours until 05.00 (which was the final recording), that the heart rate progressively increased from an admission heart rate of what appears to be just over 110 beats per minute (*raised*), to a heart rate between 150 & 140 beats per minute

Prepared by: Dr Ian Maconochie FRCPCH FFAEM FRCPI PhD

(greatly raised). The respiratory rate at admission is listed as being at 60 breaths per minute *(very raised)*, going up to within this time to lying between 80-mid 75 breaths per minute *(this is greatly increased).*

The peripheral oxygen saturations with accompanying amounts of oxygen being given at different times are given as:

19.30 hours 90% in 10 litres
21.00 hours 94% in 12 litres
22.00 hours 94% in 12 litres
23.00 hours 96% in 12 litres
01.00 hours 94% in 12 litres
02.00 hours 92% in 12 litres
04.00 hours 82% in 12 litres
05.00 hours 90% in 12 litres

This would be extremely worrying as there is a high oxygen demand and a general decline in the level of peripheral saturation of the blood.
It is also recorded under five of these values that there was recession of the chest, indicating that she was working hard despite the additional oxygen.

There is one blood pressure which was taken at the outset of 112/60 mmHg, i.e. this was taken at 19.30 hours, which was within the normal range for a child of this age. Blood tests are included which showed a raised white cell count and a raised neutrophil count, as discussed before- these can indicate infection but can be raised in other conditions.

The nursing notes state "Kirsty attended triage with difficulty in breathing, saturation 66% in air, respiration rate 60 breaths per minute. This improved to 90% with oxygen, moved to the ward, on moving 78% in air, where 10 litres per minute was given, went up to 85% and then slowly creeping up to 88-91% in 10 litres of oxygen. There was Frusemide given in triage, passed 175mls of urine on the ward, feels cold".

No improvement with Kirsty overnight, Frusemide and Ceftriaxone given at 01.00 hours with no improvement, saturations remaining around 80-90% in 12 litres

Prepared by: Dr Ian Maconochie FRCPCH FFAEM FRCPI PhD

oxygen, seen by anaesthesia to transfer to ITU for ventilation. Thereafter the ITU nursing notes detailed "admission from Puffin Ward at 06.00 hours until the death at 07.00 hours".

In summary her clinical course may be described as follows:

The initial assessment undertaken by Sr Parker gave pulse oxymetry of 66% in air, which is grossly abnormal. Dr Reddy saw her at 18.00 hours, he found raised respiratory rate, raised pulse rate and peripheral oxygen saturation of 96%; these are all abnormal features. The presence of the additional noises upon listening to the chest (crackles/creps) and the other clinical features lead Dr Reddy to consider pulmonary oedema and his plan was, in accordance with managing pulmonary oedema, to start intravenous Frusemide, to provide pain relief, to consider antibiotics and to start a fluid chart, and to discuss Kirsty with the registrar. The nursing observation notes show that there was a continued deterioration all in all and that the peripheral oxygen saturations dropped from between 94-96% to 92% and 82% at 04.00.

Another assessment by Dr Reddy did find Kirsty to be breathless with still a raised respiratory rate and a high pulse rate. The course throughout is essentially that of a worsening scenario of pulmonary oedema. I do note that there were three intravenous Frusemide doses given until her appearance in the ITU department.

The registrar saw Kirsty at 01.00 and recorded that still her breathing rate was abnormally high, heart rate was high, peripheral oxygen saturations were abnormal and this was the time for another bolus of Frusemide.

03.00 Dr Reddy reported that Kirsty was marginally improved but the parameters were still highly suggestive of an extremely unwell child.

05.00 The Registrar came to see her again and noted that she was not getting better and that her peripheral oxygen saturations were in the 80s whilst on oxygen. Her heart rate and respiratory rate were both abnormally high, she still had crackles in both lung fields.

Subsequent records shows entry by the Specialist Registrar in Anaesthetics detailing she was conscious, responding to voice and using accessory muscles, breathing fast, with a high heart rate, in other words that she was extremely ill and he considered that she should be transferred for intubation. During the process of intubation Kirsty suffered a bradycardia and then went into full cardiopulmonary arrest and subsequently died, being declared dead at 07.00.

An independent paediatrician has already looked at this case as an Independent Assessor; he has commented upon key clinical elements of Kirsty's management, the comments being part of the bundle sent to me.

I agree with the paediatrician in that she should have been transferred to a High Dependency Unit (HDU) from the very outset of her attendance. She had a known previous history of pulmonary oedema, she had a non-productive cough, without a high temperature, she was breathless, she had an increased heart rate and an increased breathing rate with additional sounds in the chest to indicate pulmonary oedema at her presentation to the ward.

As she was not in the HDU setting, the ability to monitor her was limited, but there was a continued deterioration in her clinical status, as seen from the vital signs which were measured. This deterioration was slow to be recognised by the doctors or nurses attending to Kirsty, with referral to ITU only being made when she was extremely ill.

I agree with the Independent Assessor's assessment that the notes were not comprehensive, there was no fluid balance chart as had been requested, there was no input record of fluids and there were no specific investigations which may have assisted such as a blood gas tests (venous or capillary would have been helpful).

I agree with the Independent Assessors' view that the nursing notes were scanty and infrequent and did not show that there was understanding of the underlying clinical conditions from the nursing staff.

It is clear that the clinicians involved did not entertain the possibility of a continuing deterioration in this patient; they were thinking that her condition would improve with the treatments that they had offered. These were the correct treatments but as they had not improved her condition recourse to more advanced treatment such as intubation and ventilation could have been carried out at an earlier stage.

Prepared by: Dr Ian Maconochie FRCPCH FFAEM FRCPI PhD

I agree with the following statement given by the Independent Assessor: "A more thorough and timely assessment and investigation of Kirsty's illness would have added information to the clinical picture". I agree with him that such information would have emphasised the seriousness of her condition and expedited the transfer to critical care.

In conclusion, it certainly is true that Kirsty had had previous bouts of pulmonary oedema, for which she had been successfully treated. This episode was a clear case of a repeat onset of pulmonary oedema. The failure to recognise the severity at the outset of her presentation meant there was considerable delay in her getting the sought of specialist help that she required. The absence of monitoring the measurements and a failure by the clinicians involved to appreciate the seriousness of this condition meant it contributed to this delay in Kirsty receiving the appropriate treatment which she needed. I would therefore say that Kirsty (albeit that she may not have survived this particular episode of pulmonary oedema), the delay in her getting to the sort of treatment required for her from the outset of her presentation contributed to her death.

Dr Ian Maconochie FRCPCH FFAEM FRCPI PhD
Consultant in Paediatric/Emergency Medicine

Dated: 9th May 2011

Two days after receiving the specialists report I was contacted by the Coroner's officer who informed me that the Coroner was happy with my contacting the police with regard to the contents of the report. I spoke to the police the same day, and they said that they would contact us in a couple of days in order to get a possible investigation started with regard to Kirsty's death.

The Coroner's officer Paul Roberts contacted me 16th June 2011 to inform Peggy and me that there would be a pre-inquest meeting at the County Hall Chelmsford Essex on 21st June at 3pm. It appears that things are moving along at last.

Today 17th June 2011 I received a phone call from the Police Inspector to inform me that though the hospital contributed to Kirsty's death they would not be placing charges against them because it was the responsibility of the doctors monitoring body the General Medical Council that should deal with this type of medical matter, not the Police. I could not believe that I was hearing this nonsense and immediately blasted him over the Police decision; I don't think it bothered him in the slightest. It now makes me wonder what an inquest will achieve; I suppose that we shall get some idea at the pre-inquest meeting, I am wondering if there will be anybody there that we are accusing of malpractice.

On the 21st June we arrived at the Coroners court where we were met by the Coroners officer, he gave us a copy of the pre inquest review papers that set out the proceedings for the day. These papers indicated as to whom would be called to the inquest proper. The one vital instruction set out by the Coroner is that the Chief Executive Officer of the trust attends the inquest in person. We were only in the court for an hour and so it seemed that we were on our way out again in no time. The Coroner did suggest that the inquest would only take one day. The only other people in the court that day were the legal team representing the hospital.

The one thing that the Coroner did make clear was that in accordance with section forty two of the Coroners act she was not allowed to place the blame for Kirsty's death on any one individual, it seems though that she can place the blame on the trust's service failures if she believes they were at fault in not providing the collective care that Kirsty required. We now wait for the date of the inquest.

On 26th June 2011 we received a letter from the Coroner's officer that the inquest has been called for November 25th 2011, now we can come to the end of this sad story. We have been informed that the inquest should only take one day as previously stated.

In preparation for the inquest the following address was made to the coroner in advance of the hearing and it was as follows and entered below.

Address to the Coroners court.

Dear Madam Coroner,

On the 28th August, 2003 my daughter Kirsty was admitted to Basildon hospital suffering from Acute Respiratory Distress Syndrome (ARDS) a condition caused by Pulmonary Oedema, or fluid on the lungs.

ARDS is a condition that should always be treated in a high dependency unit or in the absence of that, an Intensive care unit; there is no medical journal I have seen that states otherwise.

The Parliamentary Health Service Ombudsman stated in her report that Kirsty was a candidate for the Intensive care unit from the time of her admission though in fact she was not placed there until thirteen hours after her admission.

Kirsty though in a very distressed condition was not seen by a paediatrician until five hours after her arrival at triage.

Antibiotics for Kirsty were prescribed at 1810 hours on 28th August 2003 but not given until 0110 hours on the morning of 29th August 2003; this was a delay of over seven hours.

Though there were nurses on the ward that had known Kirsty for many years she was put into the care of a bank nurse who had never seen her previously and as a consequence Kirsty was not afforded the type observations that her condition demanded, in fact the observations were very few and far between and her blood pressure was only checked once throughout the night she died. Observations were carried out sometimes every two hours and at other times hourly, the normal observation criteria for Kirsty's problems are 20-30 minutes throughout her crisis.

Though it was very obvious that Kirsty was in very dire straits the registrar failed to contact the on-call Consultant Paediatrician until it was far too late for her recovery.

The Consultant eventually arrived at the ITU at 6.30am on the 29th August 2003 half an hour before death occurred, in my opinion this was scandalous.

Kirsty's mother was forced to stand by her bedside and watch her slowly die, in pain, frightened, de-hydrated, and without dignity for a period of thirteen hours. My wife was not with Kirsty for the final hour of her life because thirteen hours too late she was admitted to the ITU where resuscitation attempts were being made to save her.

The Trust admitted absolutely no liability in Kirsty's death, though this is always the response of medical authorities, and it was not until three years later following the Ombudsman's report that they shouldered any responsibility.

The now defunct Healthcare Commission supported the trust after providing a seriously flawed report on the night's events; this I believe misled the Coroner causing her to deny an inquest in 2005.

The General Medical Council carried out their own investigation and initially decided that the registrar should face the Fitness to Practice panel at a hearing to be held in Manchester lasting for nine days, they then cancelled that by saying, "though the doctors behaviour could be considered negligent, it was not negligent enough for him to be tried by a panel of his peers," even though Kirsty died as a result of that negligence.

There were a catalogue of errors and significant failings by the medical and nursing staff on the night of Kirsty's death, such as, not carrying out basic nursing observations appropriate for a very seriously ill child, failure to recognise the seriousness of her condition, delays in seeking and obtaining reviews by senior doctors. Some blood tests should have been repeated and blood gasses that should have been monitored were not, this would have helped as the values would be vital in the monitoring the severity of Kirsty's illness. There were clear indications that Kirsty needed care more intensive than that available on the paediatric ward, either in a High Dependency Unit or in Intensive Care, she was not transferred until her condition had already deteriorated too far for recovery. Over a period of thirteen hours during the night of 28th August 2003 the staff caring for Kirsty became very complacent, she had been in this situation many times before and they took it for granted that she would recover as quickly as on previous admissions.

Overall the standard of care was appalling for my daughter and for this the staff responsible should be ashamed of their non-commitment. If there is such a thing as death by indifference then Kirsty is a prime example of this. At home the responsibility of a child lay with the parents, when that child is placed into hospital care then that responsibility transfers to those accepting the child into their care.

There is no doubt that those responsible for Kirsty during the night she died broke their duty of care towards her.

Kirsty's death was partly due to that of indifference by all concerned in her care.

In my opinion my daughter's death was as a result of nothing less than criminal negligence.

Charles Pearce. (Father)

I received a file from the Coroners officer relating to the inquest proper on 30th June 2011; it contained one hundred and eighty nine pages of information and medical records pertaining to Kirsty's death. All those to be called to the inquest also received that same file. After a while I read every page in the file which was in chronological order and it just brought me to tears, it was nothing more than an official record of medical negligence in the death of Kirsty and it pained me so much in reading it, Peggy tried but just could not face reading it herself at that time.

IN THE CORONER'S COURT

AT CHELMSFORD

Council Chamber
Chelmsford Borough Council
Duke Street
Essex.

Friday, 25th November 2011

Before

MRS TINA HARRINGTON
(Her Majesty's Deputy Assistant Coroner)

———————

INQUEST

TOUCHING UPON THE DEATH OF

KIRSTY JAYNE PEARCE

———————

MISS N PERSAUD appeared on behalf of the Basildon and Thurrock
University Hospital NHS Trust.

Transcript of Stenographic Notes for
Sellers Legal Services,
(Official Stenographers to the Crown Court)
40-43 Chancery Lane, London, WC2A 1JQ.

1

Telephone: 020 7405 4512

ALL PROCEEDINGS

INDEX

2

Friday, 25th November 2011

INQUEST TOUCHING UPON THE DEATH OF KIRSTY JAYNE PEARCE

THE CORONER: Good morning. If you just introduce me to the parties, please.

THE CORONER'S OFFICER: Yes, madam. Directly in front of you are Mr. and Mrs. Pearce, who are Kirsty's mother and father. They have two representatives, one from the Health Care Commission and MENCAP. The lady is here to observe and support them. We have counsel in front of you for the Trust Miss Nadia Persaud, and you have your witnesses behind, and one lady member of the Press. On this side you have your own expert, madam, Dr. Maconochie, who is going to observe proceedings.

THE CORONER: Before we commence the evidence I would like to formally reopen this inquest. This inquest was opened on 20th June 2011 and adjourned until this date. We are touching upon the death of Kirsty Jane Pearce, born on 22nd February 1986. She lived with her parents and her brother at an address in Basildon.

Before we start to hear any evidence I want to spend a short

3

time explaining to all concerned here what the nature and the purpose of an inquest is. I am aware that there have been a number of other inquiries in this matter into the events that led to Kirsty's death. I have been supplied with documentation regarding those other inquiries and, of course, the findings. However, it is important for everyone here to be aware and to note that this is a new and different inquiry and I have a different remit.

It is important for the Properly Interested Parties, particularly the parents, to know what an inquest is. An inquest is an investigation into a death, it is a fact-finding inquiry conducted by me. The sole purpose of an inquest is to establish certain facts about the death, so four important questions must be answered. The four questions are who the deceased was, where she died, when she died, and how she came by her death.

At this inquest I have asked witnesses to come along to give evidence and I will be asking questions first of all and after I have finished asking my questions any of the Properly Interested Persons can ask questions. The first three questions -- who the deceased was, when and where she died -- are usually answered quite easily. The fourth question of how she came by her death is often the most difficult and most of the evidence that we will hear today will be concerned with how Kirsty came by her death.

We have dealt with what an inquest is, it is a fact-finding inquiry, I just want to explain a little bit about what an inquest is not. It is not a fault-finding inquiry. Its purpose is not to decide who, if anyone, is to blame for the death and in that respect I am governed by the Coroner's Rules 1984, Rule 42, which gives me

4

clear directions in that respect and it states, and it is helpful to note this: "No verdict shall be framed in such a way as to appear to determine any question of criminal liability on the part of any named person or civil liability."

What that means is in layman's terms is that this inquest is not a trial, no-one is on trial, and no-one can be found guilty of anything. There is no prosecution and no defence. It also means, importantly, that this inquest is not a civil trial, so there are no sides claiming compensation from the other. In this inquest there are no sides and there are no parties. I am aware that the Basildon and Thurrock University Hospital NHS Trust is represented today. However, Miss Persaud does not represent a different side, she is here to assist the inquest.

Without further ado I am going to call Mr. Roberts, the Coroner's Officer, to provide some evidence.

THE CORONER'S OFFICER, PAUL ROBERTS, sworn

Q.   Paul Roberts, your Coroner's Officer. Madam, this inquest touches upon the death of Kirsty Jane Pearce who was born into life on 22nd February 1986 and who lived at an address in Basildon, Essex. Kirsty was admitted to Basildon Hospital on the late afternoon of 28th August 2003 with difficulties with breathing. Despite some medical intervention during the night Kirsty was declared dead on the morning of 29th August 2003.

The family still had concerns over the care of Kirsty at Basildon Hospital and complained to the Health Trust, the Health Care Commission and appealed to the Health Service Primary Trust.

5

This also involved a complaint to the General Medical Council.

The medical problems that Kirsty suffered from were polyarticular JCA with valgus to both ankles, microcephaly, asthma, intercranial calcifications, complex seizures, Raynauld's Syndrome, right bilateral retinal detachment, growth failure below the third centile, learning difficulties, colitis, anaemia, osteoporosis, micrognathia, hypothyroidism and vasculitis with impaired kidney function.

A post-mortem examination was carried out at Basildon Hospital by Dr. Uza who is a pathologist at the hospital. The cause of death was found to be 1A pulmonary oedema and 1B left ventricular failure.

Madam, that is the brief facts in this case and we have the witnesses to call before you.

THE CORONER: Thank you very much. Can we please call Dr. Gangavati.

DR. RAGHAVENDRA RAMARAO GANGAVATI, affirmed

EXAMINED by THE CORONER

THE CORONER'S OFFICER: Can you state your full name?

A. My full name is Raghavendra Ramarao Gangavati and I am currently working as a locum consultant paediatrician at Leicester (inaudible).

THE CORONER: Please be seated.

A. Thank you.

THE CORONER: Dr. Gangavati, I have two statements from you, can I just clarify that? The first one appears at page 141 of the bundle of documents and is dated 21st January 2004. Do you have a copy of

6

that?

A. Yes, I do.

THE CORONER: Thank you. Then I have a recent statement that has been forwarded to me under cover of an email dated 23rd November, and it is dated 23rd November, which is a more detailed statement.

A. Yes.

THE CORONER: So those two statements have you got copies of those?

A. Yes, I got copies of both.

THE CORONER: You have had an opportunity to look at those?

A. Yes, I have.

THE CORONER: May I first of all ask you to explain to me what time you came on call, what time when you started work that day?

A. I started work at 5.00 in the evening.

THE CORONER: I have read in both of your statements that it was a very busy evening in terms of the amount of patients that you had requiring your attention?

A. Yes. As you see from my statement, I mean, that was very hard, it was an absolutely extremely busy night, both on the general paediatric and intensive care unit.

THE CORONER: Can you just tell the inquest how many registrars in your department were working that evening?

A. I was the only registrar covering the whole of the general paediatric service and neonatal intensive care unit, which also includes covering the labour ward, yes, so basically the three paediatric wards and the Neonatal Intensive Care Unit.

THE CORONER: Sorry, you speak very quickly so I got the first part of that. There were three paediatric wards to cover and?

7

A.   And Neonatal Intensive Care Unit and a labour ward and, of course, the (inaudible).

THE CORONER: Can help me with this, you say in your statement that you started your shift at 5.00 and you confirmed that today. You said this in your statement: "The handover of all patients and the NICU by the day registrars went on until about 5.45."

A.   Yes, that is right.

THE CORONER: Then you said while the handover was going on you got a call asking you to review an extremely pre-term baby?

A.   Yes, that is right.

THE CORONER: Help us with this; you went over to the NICU and you say in your statement you were not handed over Kirsty Pearce's attendance to the Paediatric Assessment Unit by the day registrar?

A.   Yes that is correct.

THE CORONER: So how was it that you came to be aware of Kirsty's presence in the paediatric ward?

A.   It was only after the on-call SHO, the Senior House Officer, Dr. Reddy, had seen her and assessed her, only after that when he called me to inform of her admission on the Puffin Ward, I believe, I am not sure about the exact time but it was after her admission to Puffin Ward, which I presume was around 7.30 that evening.

THE CORONER: Do you remember what time you spoke to Dr. Reddy about Kirsty for the first time?

A.   That was that time.

THE CORONER: What time?

A.   Approximately 7.30, after, because that was the time she was admitted to Puffin Ward so I was informed after she was admitted to

8

Puffin Ward.

THE CORONER: You say in your statement that Dr. Reddy informed you that he had made a pre-term assessment of Kirsty and he had already instituted appropriate management.

A. Yes, that is correct.

THE CORONER: He had undertaken blood investigations, the chest x-ray, and he had prescribed a dose of IV Frusemide?

A. Yes.

THE CORONER: He instructed the nurse to monitor urine output and fluid banks.

A. Yes, that is right.

THE CORONER: You go on to say in your statement you were informed this was in line with her previous management plans when she was admitted with similar problems in the past. How did you know, who informed you of that?

A. That was also Dr. Reddy because he had gone through Kirsty's notes. It was actually mentioned in his (inaudible) as well that Kirsty responds to Frusemide so he had the chance to go through her notes at that point.

THE CORONER: Then you go back on to say in your statement you had to prioritise your work and you continued with the management of the sick pre-term baby. Then your plan was to go and see Kirsty once the baby was stabilised?

A. That is correct.

THE CORONER: You go on to say in your statement that you spoke to Dr. Ware at about 10.10?

A. No, 8.10 actually.

9

THE CORONER: 8.10, but you spoke to him about the baby, the pre-term baby's conditions at this point?

A. Yes, that is correct.

THE CORONER: Did you mention to him at all that Kirsty Pearce had been admitted into hospital and she was in Puffin Ward at that point?

A. I don't recall.

THE CORONER: Then you go on to say in your statement that once you finished stabilising the baby you went to Puffin Ward to review Kirsty and you think that was at about 10.00.

A. Yes, that is correct.

THE CORONER: Can you help me with this; I think we are all clear about what you found in terms of your observations when you went to see Kirsty. Tell us a little bit, in your own words, about what your observations of her were when you went to review her at 10.00.

A. Her observations at that time showed she had a heart rate of 130 per minute, respiratory rate of 70 per minute, blood pressure of 112/60 and oxygen saturation at 94 per cent. (Inaudible) oxygen by mask and from what I can recall she was fully conscious at this time.

THE CORONER: You go on to say in the next paragraph that she had already received one dose of Frusemide at that point?

A. Yes.

THE CORONER: But she did not appear to be getting any better by 10.00?

A. Yes, that is correct.

THE CORONER: Can you help me with this; why at this stage did you

10

not feel that it was suitable to admit Kirsty to the Intensive Care Unit?

A.   Once we give Frusemide then we have to wait for a few hours before we can actually notice the action that whether it has helped and wait for at least four to six hours for it to see if it is working, and the other thing which I noticed when I assessed her at that time was chest x-ray it showed some evidence of chest infection, so my plan was at that time to start her on IV antibiotics as well and to see if that affects... makes any difference in her presentation, so at that point my plan that she had IV antibiotics and I wanted some more time to see how the effect was because especially, I mean, moving at that point that was the first time when I actually review her notes and I... reviewing her notes, I mean, I know she respond to Frusemide on previous occasion. She had always been treated with IV Frusemide and always responded to that so I wanted to give a chance to see if her... see how it works and also to give the antibiotics and see what difference that makes and then to give her again.

THE CORONER: At that point, so 10.00, what plan did you have to review her again in terms of timeframe? When did you think that you would be looking at her again to see whether the plan that you put in place was working?

A.   Yes, my plan was to see her again in about two hours' time.

THE CORONER: You go on to say that you did not get time to document your review of Kirsty at that point?

A.   Yes, that is correct.

THE CORONER: And so the medical notes that we have are limited in

11

terms of your input?

A.   At 10.00?

THE CORONER: Pardon?

A.   Sorry, at 10.00?

THE CORONER: At 10.00, yes. Help me with this; you go on to say
that at midnight you were asked to review Kirsty by Dr. Reddy?

A.   That is right.

THE CORONER: When I was asking about your plan at 10.00 you were
plan was to review her in any event and I understand that from
reading the documentation that in fact Mother was so concerned that
she asked for a further review and Dr. Reddy asked you to review her
by 12.00. You see my point? In fact, you had been called to come
and review her rather than you coming back as the result of a call?

A.   I planned to come and review her but I got busy in the Neonatal
Intensive Care Unit and meanwhile I got a call from an SHO who had
assessed her and he called me so instead of coincided my previous
plan, I mean, when I had planned and when I got the call from Dr.
Reddy.

THE CORONER: We have set out in your statement what your
observations were. There had not been much of any improvement, you
decided to give the second dose of Frusemide and, in fact, the IV
treatment you had prescribed earlier had not been given by the time
you reviewed her at 12.10, is that right?

A.   Sorry, repeat again, please.

THE CORONER: Yes, you decided to give her a second dose of
Frusemide?

A.   Huh-huh.

12

THE CORONER: You set out in your statement that the IV that you prescribed earlier had not been given to her so you instructed the nurse to give it at that point?

A. I kept tracks.

THE CORONER: Antibiotic.

A. Yes.

THE CORONER: At that point, this is obviously 12.00, 12.10. Why did you not think that admitting her to the ICU would have been an appropriate given she made no improvement? She had been hospitalised, I think, for six hours at the point?

A. Yes, I mean, as I mentioned in my statement, I mean, I got a call at that same time about informing me about the imminent birth of the pre-term baby, 24-week pre-term baby with (inaudible) prematurity within gestation, so I called Dr. Ware, the consultant on-call, on-call on that night, to inform him about the imminent birth of this pre-term baby and I also discussed with (inaudible) about Kirsty's admission and management plan and mentioned about our plan after repeating the second dose of Frusemide and Dr. Ware was in agreement with that and that was... I was advised that she normally responds to IV Frusemide and should give her a second dose and see how she responds.

THE CORONER: So just summarise for me, Dr. Gangavati, the information you gave Dr. Ware included the medication she had received thus far?

A. Mm.

THE CORONER: Did you tell him the timeframes in terms of when she had been admitted and did you give him the information about your

13

observations?

A.   I should have because that is the only way you inform the ward of the condition of the patient.

THE CORONER: I know you should have, did you?

A.   Yes, I did.

THE CORONER: Right. You say that this phone call was just after 12.00, was it?

A.   I mean, at 12.10 I reviewed Kirsty so must be some time around 12.30-ish, I don't know exact time. I mean, I believe around 12.30

THE CORONER: About 12.30?

A.   Yes, approximately, I mean.

THE CORONER: Again, we do not have any evidence to support that in terms of any documentation, nothing in the medical notes to suggest that happened?

A.   Not in the medical notes but after I saw, actually, that investigation, the GMC investigation, (inaudible) I mean, I got hold of the documents, I mean, and I saw that in (inaudible) so he did mention about that phone call.

THE CORONER: Again, can you just help me with this; obviously nothing in the medical notes, can you just explain to this inquest why that was not documented in the medical notes?

A.   Again, as I said, it was an extremely busy night that day and I had to prioritise clinical care over documentation. As I already mentioned in my statement, if documentation was given more priority then clinical care would have been seriously compromised so, I mean, I might have been called because normally when there is an extremely premature baby who is going to be imminent (inaudible)

14

called to labour ward to see whether everything is set up, I mean, and that the baby imminent, I speak to the parents, I mean, I inform them about the outcome of the baby being born that early, so I must have been rushed, I mean, to labour ward and NICU at that time and that's why I haven't time to document that.

THE CORONER: You also set out that you had never treated Kirsty before and you were aware that Dr. Ware had, he had been treating her for a very long time?

A.   Yes, that is right.

THE CORONER: To what extent, knowing that information, did that influence your decision not to ask her to be admitted into the Intensive Care Unit?

A.   Very much, because very reassured, because I never seen Kirsty before so, I mean, I ought not to have made a decision myself. I feel sure (inaudible) received so that was.

THE CORONER: You say in your statement you next reviewed Kirsty at about 3.10 a.m..

A.   That is right.

THE CORONER: Following another request by Dr. Reddy and again done between carrying out procedures on the 24-week baby, pre-term baby. Once again do you say that there was no significant improvement in her clinical condition and you decided to discuss her management with Dr. Ware again and also to request the registrar in the IT Unit to review her. Help me with this; you say here you spoke to Dr. Ware at around this time again in the presence of Dr. Reddy and nurses?

A.   Yes, that is right.

15

THE CORONER: Once again, just so that I am clear, there is no reference again in the medical notes that I can see as to what specifically took place at this point.

A. No, there is no medical notes. My plan is... I don't have a copy here, but to discuss with consultant on-call, Dr. Ware, so there is a plan and also the plan was... and the second plan was to discuss with the anaesthetic ITU registrar.

THE CORONER: I am afraid the times are not very clear but I have plan, as it were, set out says: "Plan page 34"?

A. Yes, I can see.

THE CORONER: So is this the ----

A. Yes, 3.10.

THE CORONER: 3.10. So under "plan": "To DW consultant on-call, Dr. Ware, and also to speak to anaesthetist," so you are saying that is what your plan was but that is also what you did?

A. No, my plan... this is my plan which I wrote after I examined Kirsty, but following this I discussed with consultant, Dr. Ware, and I... in my statement I mention (inaudible) that Dr. Ware advised repeat dose of Frusemide and specifically asking whether she needed to be reviewed by the ITU at that time. I mean, I was advised that she didn't need and in following the consultant's advice I did not contact ITU registrar at that time.

THE CORONER: Again, you say you did not document this telephone discussion with Dr. Ware at this time because you had to rush back to the pre-term baby?

A. Yes.

THE CORONER: You have put that this discussion with Dr. Ware had

16

been recorded by you in the medical notes at 5.00 because that was the next documentation in the notes. I just want to be clear about that, please. If we look at your notes 5.00 a.m., this is on page 38.

A.   Yes.

THE CORONER: "Not improving," and you set out the examination.

A.   Yes.

THE CORONER: Then you put: "DW consultant on-call Dr. Ware." Can I just be clear, the information that is contained at this point in the medical notes, under the 5.00 a.m. notes, is that referring to the information that you had at 3.10 a.m. or is that separate?

A.   No, the observation findings are when I saw Kirsty at 5.00 a.m.

THE CORONER: Yes?

A.   But the... I mean, because I don't document the earlier discussion with Dr. Ware I documented that. I mean, that's why I put discussed with on-call consultant Dr. Ware and then made a step and suggested repeat Frusemide because that was his advice at that point but following that the next two plans are mine, which was made at 5.00, and that is why they are starting from the margin of the page, because Dr. Ware's advice was repeat Frusemide but my plan was at 5.00 we inform the (inaudible) and it was (inaudible) and those are the plans which I made at 5.00.

THE CORONER: Right. Just so that I am clear, according to your statement you rang Dr. Ware again at about 3.00?

A.   Yes. Around 3.30, probably.

THE CORONER: At 3.30 but you recorded that in your 5.00 notes?

A.   Yes, because it was my next documentation. I mean, I couldn't

17

209

document immediately after because after I had recorded my plan to discuss with him at 3.10 and also to speak to the anaesthetist, that was my plan, and following that I spoke to Dr. Ware but then I was rushed back to the Intensive Care and ICU so I didn't get a chance to document that discussion around that time and the next time I saw Kirsty was at 5.00 and that is when I have documented that advice which I had earlier received at around 3.30.

THE CORONER: You would agree with me, no doubt, it is completely impossible to understand what happened at which point if we have observations going in and details of telephone conversations in at the wrong time?

A.   It was such a short period, it is not... it's 3.30 to 5.00, so it's not like there was a big gap, it was just one hour when I was on different places and it is not a large time gap, actually, to document. I mean, the previous advice (inaudible) which was an hour and a half back.

THE CORONER: It might have been easier to make it clear that in fact the telephone call took place at 3.30. I appreciate you are writing in at 5.00?

A.   I appreciate my documentation is not (inaudible) not been done properly.

THE CORONER: So you then went back, as you said, at 5.00, again Kirsty was not improving. Then you requested that the ITU anaesthetic registrar review her and that is recorded in your medical notes.

A.   Yes.

THE CORONER: Then this plan was made by you in the presence of Dr.

18

Reddy?

A. That is correct.

THE CORONER: Then you waited until the ITU registrar arrived and then you went back to manage the pre-term baby?

A. Yes, I did.

THE CORONER: Right. The next event is that Kirsty was transferred to the ITU, that was the next event. What, in your terms of what you did, your role with Kirsty, did you have any other interaction with Kirsty that evening?

A. Following my 5.00 review?

THE CORONER: Following the 5.00 review.

A. No, I left at around ten past, 5.10, and went back to ICU and, as I mentioned, I mean, when the anaesthetic registrar came I handed over Kirsty to him and following that point I think I was called to the ITU, I don't have any direct intervention with Kirsty because anaesthetic registrar has taken over her care.

THE CORONER: Then you received a cardiac arrest call from the ITU unit at 6.31 and then you say you rang Dr. Ware whilst the resuscitation was being carried out at 6.35?

A. That is right.

THE CORONER: So there was no telephone call from you to Dr. Ware between 3.30 and approximately 6.30?

A. Yes.

THE CORONER: Is that right?

A. Yes.

THE CORONER: When you made the decision to hand Kirsty's care over the IT Unit, which I think is about 5.00, 5.05, something like that,

did you not feel it is important to ring Dr. Ware at that point to
tell him of your decision, because it runs contrary to what he was
saying to you, certainly at 3.30?

A.   Yes, I mean, I called ITU registrar to come and assess her. At
that point I didn't know that after assessment he would take her to
ITU. I wanted to wait for his assessment.

THE CORONER: Right.

A.   And I had... I asked him to inform me about what his plan was,
so in retrospect I came to know that he had assessed her and he had
spoken to his consultant on call and had made the plan for ITU so I
wanted to discuss... wait for his assessment to be finished and for
his plan to be made and then inform Dr. Ware what was the plan but I
didn't get informed by the anaesthetic registrar that he had planned
to transfer Kirsty to ITU so that is why I couldn't inform Dr. Ware.

THE CORONER: Then I think you said that you spoke to Dr. Ware
whilst resuscitation was being carried out and then Dr. Ware arrived
at the IT Unit?

A.   Yes, that is right.

THE CORONER: Can you explain to me why it was that the antibiotics
were not administered to Kirsty after you had initially prescribed
them for her? Can you give me an explanation as to why they were
not administered in the way you had prescribed them to be?

A.   They were originally prescribed at 10.00, you see on the
regular medicine chart, but obviously the antibiotics hadn't been
prescribed by the nursing staff and I can't comment as to why there
was a delay, so I can't unfortunately comment on that.

THE CORONER: From what you told us in your second statement, in

20

fact you had contacted Dr. Ware on three occasions that evening, three telephone calls concerning Kirsty?

A. Concerning Kirsty, yes, just after midnight, after 3.00 and at 6.30.

THE CORONER: Just assist me with this; in terms of fluid to Kirsty was there any reason why Kirsty was not put on an IV fluid drip?

A. Following the discussion with the consultant, I mean, the management plan was, I think, to result in dehydration because Kirsty had excess fluid on her lungs and the plan was to get rid of the excess fluid by give her diuretics, so that was the aim of the treatment, so in doing so, I mean, her saturation otherwise was normal. I mean, even though I have not actually documented those parameters but her circulatory status was normal and the aim was to result in dehydration so why at that time we didn't want to overload her with extra IV fluid because that would defeat the purpose of giving the diuretics so in following the... because after midnight I have discussed with Dr. Ware and I have followed his management plan and in doing so I have not put Kirsty on IV fluids.

THE CORONER: Right.

A. Can I just clarify a point on the antibiotics, please.

THE CORONER: Yes?

A. The antibiotics were initially prescribed at 10.00, so if you see the regular medication chart.

THE CORONER: Yes, let us find the reference.

MISS PERSAUD: Madam, I am not sure that the full medical chart is in the bundle. We have the front page, we are just trying to find the original.

21

THE CORONER: I am grateful.

A. So I cannot (inaudible) we had actually done on the regular medication side but when I review at 10.00 and I noticed they were still not given so that's reason... that's when we wrote it up upon the stat in the front page where we (inaudible) to be given at that point so that is why it is (inaudible).

THE CORONER: Let us see if we can find that document. Right, yes, I see that, thank you. Would you like to just show the witness so he can confirm that? (Same handed) Just so you can confirm that.

A. Yes.

THE CORONER: Thank you, Dr. Gangavati. If you wait there for a moment to see if there are any other questions for you. Mrs. Persuad, do you have any questions of this witness?

MISS PERSAUD: Madam, can I go last?

THE CORONER: Of course. Mr. Pearce, do you have any questions?

EXAMINED by MR. PEARCE

MR PEARCE: If I may. Dr. Gangavati, you prescribed the antibiotics at 10.00.

A. That was prescribed by Dr. Reddy.

Q. She didn't get them until gone 1.00.

A. That is right.

Q. Were the antibiotics in the ward drug cupboard?

A. I can't comment because those are not (inaudible). I can't comment on whether they were in the drug cupboard or whether... we prescribed it and the nurses give the antibiotics so I don't know that.

22

Q.   Who would have got the antibiotics? Would it have been
collected from the pharmacy or... you don't know, really, do you?

A.   No, I don't, sorry.

Q.   There is that. How many times do you recall you actually
called Dr. Ware, you spoke to him?

A.   As I have mentioned in my statement, I went through so on that
night, I mean, the first time I recall was at ten past twenty but
that was to discuss about a baby in the ICU but the next time was
regarding Kirsty, the first time was after my review of Kirsty at
midnight, so that just after probably 12.30-ish. The next one was
at 3.30 and the next one at 6.30, so three times regarding Kirsty.

Q.   When you first became aware of Kirsty's admission I believe you
said that was about may be 9.45, no 7.15?

A.   7.30.

Q.   Are you telling me that you could not possibly go 40 yards to
have a quick look before 10.00?

A.   The baby was needed a chest drain which was an emergency. It
actually had a large pneumothorax and had to insert a chest drain,
so I have discuss ----

Q.   So you constantly were tied up, you didn't get a second to go
round the corner?

A.   No, because doing a chest drain, I mean, (inaudible).

Q.   Why did you not call Dr. Ware out? You are a paediatric
specialist registrar, why didn't you say to Dr. Ware: "I need you
here," because Kirsty, she went in very, very seriously ill, she was
so ill, in fact, that her problems getting worse but not that very
great, she was pretty poor when she first went in. She should have

23

been immediately admitted to intensive care because there was no High Dependency Unit in Basildon, why didn't you call Dr. Ware and say: "Please come out"? You were snowed under, you had all this work with different babies, you had so many admissions to the ward, but you did not call him. Why not?

A. What time do you say? At what time are you referring, sir? At 7.30 when I was informed ----

Q. No.

THE CORONER: Sorry, can I just... let us try and clarify. I think the question is, tell me if I am wrong, Mr. Pearce, the question is given that you had so many patients and a very sick patient that evening, why did you not ask Dr. Ware to come out?

A. At 7.30?

THE CORONER: At 7.30 or, indeed, any other time prior to 6.30?

A. Well, at 7.30, as I say... I mean, Dr. Reddy had gone to her case file and he had noticed that she... that this one of her recurrence of the presentation with the same problem and she had responded to diuretics every time so, as I explained in my evidence, that we had to wait for the treatment to work so I don't have call Dr. Ware at that point, I mean, because we had to wait to see if the treatment worked or not. But subsequently, I mean, as I mentioned, that I called him at those times which I have mentioned already.

THE CORONER: Okay. That is the answer, I think, Mr. Pearce.

MR PEARCE: Just one more question; it was extremely busy, we understand that, how did you prioritise the patients? What criteria were you using? How did you prioritise the care of these patients?

24

216

Where did Kirsty come into this?

A. This is a very general question.

Q. Let me just finish the question. I will make a statement; she was dying at that time so where did your priorities lie?

A. My priorities were actually, I mean, based on the clinical need of the patient. As I said, I mean, the Neonatal Intensive Care Unit the baby need a chest drain. I had to prioritise the baby at that point. That doesn't mean that... because I was already satisfied with the management plan proposed by Dr. Reddy for Kirsty. That doesn't mean that I ignored Kirsty's care. After midnight I have reviewed Kirsty at regular intervals. I have discussed the management plan with the consultant on call, so I was following his advice and, I mean, and unfortunately, I mean, there were very (inaudible) children who were like the 24-weeker who was extremely premature and that needed urgent attention by the paediatric medical team, so I had to prioritise my care to that baby, but that doesn't mean that I didn't review Kirsty. I have reviewed Kirsty and discussed with the consultant.

Q. Right. Dr. Reddy was a trainee doctor on rotation, an SHO. He really didn't have responsibility, he didn't have that warrant to take over all this business and that again is the reason why I say to you why didn't you call Dr. Ware? Dr. Reddy was not a paediatrician.

A. I said, I have called Dr. Ware.

Q. Called him out. No, I am saying why didn't you him to come to the hospital?

A. I was constantly updating Dr. Ware with what is happening and

25

he was aware of the things which were happening in the ward.

Q.   But you didn't ask him to come out to see Kirsty, did you?

A.   Things kept happening, one after the other.

Q.   You are not answering my question.

A.   Sorry?

THE CORONER: Let us put it another way; was there any point up to, say, 6.30 where you felt that Dr. Ware should have actually physically come to hospital to review Kirsty? I think that is your question.

MR PEARCE: Yes. There is only one other part to that.

THE CORONER: One bit at a time.

A.   Things kept happening one after the other. I mean, if there were three emergencies happening at the same time then I would have called Dr. Ware to come in. Because not like (inaudible) emergency situation at the same time. I mean, I was attending to different patients on a regular basis and I kept Dr. Ware updated and informed about what was happening so I can only inform at that point. I mean, I didn't specifically call him out but Dr. Ware was aware of what was happening and I can't comment on that. I mean, it is his decision whether to come in or not, I mean, but, as I say, when things kept happening one after the other and I was able to manage different patients, attending to one patient and then I was going to another patient. It was not like three emergencies happening at the same time. At that point, I mean, at the single point I was needed in two, three places then certainly I (inaudible) but I was constantly updating and Dr. Ware was aware of the situation.

26

218

THE CORONER: Your second part of question, please?

MR PEARCE: Yes, did Dr. Ware... I understand reading through all the statements that you asked Dr. Ware should you involve ITU and I think he told you no, give more Frusemide, or words to that effect, yes?

A. Mm.

Q. Is that right? So you did ask him about taking Kirsty to ITU?

A. Yes.

Q. You were told not to do it?

A. Yes.

Q. Why did he say not to do it?

A. Why?

THE CORONER: I think that is probably a question for... we will hear from Dr. Ware. I do not think this witness can properly answer that, with all due respect, Mr. Pearce. Do you have any other questions?

MR PEARCE: COUNSEL: No, that's it, thank you.

EXAMINED by MISS PERSAUD
on behalf of the Trust

Q. Dr. Gangavati, you said that when you first saw Kirsty at around 10.00 the observations were heart rate of 130, respiratory rate of 70, blood pressure 112/60 and the oxygen saturation 94 per cent on oxygen. Those are not normal observations, are they?

A. No, they are not.

Q. What do you think about the observations? How concerned were you about those observations at 10.00?

27

A.   Those observations were not normal. I was concerned but, as I already stated, I mean, we had given her a dose of Frusemide and wanted to wait and see what response she had to the antibiotic and Frusemide, so at that point, I mean, I had advice to monitor her regularly and our plan was to review her again and see her response to (inaudible).

Q.   So you were concerned about her at that time. I think you said that you were reassured by having looked at the medical records that Kirsty had had pulmonary oedema before in the past and had responded to Frusemide. Was that just from looking at the medical records or did you also speak to staff on the ward?

A.   I mean, I have looked at the medical notes but I must have, because of time constraints, I have looked at the one or two previous admissions for similar problem but the staff on the unit, I mean, they knew Kirsty very well and I may have been influenced, my decision may have been influenced by their advice as well, I mean, but I don't specifically recall this at this moment.

Q.   Okay.

THE CORONER: In might have happened, it might not, you just do not know.

MISS PERSAUD: When you spoke to Mr. Ware at around midnight and at around 3.00 in the morning do you remember if you specifically passed on to him the observations that were taken in terms of Kirsty's respiratory rate and her oxygen saturation levels?

A.   Yes, I would have given answer to that I did.

THE CORONER: He said he would have done.

MISS PERSAUD: You have been asked this question a couple of times

28

and I am just not entirely clear about your answer; the consultant on call can be called into the hospital to assist. It is clear from your statement and from your evidence that you were extremely busy. You were aware that there was a system in place for Dr. Ware to come in if necessary. Were you aware of that at the time, that you could have called Dr. Ware in to assist you?

A. Yes, I was aware but again, I mean, I think this has been a falsely... I mean, anybody can call a consultant, it is not just a registrar has to... nobody has to get permission from the registrar to call the consultant. The nursing staff can call the consultant. They didn't need permission of the registrar, so I think and looking at some of the documents it says that... permit to call Dr. Ware so I don't know where that comes from actually, so basically it is not just me who can contact the consultant. If anybody else got or any child they can call the consultant themselves so, sorry, I mean, does that answer your question?

MISS PERSAUD: Sort of.

THE CORONER: When you say the answer is that you did not at that point see the need to actually physically call him in that is the answer?

A. Yes, I didn't see the need to physically call him but I was getting his advice.

MISS PERSAUD: Yes, thank you. I think you last saw Kirsty before her arrest at just after 5.00. How was she in terms of her cognitive... was she alert? Was she talking to you? Can you remember how she was presenting at that time?

A. As I recall she was still conscious and responding, was

29

communicating at that stage, so cognitively she was still alert and responding. As I stated in my statement, this is only from looking at the document and I understand from Mr. and Mrs. Pearce's statement, even ITU, that just before she was given the pre-anaesthetic medication she was still talking and in sentences so I presume... I didn't even at that stage she was cognitively alert and responding and conscious.

Q. Thank you. My final question is in relation to you were asked about why intravenous fluids were not given. I think you said that there was a need to dehydrate her to remove the fluids, which you were doing through the Frusemide, and that you were keeping an eye on her circulation. You said that was not documented but you were looking at parameters. Can you just clarify what those parameters were because I think we only have one blood pressure taken quite early on in the admission in the notes, so what parameters were you looking at?

A. Obviously blood pressure is one of the things I looked at when giving (inaudible) at 10.00 but then following that, I mean, heart rate is another parameter for assessing your saturation so I didn't notice much of a difference in the heart rate over the next three to four hours. Her heart rate clearly remained the same so that was an indication that the saturation was (inaudible) at that stage and I would have assessed her (inaudible) is not documented but that is part of my examination, so there are other parameters like (inaudible) circulation which I may have done and blood pressure. I don't know why it wasn't done again after that or whether it was done by the nursing staff and not documented. I can't comment on

30

222

that but, you know ----

Q. So the capillary refill time, are you saying you did do it or that you may have done it? Can you recall whether you did do it?

A. As I said, that's part of my routine examination, it is a normal examination, so I don't specifically recall whether I did it or not but that is my (inaudible) examination.

THE CORONER: It is not recorded?

A. It is not recorded, I mean, again, I mean, the parameters I mean, which I recorded those were abnormal at this point and you can't recall each and every observation in the documentation with time constraints and we are not able to, actually.

MISS PERSAUD: Thank you very much.

THE CORONER: Thank you very much, Dr. Gangavati. Has anyone any objection to Dr. Gangavati being released from the inquest? Dr. Gangavati, you are free to leave this inquest. Thank you very much for coming along to give evidence.

A. Thank you very much.

(The witness withdrew)

DR. STEPHEN JOHN WARE, sworn

EXAMINED by THE CORONER

THE CORONER'S OFFICER: Would you state your full name, please?

A. My name is Stephen John Ware.

THE CORONER: Please take a seat. Could you first of all give the inquest your professional qualification and experience, please, Dr. Ware?

A. My qualifications are I have two degrees, two qualifying

31

degrees, Bachelor of Medicine, Bachelor of Surgery. I am Member of the Royal College of Physicians, I am Member of the Royal College of Paediatrics and Child Health and I have a Diploma in Child Health and I was appointed Consultant Paediatrician at Basildon Hospital and, at the time, also Southend in 1980.

THE CORONER: I wonder if you could help me. I have two sets of documents from you, Dr. Ware, one letter dated 3rd July 2011 and then I have a subsequent document from you which appears at pages 148-149 of the bundle, which is a relatively short statement dated 15th January 2004, in fact it is in letter form. Have you had an opportunity to read these?

A.   Yes, I have.

THE CORONER: I am very grateful?

A.   Perhaps could I just make one comment. I actually in the letter I said that my registrar phoned me at 5.00.

THE CORONER: Yes?

A.   That was clearly wrong. I must have got that time from the notes and that I don't have, I am afraid, at night. I don't necessarily know what the time is, so that should probably have been 3.30, I think Dr. Gangavati said.

THE CORONER: Can we just be clear; first of all, we are all aware you were on-call that particular evening, Dr. Gangavati has given us some evidence that in fact he called on three separate occasions during the course of that night or the early hours of the morning, can you specifically recall those telephone calls?

A.   Yes, I have a call in the letter, the call to which I referred in my letter and, of course, the one as a result of which I came up

32

to the hospital. I don't... it is a while ago but I don't actually specifically recall one (inaudible).

THE CORONER: It may well have taken place, you just do not specifically recall?

A. I don't recall it, no.

THE CORONER: Dr. Gangavati said that he had the first telephone call to you was about 12.30 a.m., so about 12.30 in the early hours of the morning of 29th August. He spoke to you specifically about Kirsty, details of his observations and you recommended continuation of the treatment that had always been given to Kirsty when previous episodes of the same nature occurred, do you specifically recall that?

A. The telephone call at 3.30 in the morning?

THE CORONER: Yes.

A. He told me that Kirsty was not responding to her usual treatment, and I knew that she had been in the ward since tea time, I think.

THE CORONER: Right.

A. He asked me whether we should continue with her conservative treatment, that is to say medical management, or whether we should make referral to the intensive care registrar and I told him to give a third dose of Frusemide and not to alert the intensive care department.

THE CORONER: Can you help me on what basis you made that decision?

A. It was a... I was misled by her previous history. It was a bad decision and one I found very hard to come to terms with and if my advice had been different may be the outcome would have been

33

different but Dr. Gangavati, in not calling the ITU department at that time, was acting on my instructions.

THE CORONER: Can you help me with this; you said that you were misled by the previous history, can you specifically explain to me what you mean by that?

A. Well, this condition of recurrent pulmonary oedema is a very rare thing, it is not something one sees in childhood. In Kirsty's case it had been extensively investigated, I believe she had admissions all over the world, I think, did she not, Charles?

MR PEARCE: Yes.

DR. WARE: And nobody came up with an explanation, but on each occasion, and I think there were more than 30 occasions, I think you said, when she actually had been admitted with this condition. On each occasion she had responded to simple medical measures. Perhaps I should say that pulmonary oedema is an extremely serious and dangerous condition and if I were to hear of a patient who I had not come across before who had pulmonary oedema I would give clear instructions to get a bed ready very quickly on the Intensive Care Unit and to alert the anaesthetist. Indeed, when Kirsty first started having these episodes that is where she ended up but when the pattern of her illness became established she was, when this happened, she would be admitted straight to the children's ward, wouldn't she? As I say, on each occasion she had responded, she never needed intensive care and I think there had been, Mr. and Mrs. Pearce will tell you, there were episodes prior to this where she was actually worse. There was one occasion ----

MR PEARCE: Yes.

34

DR WARE: But I will talk about that after.

THE CORONER: Yes, I will ask you about that. So there was?

A. She certainly was not the illest she had ever been on that occasion, so the fault is mine, quite clearly, and I gave bad advice. Perhaps I should make one or two other sort of comments. First of all, the question of my coming in, this is something that consultants do ----

THE CORONER: Yes?

A. ..... when things are tight. There's not a problem about that. The decision to do that is made by the consultant and I have to say that I wasn't aware just how (inaudible)... it was 3.30 in the morning, I hadn't really clocked just how busy Dr. Gangavati had been. What else was there I wanted say?

THE CORONER: While you think of that can I ask you about fluids, because the issue about fluids has been raised? I just want to ask you about this; is there any reason why... I think Dr. Gangavati gave evidence to explain why he would not have prescribed an IV fluid.

A. I think what he said is very reasonable. Management... what happens with pulmonary oedema is that the lungs are packed with fluid and there are two ways of approaching this. One is to remove the fluid from the body, the whole body becomes dehydrated. Then if the child does not respond to this then they need a ventilator to physically blow the fluid out of the lungs and so dehydration, or a degree of dehydration, is actually part of the treatment.

THE CORONER: Had you used that method before, so in the past you had not used IV fluids, you had dehydrated her?

35

A.   Not in Kirsty's case. I had not actually... I knew Kirsty for
a variety of reasons, but she was well known and loved in the
department. Somebody was asking recently just now about whether the
nursing staff would have been consulted. Nursing staff are, of
course, all consulted about famous patients, and I would do it
myself if I was unfamiliar with a patient. Nurses were an extremely
important source of information and judgment in matters of this
kind, but I obviously knew Kirsty well having met her on ward
rounds (inaudible) her episodes or when she had been in hospital for
a number of other reasons I might well have met her. Of course, we
discussed her in the department and she featured in a number of our
case presentations but I was never actually involved with... I don't
think I ever made an important decision about any aspect of her
management prior to this disastrous night.

THE CORONER: Do you recall specifically whether you were informed
what time Kirsty had been admitted? So by 3.30 in the morning you
had that specific ----

A.   I think I had. I think I had that... I must have been... yes,
I certainly had that in my head.

THE CORONER: Thank you, I have no further questions. There may be
some questions.

                    EXAMINED by MR PEARCE

Q.   Thank you. Dr. Ware, you have referred to Kirsty, you didn't
think she was any more seriously ill than previous occasions, I
think, in your statement. You didn't recall that she had been any
worse than at that time. You are not aware that, I think, three to

                          36

four years previously she had actually the same thing and she was

heading for where she ended up this time but what happened on that

occasion was it was daylight hours, her consultant, Dr. Jackie

Asquith, was in attendance, there were two registrars, there was a

cardiologist with a monitor and two nurses. Even then it took seven

days to pull Kirsty round, so by not getting admitted into IT the

fact was condemning her to death. That's my view.

A. Was she admitted to ITU on that occasion.

Q. No, she was admitted to the side ward on Puffin Ward where she

was dealt with by the consultant, by the two registrars, by the

cardiologist and by the nurses. One of the doctors registrars was

Epi, Dr. Epi?

THE CORONER: Sorry, Mr. Pearce, I am not quite clear what your

question is. What is your question?

A. My question is why didn't she get him... why didn't he get her

into... I am just trying to state how bad she was previously.

THE CORONER: Yes, I understand you are using a previous incident to

highlight but what is your question?

MR PEARCE: Dr. Ware is not aware of this. He wasn't aware of this.

Dr. Ware was Kirsty's doctor for, may be, three years before we

went on with Dr. Eastern. You saw her in your clinics many times

but I didn't believe, actually, you ever saw her in crisis ----

A. No, I don't think ----

Q. ..... in the whole 17 years. What I am trying to get across she

had been as bad as this but because the expertise they pulled her

round, but it took seven days.

A. Sorry, your question was why did I not send her to the ITU?

37

Q. Yes, why didn't you send her to ITU, because she was in terrible distress?

A. It was bad judgment on my part.

Q. So you accept that. We accept that because you knew that ----

THE CORONER: Dr. Ware has said that it was a bad decision.

MR PEARCE: The only other question I have got really is the fact that we had the complaints meeting with you, if you recall. I did say to you at that time how many times did Dr. Gangavati call you? You said he called me at 5.00 a.m.

A. Yes, I just said (inaudible).

Q. He actually told Dr. Asquith that he was in constant contact with you, so I wonder if you can clarify what constant contact means?

THE CORONER: I think ----

A. It is a hard question, it's a while ago.

THE CORONER: We have tried to clarify that, you cannot specifically recall the phone call at 12.30, as I understand it. You specifically recall the phone call you think might have been at 3.30 because you have 5.00 in the notes, I think you told me, and then you accept that you were called just prior to your arrival and you came on the strength of that call. I think that is my understanding of the evidence, Mr. Pearce.

MR PEARCE: Yes, I think sometimes when asking questions it is very difficult to put them in the context that they should be.

THE CORONER: No, that is perfectly fine.

MR PEARCE: It is difficult.

THE CORONER: It helps if I hear what your question is and then

38

assemble it for the witness. Do you have any other questions?

MR PEARCE: No, thank you.

THE CORONER: Mrs. Pearce, any questions?

MRS PEARCE: No, thank you.

THE CORONER: Miss Persaud?

MISS PERSAUD: No, thank you, madam.

THE CORONER: Thank you. Does anyone have any objection to Dr. Ware being released? Thank you very much, you are free to leave this inquest.

            (The witness withdrew)

            ALEXANDRA CORTHINE, sworn

            EXAMINED by THE CORONER

THE CORONER'S OFFICER: Can you give the court your full name, please?

A.   Alexandra Corthine.

THE CORONER: Your professional address, please?

A.   Basildon and Thurrock Health Authority.

THE CORONER: I wonder if you could assist me with a number of matters. Help me with this; first of all, I have one statement from you which starts at page 145A. It is a very short letter dated 20th January 2004. Have you seen a copy of that?

A.   Yes.

THE CORONER: You have familiarised yourself with it. I think it is a typed-up copy of the manuscript statement which appears on the following pages, and that appears on the signed on the same date?

A.   Yes.

            39

THE CORONER: Do you have a copy of that?

A. Yes.

THE CORONER: Can you first of all help me with this; the contents of that statement that is signed by you, are they true and correct?

A. Yes.

THE CORONER: One of the matters I think you might be able to help me with is, first of all, as I understand it you were not a full-time employee?

A. No.

THE CORONER: You were a bank nurse on that evening in question?

A. Yes.

THE CORONER: At the time of this incident what was your experience in paediatric nursing?

A. I had worked at Southend Hospital on the paediatric department as a general nurse, adult nurse, then I did my conversion in 2000 at Basildon Hospital, 2000-2002, and then that is... I liked the ward and that is when I went there to do bank nursing and since then I now work on Puffin full-time or part-time.

THE CORONER: So you are now, as it were, an employee of the Trust?

A. Yes.

THE CORONER: I would be very grateful if you could help us with this; we know from the medical notes that Kirsty was prescribed some antibiotics by Dr. Reddy and it does not appear that she was given those antibiotics after they were initially prescribed. I think that it was picked up by Dr. Gangavati when he came to review Kirsty at 12.00. Can you assist us as to why those antibiotics were not given?

40

A.   I am sorry, I can't, and as a bank nurse I wouldn't be giving

IV antibiotics anyway.   I don't... I honestly don't know why.   I

can't remember if I know.

THE CORONER: You cannot explain why the antibiotics ----

A.   No.

THE CORONER: ..... were not administered?

A.   No.

THE CORONER: You would not have had the authority to be able to do

it?

A.   No.

THE CORONER: Who would have been given the role that evening of

administering ----

A.   The nurse in charge of the ward.

THE CORONER: I have seen the nursing notes.   I do not know, have

you seen a copy of the nursing notes?

A.   No.

THE CORONER: I wonder if you can just go to them.   As I recall

there are just two entries.

THE CORONER'S OFFICER: I have it here, madam, page 49.   (Same

handed)

THE CORONER: Thank you, I am very grateful.   Were these notes

completed by you?

A.   No.

THE CORONER: Did you complete any notes?

A.   No.

THE CORONER: Nothing at all?

A.   No, the nurse in charge.

41

THE CORONER: These notes would have been made by the nurse in charge?

A. By the nurse charge, yes. It's got on the bottom here that I was her named nurse but I was never her named nurse. The named nurse is someone who sees them through from start to finish. As a bank nurse I was there few and far between so I don't know how that has been put on there.

THE CORONER: Let us just stop there, so you were not her named nurse ----

A. No.

THE CORONER: ..... despite what the medical nursing notes say?

A. Despite what that says on there.

MISS PERSAUD: Madam, the original reference does not have that at the bottom. I do not know who wrote that on.

THE CORONER: All right. That is helpful, thank you. (Same handed) Right. It does not appear that was on the original notes so I have no idea how that got there and we may never know but we will move on from that. These are not your notes?

A. No.

THE CORONER: Can you just help this inquest; what was your role that evening? You said you were a bank nurse so what was your role that evening?

A. Bank nurse.

THE CORONER: What was your role that evening particularly in the care of Kirsty?

A. Mrs. Pearce had called me over at the early part of the night to help her put Kirsty on the commode and then it sort of seemed

42

from there I just went over every time Kirsty needed the commode. I

was doing observations on her and the other nurses on the ward.

THE CORONER: Did you have any other specific role so far as Kirsty

was concerned?

A.   No. I phoned the doctor ----

THE CORONER: Yes.

A.   ..... for Kirsty because of her observations.

THE CORONER: When Kirsty came on to Puffin Ward did anyone

specifically explain to you what Kirsty's problems were?

A.   I don't recall. I know she had multiple problems but I don't

recall... can't recall if it was ever said about her pulmonary

oedema. I can't remember.

THE CORONER: You knew she had a problem?

A.   Yes.

THE CORONER: I think she was very well known to the nurses on that

ward?

A.   Yes.

THE CORONER: But not specifically known to you?

A.   No.

THE CORONER: Had you ever nursed her before at all?

A.   No.

THE CORONER: Are you specifically able to recall how many times Dr.

Gangavati rang the consultant on call?

A.   No.

THE CORONER: You are not able to recall that?

A.   No, not aware, sorry.

THE CORONER: Are you able to recall for me how busy it was in the

43

hospital that evening, specifically on the paediatric wards?

A.   I think the triage was exceptionally busy. One of the staff nurses, the regular nurses from the ward, was up there for quite a long time of the night. Just getting hold of the doctor sort of was an indication that it was busy.

THE CORONER: Any other observations about how busy it was that evening?

A.   No, I can't say.

THE CORONER: You cannot say. Did you have any specific difficulties getting hold of the registrar or, indeed, the Senior House Officer that evening?

A.   When I phoned the SHO he said for me to get in touch with the registrar, which I did, and he was busy as well but the only time I spoke to the registrar was... he had already reviewed Kirsty, which must have been the 12.30 review, and I phoned him again. Mrs. Pearce asked me and I did phone him again, and he said he had already reviewed her, what did he want me to do so I said, you know, Mrs. Pearce would like him to come back but obviously he was really busy as well.

THE CORONER: Do you remember when that was?

A.   About 1.30 I think I got here. I can't remember the exact time.

THE CORONER: You cannot remember?

A.   No.

THE CORONER: So he indicated to you he could not come back because he was too busy?

A.   Yes.

44

THE CORONER: Do you recall what condition Kirsty was at that point at about 1.30?

A. Her oxygen saturations were just about 94, 92, 94 but in high oxygen, she was in a lot of oxygen to maintain those saturations. Her respiration rate was high as well but she was talking and we were able to get her on and off the commode, me and Mrs. Pearce.

THE CORONER: Give me a moment, please. I do not have any further questions of you, thank you.

EXAMINED by MR PEARCE

MR PEARCE: When you came on, when you took over Kirsty's care, I assume you took over her care, what instructions can you remember what you were given regarding observations?

A. Well, because Kirsty was on the saturation monitor it would have been two hourly observations, as with all the children on the saturation monitors.

Q. Because I see on the record, the observation chart, they were done sometimes one hour, two hours, but not the appropriate time that would be sort of recommended for Kirsty's problems. I mean, from my understanding she had every half hour, she was in such dire straits. Did you much to do with Kirsty that night?

A. Just really with your wife.

Q. Yes, the reason I ask this is when my wife at one stage went to the nursing station and said can you help me to lift Kirsty up, she was in desperate need, she was puffing like a train, as we said, she was flat on the bed, she was asked to wait, so what she had to do... I am only telling you this because it is shown how busy you were

45

THE CORONER: The question for this witness, this nurse, is what her role specifically was that evening.

MR PEARCE: Yes, what was your role exactly?

THE CORONER: Let us try and break it down. I appreciate you have some issues. I think I asked you this but it would be helpful if you just explain to Mr. Pearce what your specific role was, and that is in relation to Kirsty that evening. Were you a given specific role?

A. No, no, no, not at all. I weren't allocated patients back then.

THE CORONER: You were a bank nurse?

A. Yes.

THE CORONER: This is generally on that ward?

A. The children's... I was with all the children and I just happened to get with Mrs. Pearce at the beginning of the night of putting Kirsty on the commode.

MR PEARCE: Excuse me, I am not trying to get at you, believe me. You weren't really given any instructions as to Kirsty's care?

A. No.

MR PEARCE: That is all.

THE CORONER: I think that is all, thank you very much. Miss Persaud?

MISS PERSAUD: No, thank you, madam.

THE CORONER: Does anyone have any objection to this witness being released? Thank you.

(The witness withdrew)

46

DR. IAN PRESTON MACONOCHIE, sworn

EXAMINED by THE CORONER

THE CORONER'S OFFICER: State your full name, please.

A.   My name is Dr. Ian Preston Maconochie.

THE CORONER: Your professional address?

A.   I work at St. Mary's Hospital in London.

THE CORONER: I am very grateful. Do take a seat.

A.   Thank you.

THE CORONER: Dr. Maconochie, you have been instructed to provide us with expert opinion. I wonder if you could just outline for us the experience and qualifications as an expert in this particular area?

A.   Certainly. I am a Fellow of the Royal College of Paediatrics and Child Health, a Fellow of the Royal College of Physicians and I have Ph.D. which relates to meningitis and meningococcal disease. I am a Member of the United Kingdom Resuscitation Council, Editor of the United Kingdom and European Paediatric Life Support. I have written papers about things like CEW scores, which you may wish to touch upon, which is about vital signs and the indications for seeking help.

THE CORONER: Thank you very much. You have outlined in your report dated 9th May 2011 the events of that evening and, indeed, you have outlined the information that you have been given in order to come to an opinion. You have also now heard evidence from Dr. Ware, Dr. Gangavati and, indeed, to a limited extent Nurse Corthine. I wonder if you could assist the inquest in this way to begin with; does that alter any information that you provided to the inquiry in the form

47

239

of this report?

A.   No, it does not. There is an additional note I would like to make which centres around the importance of the antibiotics and the potential of infection that has been raised. Certainly there were indications suggesting from the blood tests that there might be infection shown as the while cell count was elevated. Another indicator which is called C Reactive Protein, which can either be extremely high or, in very severe illness, may be low. They both indicated that there might be infection on board.

I noticed at the same time that the pathologist's findings were that there wasn't infection within the lung, so it just really to say that in considering this I don't think that the delay as such in the administration of antibiotics contributed.

THE CORONER: Right. I wonder if you could first of all outline for us what your findings were, please?

A.   Yes, certainly. I had an opportunity to look at the notes and also to see that they had been examined by other independent paediatricians as well and many of those findings independently of, and in conjunction with, if you see what I mean. I think that some circumstances that surround this case is an expectation that Kirsty was going to improve, a hope based on previous experiences, and then unfortunately delay being able to get to the appropriate treatment. As I conclude, I don't think anyone can say that this might not have been the episode when things may have gone wrong anyway but I think that the delays contributed significantly to her death. In all honesty I can't say that she might not have died anyway from this episode but I think there are contributory factors. I think

48

many of those look at the systems basis and I think some of those
have been addressed by the Trust, certainly by some documents that I
was handed earlier on.

THE CORONER: Yes, I will ask you about that.

A.   Thank you, madam.

THE CORONER: Basically your findings are that there were delays
which contributed to her death?

A.   Yes, madam.

THE CORONER: And the delays are based on system failures as opposed
to anything else that is specific, is that your position?

A.   My position is that I think that often with these cases there
is a sequence of errors that occurs and there is a principle, it
sounds a bit trite, but with Swiss Gruyere cheese sometimes all the
holes line up so you can put something through the whole block of
cheese, if you see what I mean, in other words there is a series of
malalignments that occurred.

THE CORONER: In your opinion what were those malalignments?

A.   Yes, firstly there is the working environment, the busyness
that there was on the night and there was demand for the staff to be
in different places. From what I have heard from the inquest has
much, much greater clarification about the communication that
occurred which was not evident to me from the medical notes. Again,
as always, medical and nursing documentation is extremely important
for care. That is a given. With that it has been made clearer to
me that there certainly was communication between the registrar and
with Dr. Ware.

     I think the other aspect is this expectation that things will

49

get better. There is almost an optimism and there is a hope that patients improve. Sometimes you can linger too much on the hope before actually stepping in to say: "We have got to do something now," and that's, I think, mitigated in part by, for example, these vital signs and scores which may be for the future. I know it is not helpful for Kirsty but, again, sort of from a preventative point of view in the future I think that is important.

THE CORONER: You say in your report at page 179 of the bundle, it is the penultimate page, the third paragraph: "I agree with the paediatrician that Kirsty should have been transferred to a High Dependency Unit from the very outset of her attendance." Can you just explain to this inquest why you formed that view?

A.   Certainly. In the rest of the paragraph I state that she had known previous history of pulmonary oedema, and I had not anticipated quite as many as that. That she had features currently of another episode of pulmonary oedema. She had quite disturbed vital signs, as has been mentioned. I think in order to deal with her she would need monitoring that really could be best carried out on the High Dependency Unit or in the ITU setting, in the case of Basildon from the resource point of view, because very frequent monitoring is required.

The nursing level or staffing, for example, in an ITU is one nurse at least to one patient. HDU is one nurse to at least two. On a busy ward, particularly on average, it is about -- I can't speak precisely for Basildon -- but usually it is something like to 1:4 particularly if new patients are being admitted on the night and so on, so I think it is difficult sometimes to actually have the

50

degree of monitoring that is required.

That is a very important point that Mr. Pearce made was that she had had a previous episode which had taken a lot of resource and intensive management in a side ward, and I am sure there was a lot of monitoring at that time, in the daylight hours, so there is opportunity to have continuous monitoring and high levels of input from, again, experienced consultant to SPRs so, again, it is the setting that we are in, the resources that you have, what is required for the patient, and also in the context of what is going on with other patients at the same time.

THE CORONER: You set out again on the same page, penultimate page, three paragraphs up, you agree with the independent assessment saying that the notes were not comprehensive on the fluid chart and there was no input record of fluids, there was no specific investigations which may have assisted, such as blood gas tests. Can you specifically help me with that part; what assistance would have been given by blood gas tests?

A. Yes, very good question. Underlying pulmonary oedema has been stated. The lungs become flooded with fluid and because there is fluid within the gas exchange part of the lung you specifically can't move oxygen and carbon dioxide efficiently any more because there is a film of sort of exudate fluid that comes out from the blood into the lung, so you can see deterioration, for example, in that particular exchange to the extent that that is highlighted by the peripheral oxygen saturation levels. Again, I think there is a chart here to show that they were kept in the 90s, mid to low 90s by dint of high flow oxygen.

51

THE CORONER: That is right.

A.   So she actually had a considerable amount of oxygen to maintain such a saturation which is borderline anyway, so that is another example that the gas exchange is not occurring as efficiently as it should within the lung, so that is why a gas sample would be helpful.

THE CORONER: You also say that you agree with the independent assessment that the nursing notes are scanty and infrequent. We have already looked at the nursing notes, I see two or may be three entries for the whole period.

A.   Yes.

THE CORONER: What would you have expected to see?

A.   Again, the stance that I would take would that would be required, for example, for an HDU-type of setting, so it is not to blame the nursing staff as such but it is in the context of the level of observation and care that I think would be delivered in that HDU setting.

THE CORONER: You also go on to say that you agree with the statement given by the independent assessor a more thorough and timely assessment and investigation of Kirsty's illness would have added information to the clinical picture. I wonder whether you would be so kind, Dr. Maconochie, just to provide us with a conclusion, summary of your conclusions of this investigation that you carried out?

A.   Firstly, I should say that what I have not put into my report is I think there was, and listening here, I think Kirsty was a well-known and very well-liked child on the ward. I think there had

52

244

been strong relationships for a long time, so I think there was an element of disappointment, anger, upset, obviously, on all the people who were involved. I think that is important to note.

Kirsty also had very complicated medical conditions. She saw specialists at Great Ormond Street, I think she had been to specialists in Florida as well. It should be mentioned that some of those problems I think had actually worsened, for example the renal function had decreased, so her ability to handle fluid may not have been what it had been earlier in previous episodes of pulmonary oedema. As has been mentioned... again, I don't think anyone would have given her intravenous fluid but we would want to give her Frusemide to, as it were, drive the excess fluid within the lung out. That depends on good renal function and her renal function was below par and had been noted as such in one of the outpatient statements that I saw.

I have just seen a fluid chart today again and, yes, there was some renal... there was some urine output, which is good, and is monitored, which is excellent, but in order to get to the stage of having pulmonary oedema you really have to remove litres or more of fluid, so she had not got to the stage where the diuretics had had an effect upon the clinical condition. It had not removed enough of the fluid for her symptoms to improve, so I agree that the use of Frusemide was, yes, it was good, the idea was sound, it is a question of then seeing about the escalation of treatment and when you go in to intervene.

I think that is what this case is very much about. It is when do you step in. I think that decision is hard sometimes. It is

53

hard on the previous knowledge that she has, but by a scoring system, I think that was set as a consequence of this investigation, there is an objective measure that can be used.

THE CORONER: Thank you very much. It is fair to say in the final paragraph of your report you set out your conclusions. Has anything has been said or you read today that alters those conclusions in any way?

A. I don't think so at all.

THE CORONER: You have been shown some documentation, I think you had seen the recommendations that were made ----

A. Yes.

THE CORONER: ..... by the Health Ombudsman, you have seen some documentation there today. This document which is headed "Paediatric Department Induction Programme"; a document which is headed up "Children's Early Warning Tool"?

A. Yes, indeed.

THE CORONER: And another document which is a training document I think that is attached to the induction programme?

A. Absolutely, madam.

THE CORONER: Then there was a third document, which is Guideline for the Care of Critically Injured Children. Can you help me with this, in terms of that information that you had received does that in any way go towards the recommendation, or any recommendations, that have been made by the health ombudsman?

A. I have not specifically gone through each one of the recommendations but I think the principles are very, very sound. In terms of induction programmes the doctors have explained to them

54

about the protocols that there are. There is the document, as you say, for the Guideline for Care of Critically Injured Child, again which on a sort of initial inspection looks very comprehensive and involves medical staff and nursing staff, I think, and the warning score.

THE CORONER: Yes?

A. Again, in order to have trigger factors, independent trigger factors, that are based on the child or young person's behaviour and vital signs. Again, those are very useful tools.

THE CORONER: Is there anything else specifically that you feel is missing that perhaps could assist the agencies in improving matters, lessons that could be learned from this case?

A. Sure. As I say, firstly the documentation, the use of pro formas or set format, and this is from the recommendations such address the Lamming Report about integrated medical and nursing notes, so allowing anyone the contribute to the account of ----

MISS PERSAUD: I am sorry to interrupt but I wonder whether Dr. Van Meijgaarden could go first because there are some additional points and then may be Dr. Maconochie can come back when we hear the system changes from the Trust.

THE CORONER: Would prefer to do that?

DR MACONOCHIE: That would be interesting, I am waffling away and it might have been done already.

THE CORONER: I would be grateful. I have not seen a statement.

MISS PERSAUD: She has not done a statement but she is replacing Maggie Rogers to explain system changes.

THE CORONER: Yes, I had understood that. That is fine. I have not seen anything specifically.

MISS PERSAUD: No. She produces these documents.

THE CORONER: It might be helpful then, Dr. Maconochie, can I, if you would not mind, just waiting to hear that evidence. Certainly in terms of your report there is nothing else that you would wish to add?

A. No, I think all aspects have been very thoroughly covered, thank you, madam.

THE CORONER: What we will do then is ask anyone if they have any questions about the evidence you given thus far. Mr. Pearce, do you have any questions of Dr. Maconochie?

EXAMINED by MR PEARCE

Q. Just one really, I am sorry to harp on this a little bit, when Kirsty passed away she was dehydrated. What could have been done to remedy this considering she was suffering from pulmonary oedema?

A. Yes, so I think the reason why she was dehydrated was because she had been breathing so fast for such a long period of time her breath rate was high and ordinarily when we breathe we have moisture that comes out in our breath, so her lips would been dry and her mouth would have been dry. Overall would she have been dehydrated? I am not sure. The purpose of ventilating, again, this is to drive the fluid back from within the lungs into the circulation.

Things that could have been done; she could go on to intubation/ventilation, she could have potentially had an infusion of Frusemide, another step up. She would have been asleep, she would have been sedated. She would probably have had a urine

56

catheter put in and also measuring of her blood pressure, continuous monitoring of her blood pressure, so the monitoring would have increased enormously.

Was she dehydrated? To come back to your answer I don't think necessarily we know she was dehydrated. I think there were signs with her mouth and she showed her mouth to be dry, but I suspect that overall she probably was not dehydrated.

Q. Though, in fact, the ITU registrar stated that in his report ----

A. Yes.

Q. ..... that Kirsty was dehydrated, so naturally enough I am going along with that and accepting that because, you know, our own feelings where she was. I mean, she had, you're talking about the breathing, speed of breathing, I mean, she was breathing like that from 3.00 in the afternoon.

A. Yes.

Q. And there was really... it was high all the way through.

A. Yes.

Q. All the way through.

A. Absolutely.

Q. So what happened then, I must ask you this, because she had this constant breathing pattern did that in fact send her into shock and to cardiac arrest?

A. No. It is a good question. The breathing rate, fast breathing rate is one to try and improve the oxygen delivery within the body. It also... she may have... did she make any noises like grunting at all?

57

Q. No, just really the bubbling of the chest.

A. So by breathing fast what you are trying to do is move air in and out as quickly as possible but without there being more fluid coming into the lungs. If you breathe fast, if you take a breath, deep and long breaths, the pressure inside the lung goes up and down far more. If it goes up and down in the lung far more, low pressure more fluid can enter in, so that is one of the reasons.

Q. Our feelings were that it was very fast and shallow.

A. Yes.

Q. Yes?

A. Yes.

Q. That was the thing we looked at. The only other question I have to ask you is wouldn't it be right that if she had been put into an ITU, because there was no HD room there at the time, it would have allowed the body to rest? If she had been ventilated the body would have rested. As it was she was fighting.

A. Sure.

Q. Fighting hard.

A. So as my conclusions are, I think that delay contributed to her death. As I say, I cannot say hundred per cent that this might not be the day that she could have died.

Q. As parents you stand there and you say: "Why don't you do this? Why don't you do that?" You know... within yourself you know what they should do and, as I have always said, they take the responsibility, they should have done... sorry, but thank you anyway.

A. Thank you, sir.

58

THE CORONER: Thank you very much, Dr. Maconochie. I may ask you to provide us with a little bit more information in due course but if you would not mind just going back to your seat?

A.   Thank you so much.

(The witness withdrew)

DR BIRGIT ELIZABETH VAN MEIJGAARDEN, sworn

EXAMINED by THE CORONER

THE CORONER'S OFFICER: Would you give your full name, please?

A.   Dr. Birgit Elizabeth van Meijgaarden.

THE CORONER: Could you give the court your professional address, please?

A.   Basildon Hospital.

THE CORONER: I understand you are going to assist us with improvements essentially that have been made as a result of some recommendations that you received. I have a document dated 13th December 2006 which is an essential action plan and the progress report. Do you have a copy of that in front of you? That is dated 13th December 2006 and it appears that the author was Maggie Rogers. Do you have that document? It is page 152. First of all, if you could assist us with this, doctor, how familiar are you with the improvements that have been made as a result of the recommendations?

A.   I am actually quite familiar with them. I arrived... I was appointed in the Trust as consultant paediatrician in 2005 and very much from the beginning I had heard about Kirsty's name and the findings that have come out and actions plans that were implemented over the years after her passing away, so I have been aware there

59

were also things, improvements being made following that.

THE CORONER: Can you tell this inquest what had your role been within that?

A. I initially was one of the general paediatricians within the department. Subsequently to that, in 2009, I became Unit Training Director and that has the responsibility of ensuring that all junior doctors are trained and that training is safeguarded. In the last month I was appointed as the Clinical Lead for the paediatric department.

THE CORONER: Could you outline for me, please, in summary form what improvements have been made as a result of the recommendations?

A. I think there were a significant number of changes that have come across over the years and are continuing to be improved. First of all, there was the actual action plan that was followed and all the changes in that action plan.

THE CORONER: Yes, I have a copy of that, that is page 155, which is dated 7th September 2006, is that right?

A. Yes, that is correct. In that action plan there was a series of actions and progress reports which continue on all the pages after that and progress reports.

THE CORONER: There is a progress report dated May 2007. I just want to make sure I have everything.

A. The recommendations were first about the need for being able to... for staff to be able recognise the ill child and deteriorating child better, and this is the early warning tool that Dr. Maconochie was referring to. The trust adopted the CEW Score which is the Children's Early Warning Score, which is the type of... more

60

252

objective scoring tool available to look at the different elements

of the child's care.

THE CORONER: That is a helpful document?

A. Yes.

THE CORONER: That is the one?

A. Yes, so in that score it allows the different elements like

behaviour, cardiovascular marker parameters and respiratory

parameters to be reported in an objective way and being linked to

age-appropriate parameters around the fact that observations vary in

children's different ages. With that it has a set of actions to go

alongside the score and that could be relative simple escalation of

doing scores more frequently all the way up to the need for urgent

intervention, escalation of care, including the fact that a

registrar... the minimum of registrar has to see a patient within 15

minutes but also includes the escalation to consideration for

calling the anaesthetic team or the consultant being informed, and

any member of staff at any time can follow any of the actions on the

escalation plan, so could pick up the phone and it is quite clear

what is expected and this is what is now in the induction programme

that you referred to briefly earlier. It has been highlighted to

all junior doctors, SHOs and registrars in their train programme

when they start their induction. It is mandatory and it is... they

are not doing any other jobs at that time and everybody will go

through a lecture on recognising the sick child and how to use

these warning tools.

THE CORONER: At the bottom of that document is the date 26th

January 2006, do I take it from that, then, that that is the date

61

after which we see this programme being implemented?

A.   Yes, so this is when the document was written, of course. There was a phase of education that went on for all the staff and that is ongoing with reeducation on a regular basis.

THE CORONER: Thank you. You mentioned the Children's Early Warning Tool, you talked about the mandatory induction programme now in place, are there any other recommendations?

A.   Yes, there is the training tool for junior doctors, mid-grade doctors and nurses being trained, the same warning tool. Then the second recommendation was along the need for medical staff, particularly middle grade and senior staff, to have advanced paediatric life support skills, which is recommendation No. 2 on that.

THE CORONER: That is the acute paediatric life support system. Mr. Pearce very helpfully sent a link or sent the Coroner's Department a link.

MR PEARCE: Yes, this is a thing that was spoken about a lot after Kirsty passed and well, you know, I can ask in a minute about that.

THE CORONER: This is something that has been implemented to?

A.   This was already available but has become much more widespread and the Trust has insisted, correctly so, that all consultants are up to date with their APLS training. Nearly all registrars are fully trained or will be trained in the first year that they are with us in our department. Also, we have advanced training for senior nurses, so they go through the same course, and intermediate courses are being held for the more junior nurses.

THE CORONER: So APLS is now, if you like, an expectation?

62

A.   It is an expectation for trainees at registrar level to have,
for all consultants to have, all consultants and anaesthetists who
come across children are to be trained as well, yes.

THE CORONER: Thank you.

A.   So the third recommendation was about having appropriately
equipped space for monitoring children in serious conditions. When
I arrived, shortly after, we had the opening in the dedication of
Kirsty of our HDU facility, which a designated cubicle on the ward
opposite the nurse's station which is for the sole purpose of
children requiring more intense monitoring and HD care whereby there
is specialist equipment in the room whereby there is one-to-one
nursing care provided and there and designated observation charts,
which was discussed previously as well.

     Then the fourth item was about the induction, which I have just
mentioned. So clinical note audit should be part of medical staff
induction, so the Trust clarifies some of the record keeping. This
forms part of the induction training again within the Trust
parameters and this is highlighted during the talks in the, although
not set as a specific item, it has been highlighted as one of the
items in the talks given in the department on induction as well.

THE CORONER: That forms part of the training?

A.   Yes, yes, absolutely.

THE CORONER: I think another one of the areas of concern was
sufficient numbers of staff and their skills?

A.   Yes. So we have increased our staff numbers, so there are now
eight consultants in the department where I think there were
previously five in the period when Kirsty was cared for. The middle

63

grade cover has increased. We now have two registrars on in the evening until 10.00-11.00 to help support the different demands of the different areas, and there is always a large demand in the assessment area in evening hours, so there are now two registrars available in that period to help cover.

Also there have been changes in the nurses parts with clear handover named nurses, so it is much more clear who is responsible and who needs to lead.

Then from that I think there was issue about medical notes. There are now fully integrated medical notes with nurses and doctor recommendations and the care plans, etcetera, all being part of the same set of notes and being contemporaneous.

THE CORONER: It is all about communication?

A. Yes, yes, and there are new nursing care plans in place as well. That come in to help with that as well.

THE CORONER: Any other changes that have been put in place?

A. No, I think the... we have the facility of having warning tools and training. I think also the Trust has appointed a Learning Disability Nurse Advisor for the Trust who basically is support for the families as well as all staff to be able to help when those children with complex needs to ensure that there are care plans available to actually address their needs.

THE CORONER: Thank you very much, that is very helpful. Mr. Pearce, do you have any questions?

EXAMINED by MR PEARCE

MR PEARCE: Yes, I would like to... the APLS was recommended by the

64

Ombudsman in her report that everybody dealing with critically ill children should get this accreditation. From the figures I see at the moment I see something like 11 per cent of staff have that at Basildon.

A.   11 per cent of which staff?

Q.   Of the APLS that are dealing with the paediatric department.

A.   Well, per shift the senior nurses, so senior nurses are APLS trained. The registrars and consultants are APLS trained. Often SHOs have already had APLS training or EPLS training. From the more junior nurses we provide training via the appointment of a clinical nurse practice facility to provide ongoing training as well. She was appointed (inaudible) for about it is medium life support, it may be not the highest level possible. All these things, all these training forms and medium life support, it is life support, etcetera, are all in relation to being able to recognise and act and are very much part... the training alone goes in conjunction with all the other work that has been done by being able to use the CEW Score and being able to provide an overall care, so per shift there will be people available. Not all nurses will be trained at that level because it might not actually be appropriate to train them at that level because they might not, depending on the level of nursing degrees they have got, it might not be appropriate.

Q.   Yes, I mean, whenever there is a crisis such as Kirsty's we can all come up with questions such as well, you know, now, no doubt, when dealing with patients such as her, you would ensure that there was a nurse who knows her, that will deal with her, as opposed to a bank nurse who knew nothing of her?

65

A.   Absolutely right, I fully agree with that.

Q.   Is that one of the improvements?

A.   That is why we say we now have named nurses for the children.
Per shift there are very clear handover rules and any child that
requires a high level of care is being specialed or being nursed
one-to-one and if it is serious enough will be one-to-one on the
ward or it could be one-to-one, if they need other facilities, in
the HDU cubicle.   It would be in the HDU cubicle, yes.

Q.   Thank you very much.

THE CORONER: Mrs. Pearce, do you have any questions?

MRS PEARCE: No, I am fine, thank you.

                    EXAMINED by MISS PERSAUD

                     on behalf of the Trust

Q.   You explained, thank you very much, the acute tool and how that
works. One of the other recommendations that the Ombudsman had was
in relation to the actual observation chart, I think the comment was
that the chart that we had in place at the time was too simplistic,
it did not have enough detail on it. Have the charts on the
paediatric ward, as opposed to the High Dependency because they have
their own charts, have they been updated as well?

A.   Yes, they have and also the lines, so there is actually a space
on the chart to actually record the CEW Score for every single
observation in there and it has more facilities to put other
observations like saturations and gases that might have been taken.
They can all go on the similar chart, yes, so the observation
charts in general have increased in the ability to capture

                              66

information.

Q. You said that the acute scoring can result now in triggers to the ITU department directly or the consultant?

A. Yes.

Q. Can the nursing staff actually trigger all the way up to the ITU?

A. Yes.

Q. And the consultant?

A. Yes, definitely so, and that is actively encouraged that if, for example, it is quite clear the registrar has to come and see the patient. If the registrar can't see the patient they have to call the consultant out to come instead. The nurses are actively encouraged if things are very busy and they feel that there isn't enough manpower on the shopfloor to escalate that via the chain of command to the consultant and I have been called in the past to say: "It's very busy, we need a hand, there's problems."

Q. Thank you much. We heard a lot of evidence about records not being recorded or insufficient medical record-keeping, is there training provided to both doctors and nurses in relation to record-keeping?

A. This item, of course, over the years has become much more recognised as having been poor in previous practice, and not just in our Trust but actual all over, so it is very much ingrained now in the training and medical student and it is highlighted again during their foundation years and dedicated sessions. It is part of the junior doctor induction. Nurses, of course, regularly are being updated. We hold regular audits of the medical notes, looking at

67

the type of information that is there and the integrated notes. It has definitely helped to improve communication, being able to actually very quickly get more feedback from what other people have felt from the nursing point of view, so actually that improves the care.

Q. Are records audited to make sure that the standards are improving?

A. Yes. Periodically at intervals and we have got those audits available in our Trust and the audit department, yes, they are being undertaken.

Q. Is it right that those audits will be checked by external agencies such as... the NHS Litigation Authority has the CMST Standards, that is the Clinical Medical Scheme for Trust Standards?

A. Yes.

Q. A requirement of that is audit so would you have external bodies coming in as well?

A. Yes, I mean, these audits are all registered within our Trust and form part of our clinical covenants and all those documents are available for external agencies to use in order to make their assessment, yes.

Q. We have heard that Kirsty had a number of medical problems, complex medical problems?

A. Very much so. I never met her but, yes, definitely.

Q. This is one of the many of the records for Kirsty, so if a doctor is coming to her care completely afresh is there any way, is there now a summary put in front of the file so the doctor can easily see the main components of ----

68

A.   Yes, there has been much more common practice for children with

complex needs or a variety of illnesses or particular unique

illnesses to have a designated or more individual action plan

written, so it could be that is a little bit dependent on the type

of problems the child's got and how the child might present. For

example, children who've got metabolic problems, they typically

would have their emergency regime in the front of the notes and

parents will also have a copy as well, what to do in an emergency to

actually hand to whichever doctor they see. So in children who

start to get files that big, the common practice is to have

summaries and problem lists and significant issues for the care of

that child in acute stages to have that available at the front, yes.

Q.   Thank you very much.

THE CORONER: I wonder if I can ask you a question arise out of

that? I have seen reference to that fairly early on after Kirsty's

death. That was one of the issues that was brought up. Can you

tell me when that was implemented?

A.   I don't think there is as such... I don't know of any

implementation date and the problem is that it is very difficult to

make it standardised because if you knew ----

THE CORONER: No, it is an individual, tailor-made ----

A.   Absolutely.

THE CORONER: ..... summary, but the whole process of doing that

appeared to occur after Kirsty's death, certainly from my reading of

the documentation.

A.   Yes, that became much more commonplace to do after that and

particularly because children like Kirsty who have direct access, so

69

when they have complex illnesses that require, particularly in cases where there is unusual presentations or medical problems, that require people who might not be familiar with the case to take actions in a certain order in a certain way, then, yes.

THE CORONER: So far as you are aware that improvement occurred relatively shortly after, I am not asking for a specific date.

A.   Yes.

THE CORONER: Does anyone have any questions arising from that? Mr. Pearce, do you have any questions arising from that?

MR PEARCE: No, I don't think so, thank you.

THE CORONER'S OFFICER: Madam, Mr. Pearce would like you to have sight of this document. It is a list of complications that Kirsty had.

THE CORONER: I think I might have a list in my bundle. Let me look at this one. Yes, I think I have this document, I believe.

MR PEARCE: This is a thing that I made up myself.

THE CORONER: Yes, I appreciate it came from you.

MR PEARCE: If Kirsty had a problem I would add it. Whenever Kirsty was admitted I would hand one of these to the doctor who was treating her and Dr. Asquith, who was her paediatrician, was going to put something on the front of the folder and if it didn't get to you I apologise, but that is the kind of thing that is very useful.

THE CORONER: I agree, it is very practical, it is a pragmatic approach. Very useful.

MR PEARCE: Anyone can understand it.

THE CORONER'S OFFICER: Madam, it is page 1 of the bundle.

THE CORONER: Yes, I knew I had seen it.

MR PEARCE: You have got it, have you?

THE CORONER: I have, it is in my bundle. I will hand that back.
Thank you very much. Thank you very much, Dr. Van Meijgaarden.
Does anyone have any objection to this witness being released? You
may return to your seat.

DR MACONOCHIE: May I just ask a question?

THE CORONER: Of course you may, I do apologise.

DR MACONOCHIE: It is just the last one, the Ombudsman's
recommendation before being completed just for finalisation,
establishment of a professional liaison with the regional paediatric
intensive care (inaudible) and resource provide training
(inaudible).

A. That has happened. We got a PIU consultant apart from this
Clinical Practice Nurse Facilitator with links in with the PIU
consultant, the CAT team regularly comes and gives us study days as
part of that.

DR MACONOCHIE: I am very grateful. Thank very much.

            (The witness withdrew)

THE CORONER: Dr. Maconochie, I will not call you back unless there
is anything else that you wanted to add to that information?

DR MACONOCHIE: I wanted to thank you. I have taken brief notes, it
is fascinating and I will use some of those documents to report
back, thank you very much.

THE CORONER: That has been very helpful, thank you very much. That
concludes the live evidence. There is one more piece of evidence at
this inquest that I wish to read out. It is a rule pursuant to Rule

71

37, it is a statement from Dr. Reddy who we have heard mention of
during the course of this inquest. The statement appears at page
150 in the bundle.

He says: "I assessed Kirsty in Puffin Ward on 28th August 2003
at 6.00. I had met Kirsty on only one occasion previously when she
came to Puffin Ward to have some blood tests done. I gathered from
Kirsty's medical notes that she had multiple problems. She had been
complaining of persistent bouts of cough and worsening shortness of
breath since that morning. She had already been treated with 5mg of
Salbutamol nebulisers, Frusemide and (inaudible). She did not
complain of any other symptoms at that stage. On examination she
was breathless, unwell, lying in bed with three pillows. Her
observations revealed that her 02 saturations were only 66 per
cent, picking up to 96 per cent on 10 litres of 02 with the
breathing mask. Respiratory rate was 40, pulse was 130 and
temperature was 37 degrees. Examination of chest revealed bilateral
crepitation up to mid zones. Cardiovascular examination revealed
normal (inaudible) pressures. Heart sounds, no murmurs. Abdominal
examinations unremarkable. My impression at this stage was of
pulmonary oedema and lower respiratory tract infection."

He sets out that the chest X-rays showed evidence of pulmonary
oedema and evidence of infection on the right side. She deals with
blood samples that were taken and the urine dipstick. Blood
portrays protein, nitrates (inaudible). Having referred to the
medical notes it is evident that Kirsty had had previous similar
problems. In similar situations she was treated with Frusemide and
she seemed to have responded to it. Having discussed with the

72

registrar it was decided that the initial management plan should also include intravenous antibiotics for suspected chest infection along with Frusemide.

"At 12.00 29th August 2003 Kirsty did not seem to have responded to this treatment even after four to five hours though clinically the crepitations seemed to be less prominent and her O2 saturations were 98 per cent in 12 litres of O2 with a breathing mask. Following my request on-call registrar Dr. Gangavati assessed Kirsty at 12.10 and then spoke to Dr. Ware. It was decided to repeat (inaudible) and Frusemide intravenously. I assessed Kirsty at 3.00 and found that she had made only marginal improvement. I informed registrar who came to review Kirsty. He agreed that Kirsty had made no improvement. Dr. Gangavati discuss with Dr. Ware and he decided to repeat another dose of Frusemide intravenously.

"At 5.00 Kirsty seemed to deteriorate. Her O2 saturations dropped to 80s on 10 litres of O2 (inaudible). She was in distress. Respiratory rate had increased to 60 per minute hence registrar contacted the ITU registrar. Kirsty was then assessed by the ITU registrar. He discussed with the consultant on call for ITU. A decision was made to transfer Kirsty to ITU. Cardiac arrest (inaudible) to ITU. At 6.31 on arrival to ITU Kirsty was already being resuscitated by the medical team. Following discussions with Dr. Ware cardiopulmonary resuscitation was stopped after 40 minutes as no progress was made."

He signed that and that is dated 20th January 2004.

That is the all the evidence that I propose to read and, indeed, hear in this inquest. However, what I propose to do is I

73

will hear any legal submissions that Miss Persaud may wish to make in a moment. I would propose to provide a narrative verdict which I will propose to do after summarising this case after approximately 1.45. Miss Persaud, do you have any legal submissions you would wish to make?

MISS PERSAUD: Madam, my submission would be that in terms of short form verdicts the only appropriate verdict would be natural causes, but the submission on behalf of the Trust that in this case a narrative verdict would be more appropriate. Madam, I would just refer you to the decision in the case of Lewis and that anything that goes into that narrative verdict must be on the basis that there is evidence that contributed on the balance of probabilities to the cause of death. Madam, would you like me to address you in relation to any riders?

THE CORONER: No, I think that has been most helpful, thank you very much. I now propose to rise and, in fact, if you are back in the building by about 1.45 then I will call you when I am ready to provide you with the summary and narrative verdict.

(The court was adjourned)

SUMMING-UP

THE CORONER: I now propose to summarise the evidence. The evidence has been given in a fairly short period of time and therefore I do not propose to summarise in a huge amount of detail but just what I consider to be some of the salient points. It is fair to say that I have read all of the documentation that has been given to me in this case, and there has been a wealth of documentation. I will not

summarise that but suffice to say that this death has been
investigated by a number of different agencies and there has been a
wealth of documentation.

In terms of the evidence that I have read and heard today, I
have heard the evidence of Dr. Gangavati. Some of the important
information he gave to us today was that he had rung Dr. Ware about
three times that evening. He recalls specifically three occasions.
He told us that the first occasion he rang Dr. Ware was about 12.30
a.m. in the morning of 29th August. He said that he was extremely
busy that evening and that morning and he did not note the phone
call in the medical notes.

He told us that he was very reassured by the information Dr.
Ware gave to him as to the treatment that he had prescribed. He
told us that he rang Dr. Ware again at approximately 3.30 a.m. that
morning and Dr. Ware clearly indicated to him that he did not need
to contact the ITU team and that he was to continue the treatment
that had been going on or ongoing in the previous hours.

He then handed over to the registrar of the ITU at
approximately 5.15 that morning. He said: "I wanted to wait for
the registrar, I wanted to wait for him to carry out the assessment
and then for them to inform me." He then went on to say: "I didn't
get any information back from the registrar and she, I understand,
was sent to the ITU." He also told us that the antibiotics that had
been prescribed were not administered.

Mr. Pearce asked a number of questions of Dr. Gangavati. He
was asked how he prioritised the patients and he said it was based
on their clinical need. He also said, in answer to questions from

Mr. Pearce: "I was satisfied with the management plan for Kirsty.
I was following the advice of the on call consultant." He also went
on to say that he was updating Dr. Ware.

In answer to questions from Miss Persaud he said that he was
reassured by the medical records that she had had this condition
before of pulmonary oedema. He also explained that he was following
essentially the treatment programme that had been put in place
before. He did say that the observations that had taken place he
passed that information on to Dr. Ware. In terms of her
presentation at 5.00 that morning he said she was still talking in
sentences. In terms of fluid intake and some specific questions
about fluid intake he said that he did not feel that IV fluids
should have been given because there was a need to dehydrate her
because of her condition.

Dr. Ware also gave evidence. He specifically recalls the
telephone call at 3.30 that morning although his statement had said
5.00. He feels that that time is probably from the medical notes.
He did not specifically recall the telephone call earlier. He told
the inquest that he was told at approximately 3.30 a.m. that Kirsty
was not responding to her usual treatment and that Dr. Gangavati had
asked whether he should continue with that treatment or refer to ITU
and that Dr. Ware's own specific information that he gave to Dr.
Gangavati was that he said to administer a third dose and not to
refer to the ITU. That is the third dose, I believe, of Frusemide.

He said specifically: "I was misled by her previous history.
It was a bad decision." He then gave evidence about the previous
admissions. He recalled there were about 30 previous admissions of

76

the same type of illness and on each occasion she had responded well to conservative treatment. He described the pattern of what normally happened when she was admitted. He specifically referred to an episode where, in fact, she was worse than she was on this particular occasion. He said specifically: "The fault is mine, I gave bad advice."

He then referred to the fact that consultants when they are on call do come into hospital. The decision to do so is made by the consultant himself. He said -- he used the word 'clock': "I didn't clock," I take it that is I did not recognise, "how busy Dr. Gangavati was." He also told the inquest that he had never personally made any important decisions about Kirsty's medical management apart from that night.

There was then discussion about an incident that occurred three to four years previously which is an intervention where it was during the day and there was a significant amount of medical intervention at a high level on a side ward off the ward that Kirsty was in that evening.

We then heard evidence from Nurse Corthine. She was a bank nurse that evening. She had worked in the Southend Hospital as a paediatric nurse. She was not able to say why the antibiotics were not administered. She was not herself able to administer them. She was not the nurse in charge of the ward. She was asked specifically about the nursing notes and she said that she was not the person who would have written the notes up, it would have been the nurse in charge of the ward.

She said specifically: "I was not her named nurse." That

77

question arose because the documentation, which appears to have been annotated post the document being written up, says that the named nurse was Alex, on the bottom. That appears to have been a later addition. She told us about her very limited role with Kirsty's care that evening and that predominantly appeared to revolve around helping Mrs. Pearce to assist getting Kirsty onto the commode. Also she was doing observations on her with other nurses on the ward.

She also told me that she had rung the doctor for Kirsty because of the observations. She gave evidence that triage was very busy that night. She was not able to provide us with any further information about that. She also told me that she had rung the SHO and he himself was busy and he said she should get hold of the registrar. The registrar himself had indicated he could not come back because he was too busy.

The next witness was Dr. Ian Maconochie and he was specifically asked to give evidence and to provide a report on behalf of Her Majesty's Coroner. He said of the delay in administering the antibiotic he did not feel that that contributed to her death. He was able, though, to provide us with a lengthy report and summarised that report today in evidence. He said as a backdrop to this the evening's events that there was an expectation that Kirsty was going to improve and that was based on her previous medical history and treatment.

He said there was a sequence of errors, a series of misalignments and he described some of those misalignments; the working environment, the demand on the staff, communication between medical staff, as I already mentioned the expectation that she would

78

recover, the hope that patients would improve before stepping in earlier and, of course, he also mentioned the medical notes, the lack of proper medical notes.

He referred to the previous episode which had occurred at that same hospital where, in fact, Kirsty was very ill but that, he said, had taken place during the day. It was high levels of input and that highlighted the setting and resources that were required to deal with Kirsty when she became that ill.

He also set out for the inquest that Kirsty had very complicated medical conditions and he highlighted for us something which I considered to be of note, that some of those problems had worsened, and particularly her renal function. I have to set that against the information that I have read because I have read in some respects Kirsty was improving. I note in particular that her mobility had improved, I think that is a very significant fact for both Kirsty and her parents, and that she was hoping to have a hip replacement operation and I have noted that, but that must be set against, I think, the point that Dr. Maconochie made that some of her medical conditions had worsened and it is whether those medical conditions that had worsened, whether they were recognised.

There is some evidence about the fluid intake. The parents are concerned, and understandably so, that Kirsty was dehydrated. Dr. Maconochie appeared very much to agree with the method that had been used by the hospital that evening, that Frusemide would have been given and the whole point would be to try and dehydrate the patient to assist them to get better. He said the principles were sounds.

Then we turn to Dr. Meijgaarden. We know that certain

79

recommendations have been made and an action plan has been set out and it is exhibited in the bundle. There are a number of recommendations and a number of actions that have been taken. I do not intend for the purposes of this inquiry to set them all out, but just highlighting some of the very important ones, there is an early warning tool now that is put in place and was put in place, it appears, relatively shortly after Kirsty's death to assist the medical staff when treating very sick children.

I understand also, and I am heartened to hear, that there is an HDU unit dedicated to Kirsty and one hopes that the advent of that unit being available will assist other very sick children. I am also heartened to hear that there is a special learning development nurse that is available for treating children who have complex needs, including learning difficulties. I am told that nurses are actively encouraged now to call consultants when they have any issues.

There are now integrated notes to help with communication and I had seen, and I was shown another copy, of Mr. Pearce's own tailor-made note or summary of Kirsty's illnesses and, indeed, medical treatments that she had, and I understand that something similar is now available for children with complex needs. It seems to me to be a very pragmatic tool, a very useful tool to have on the front of any sick child's notes.

I am aware that the Trust has recognised now a number of failures from the events of that evening and it is to their credit that they have implemented those recommendations. I do not, therefore, propose to make any Rule 43 recommendations. I asked specifically the question of Dr. Maconochie whether he would add anything to those recommendations and he would appear to be satisfied as to the implementation of those recommendations in an appropriate manner.

NARRATIVE VERDICT

THE CORONER: Kirsty Jayne Pearce, born on 22nd February 1986, was suffering from pulmonary oedema when she was admitted into hospital on 28th August 2003 at about 6.00 p.m.. There was a failure to recognise the seriousness of her condition which led to a delay in transferring her to an appropriate ICU or HDU unit. There was an absence of monitoring vital medical information. The nursing and medical notes were scant. Albeit that she may not have survived this particular episode of pulmonary oedema, the delay in getting the sort of treatment that was required from the outset contributed to her death at 7.00 a.m. on the morning of 29th August 2003.

That is the verdict that will be recorded on the documentation. Mr. and Mrs. Pearce, I would particularly like to say that this inquest is very glad that you pursued this matter in the way that you have done. It is a great credit to you and it is a great credit to your daughter. I have read in some detail, I have not read all the information about Kirsty, but she was much loved and a much respected young lady and she contributed during her short life to assisting a number of people and I know that her views were sought on a number of different issues, so thank you very much for highlighting that and the Coroner's Division is most grateful. I will now rise.

81

273

(The court was adjourned)

The Coroner has made it quite clear where the responsibility lies for Kirsty's death; it is as I have always claimed for over eight years.

The verdict has ensured that the justice we have been seeking for such a long period of time has been found through the Coroners court.

I believe that a proverb from one of England's great novelists is very appropriate with regard to the trials and tribulations I found over such a long period of time, it is as follows;

IF AT FIRST YOU DON'T SUCCEED
TRY, TRY, TRY AGAIN.

From; The Children of the New Forest.

By Frederick Marryat. 1792-1848

Rest peacefully forever Kirsty Jayne.

Final Comments

THOUGH EIGHT YEARS HAVE PASSED SINCE MY DAUGHTER KIRSTY'S death I still remain extremely angry at the failures of the doctors and nurses charged with caring for her during the night of her final illness.

There was no teamwork and nobody appeared to have any idea as to what they were dealing with.

The Medical and Nursing teams failed to recognise how serious her condition was and the plight she was in from the word go of her illness, they took it for granted that she would survive as she had done so many times previously.

The nursing observations and medical procedures necessary in the care of a very seriously ill young girl were never carried out and so consequently Kirsty failed to receive the care that she required for the major part of her stay in the hospital, because of this she suffered unnecessary pain and suffering for fourteen hours with her mother at her bedside for thirteen of those very frightening hours watching her slowly die.

Instead of observations being carried out every thirty minutes as should have been the case for Kirsty's type of illness the intervals invariably were between one and two hours and this was totally inadequate and so consequently a true picture as to the seriousness of Kirsty's illness could not be arrived at.

There were various tests that should have been carried out and others that should have been repeated but because of the inferior standard of care these were not dealt with.

One of the biggest problems for me was to know that when my daughter died she was dehydrated; I felt that this was scandalous, the reason for this dehydration was that no fluid maintenance was carried out in the ward by doctors or nurses; a fluid balance chart was requested but not implemented so this further clouded the issue by not knowing what Kirsty's fluid balance was.

The on call Consultant Paediatrician told me at a meeting after Kirsty's death that the registrar had not contacted him until five o'clock in the morning, that was twelve hours after Kirsty's admission, the registrar said that he made more than one phone call, I believe the Consultants version because this tied up with what was in the medical notes.

There is a saying in the caring profession and that is "if it is not in the notes then it did not happen" and there is nothing stronger than the written word.

The end result for Kirsty was that the combination of acute respiratory distress triggered by pulmonary oedema, dehydration and poor medical and nursing care was to culminate in a devastating loss of life that could have been saved in the right hands, the people responsible for this will never be forgiven.

When a trust is accused of the poor management of a disabled and vulnerable patient great haste is made to ensure that the complainers are assured that none of the staff responsible for the care of that patient are responsible when things go wrong, sometimes they are backed up by the very people that are there to ensure fair play.

In the case of Kirsty it was more difficult for the trust because Peggy and I are both trained nurses now retired, as the saying goes, "pulling the wool over our eyes" was not quite so easy for the Trust.

The now defunct Healthcare Commission decided that in Kirsty's case there were no grounds to take my complaint any further because the Trust had addressed any shortcomings that had come to light during their internal investigations.

The Health Service Ombudsman dismissed the Healthcare Commissions report describing it as seriously flawed and condemned the poor care for Kirsty on the night she died, it was decided that the care was below average.

The General Medical Council that proudly boasts that their function is to regulate doctors and to ensure good medical practice fell very short in their commitment to Kirsty when they initially told us that the doctor caring for her the night she died would face a hearing in front of the Fitness to Practice panel but then soon after came back to us informing us that the hearing was cancelled because they felt that though the doctors behaviour was negligent it was not negligent enough for him to face his peers, I was shocked at this because that negligence had caused the death of my lovely daughter.

The behaviour of the General medical council was disgraceful and only went to show the lack of commitment they have for patients and the public in general.

It is only because the Health Service Ombudsman and Dr Ian Maconochie the Specialist Consultant in Paediatric emergency medicine found it was right to support our claims that the Coroner has granted an inquest on behalf of Kirsty, this is eight years after her death.

The one genuine apology for the awful input by the Healthcare Commission was received from their CEO Anna Walker for the very bad handling of Kirsty's case and the further distress caused to both Peggy and myself as a direct result of their very poor report.

The only people to be thanked for showing honesty and fairness are the Parliamentary Ombudsman, Dr Ian Maconochie, Anna Walker, and Mrs Caroline Beasley-Murray the coroner for Essex and Thurrock.

Charles W Pearce.

GLOSSARY OF MEDICATIONS

The everyday medication routine for Kirsty was as follows:

NEBULISED SALBUTAMOL (AN INHALED TREATMENT FOR ASTHMA and an aid to improve lung function)

Tegretol Retard (to treat epilepsy)
Sodium Valproate (also to treat epilepsy)
Omeprazole (to reduce stomach acidity)
Losec,
Sytron
Salamol Steri-Neb
Frusol (a diuretic introduced to help prevent or reduce the severity of the episodes of pulmonary oedema; this was given orally, but the more severe episodes treated in hospitals required that it be given intravenously)
Amiloride (also a diuretic)
Iron supplements
Calcichew D3, a calcium and vitamin D supplement
Co-Codamol (a painkiller)
Magnesium Glycerophosphate
Lactulose (a laxative)
Ranitidine (to reduce stomach acid production)
Thyroxine (to replace the deficient hormone levels)
Feldene Melt (an anti-inflammatory painkiller for arthritis)
Twice weekly subcutaneous injections of Enbrel (a cytokine inhibitor that modifies and dampens the body's immune system in inflammatory conditions, such as arthritis)
Twice monthly infusions of Pamidronate administered in the hospital to help maintain bone strength

GLOSSARY OF MEDICAL TERMS

THE FOLLOWING PROBLEMS WERE THE ONES THAT KIRSTY SUFFERED from during her lifetime. I have used many sources in developing this glossary. Among them are *The Living Textbook on Medicine, The Living Textbook of Paediatric Medicine, Black's Medical Dictionary, The British Medical Association of Medicines and Drugs, Gray's Anatomy, The A-Z Families' Medical Advisor*, Kirsty's actual medical history, and discussions with Professor Patricia Woo and Professor Mike Dillon in clinical meetings.

Aicardi-Goutieres Syndrome

Aicardi-Goutieres syndrome is a rare genetic disorder. It is also known as Cree encephalitis and pseudo-Torch syndrome, both of which were once considered separate disorders. The disease is very rare, and my understanding is that only fifty cases have been described.

Aicardi-Goutieres syndrome typically has onset in the first year of life, usually at the age of around four months. Early symptoms include irritability, feeding difficulties, sleep disturbances, and recurrent fevers in the absence of any evidence of infection.

It is frequently accompanied by slowing of head growth, and microcephaly, seizures, and chilblains are also evident. These problems were associated with Kirsty's presentation.

The course of the disease is severe and progressive; death occurs in 25 per cent of patients before seventeen years of age. Those who die at this young age tend to be the ones with the most serious impairment.

Possible symptoms associated with Aicardi-Goutieres syndrome are listed below. Not all of these symptoms are present in every case.

Microcephaly: abnormally small head.

Early progressive encephalopathy: abnormalities of the brain.

Lack of progress of motor and social skills; no, or very poor, contact with surroundings.

Feeding difficulties.

Irritability.

Vomiting.

Spasticity: presence of spasms.

Dystonia: abnormal muscle tone, characterized by prolonged, repetitive muscle contractions that may cause twisting or jerking movements of the body or a body part.

Visual inattention.

Ocular jerks: abnormal eye movements.

Sterile CSF lymphocytosis: cerebrospinal fluid that has elevated levels of lymphocytes (a certain cell of the immune system), but in which there are no indications of infection (sterility).

Skin lesions of the toes and/or fingers, earlobes looking like chilblains (itchy red swelling of the skin), puffy hands and feet, and cold feet.

Intracerebral calcification: presence of calcium deposits on a particular area of the brain.

Kirsty suffered from ten of the above-listed problems. One thing that I was very grateful for was the fact that Kirsty was not mentally retarded.

Mental retardation appears to be one of the many manifestations of AGS.

The following are not usually associated with Aicardi-Goutieres syndrome. Though Kirsty was affected by them, they were separate problems that had their own manifestations.

Retinal vasculitis.

Rheumatoid factor positive destructive arthritis.

Renal vasculitis, leading to reduced filtration rate.

Periodic pulmonary oedema.

Kirsty's death was not related to Aicardi-Goutieres syndrome, however. Kirsty died from pulmonary oedema leading to left ventricular failure; these two symptoms are not associated with Aicardi-Goutieres syndrome.

Anaemia

In anaemia, the level of haemoglobin in the blood is below the normal range. Haemoglobin is the iron-containing molecule in red blood cells that carries oxygen around the body. So in those with anaemia, less oxygen is delivered to their tissues.

Iron is needed to make haemoglobin. A shortage of iron is the most common cause of anaemia in the United Kingdom, known as iron-deficiency anaemia. This may be due to blood loss, either sudden, such as when a stomach ulcer bursts, or over time, such as when a woman has heavy periods. A lack of iron may also be due to a dietary deficiency. People with chronic diseases, such as cancer, inflammatory bowel disease, kidney failure, and rheumatoid arthritis (Kirsty suffered this), may also suffer from anaemia.

Some people with anaemia don't have any symptoms for months. When symptoms do appear, common ones include lethargy, weakness, dizzy spells, and feeling faint. As the anaemia becomes more severe, shortness of breath, palpitations, headaches, sore mouth and gums, and brittle nails may cause problems. People with anaemia may look pale and find that others around them notice they look unwell.

Asthma

Asthma is a common chronic disease involving the respiratory system, in which the airways occasionally constrict, become inflamed, and are lined with excessive amounts of mucus, often in response to one or more triggers. Asthmatic episodes may be triggered by exposure to an environmental stimulant, such as an allergen, tobacco smoke, cold or warm air, perfume, pet dander, moist air, exercise or exertion, or emotional stress. In children, the most common triggers are viral illnesses, such as those that cause the common cold.

Airway narrowing causes symptoms such as wheezing, shortness of breath, chest tightness, and coughing. The airway constriction responds to bronchodilators. Between episodes, most patients feel well but can have mild symptoms and may remain short of breath after exercise for longer periods of time than an unaffected individual. The symptoms of asthma, which can range from mild to life-threatening, can usually be controlled with a combination of drugs and environmental changes.

Colitis

Colitis is a chronic digestive disease characterized by inflammation of the colon, one of a group of conditions that are inflammatory and autoimmune. It affects the tissue that lines the gastrointestinal system (the large and small intestines). It is classed as inflammatory bowel disease (IBD).

General signs and symptoms of colitis include pain, tenderness in the abdomen, depression, rapid weight loss, aches and pains within the joints, and fatigue. There are many other problems with colitis, which makes it a very debilitating disease.

Epilepsy

Epilepsy is a recurrent and paroxysmal (spasm, fit, or convulsion) disorder starting suddenly and ceasing spontaneously due to occasional, sudden, excessive rapid and local discharge of the nerve cells in the cortex (grey matter) of the brain. In childhood, up to 5 per cent of individuals have one or more fits before the age of twelve, but in many children the prognosis is good. Epilepsy always arises as a disorder of the brain, commonly of microscopic size, but it is not itself a disease. Its cause is established by laboratory tests and brain scanning. Fits can be the first sign of a tumour or follow a stroke, brain injury, or infection.

A single epileptic fit is not epilepsy. The people who have just one fit may never have a repeat and by definition are not epileptic.

There are other, more serious fits, as those suffered by Kirsty, that are caused by the extra pyramidal side effects from a reaction to drugs or the aftermath of a stroke.

Hypothyroidism

Hypothyroidism is caused by insufficient production of the thyroid hormone by the thyroid gland. The thyroid gland secretes two hormones, thyroxine and triodothyronine, which are responsible for the metabolic activity of the body. Cretinism is a form of hypothyroidism found in infants.

Hypothyroidism may result from developmental abnormalities of the gland or a deficiency of the enzymes necessary for the synthesis of the hormones. It may be a feature of endemic goitre and cretinism, but the most common cause of hypothyroidism is the autoimmune destruction of the thyroid known as chronic thyroiditis. It may also occur as a result of radioactive iodine treatment of thyroid overactivity and is occasionally secondary to pituitary disease, in which inadequate TSH (thyroid stimulating hormone) production occurs.

The term *myxoedema* was introduced in 1878 to describe the swelling of the skin and subcutaneous tissues that characterized severe forms of hypothyroidism.

Since thyroid hormones are responsible for the metabolic rate of the body, hypothyroidism usually presents with a general slowing up. This affects both physical and mental activities. The intellectual functions become slow, the speech becomes deliberate, and the formation of ideas and the answers to questions take longer than in healthy people. Physical energy is reduced, and patients frequently complain of lethargy and generalized muscle aches and pains. Patients become intolerant of the cold, and the skin becomes dry and swollen. The larynx also becomes swollen and gives rise to a hoarseness of the voice. Most people gain weight and develop constipation. The skin becomes dry and yellow due to the presence of increased carotene. Hair becomes thinned and brittle, and baldness may develop. Swelling of the soft tissues may give rise to a carpal tunnel syndrome (pain and tingling in the fist and fingers of one or both hands) and middle ear deafness.

Diagnosis of hypothyroidism is confirmed by measuring the levels of thyroid hormones in the blood, which are low, and the pituitary TSH, which is raised in primary hypothyroidism.

Intracranial Calcification

Intracranial calcifications are a condition in which calcium and sometimes iron (ferro calcification) deposit on the walls of blood vessels in brain tissues. This occurs either within normal brain tissues or in abnormal pathologic tissues. Intracranial calcifications are usually asymptomatic (lacking any symptoms of disease, whether or not a disease is present), but some patients do have symptoms, such as abnormal movement or cerebellar symptoms. Other signs and symptoms depend on underlying disorders. Doctors thought that Toxoplasmosis was the cause of Kirsty's cerebral calcifications, though this was never proven.

A CT scan, magnetic resonance imaging (MRI), and occasionally plain skull films can confirm intracranial calcifications. Management of an underlying disorder sometimes leads to the resolution of calcification.

Microcephaly

Microcephaly is a medical condition in which the circumference of the head is smaller than normal because the brain has not developed properly or has stopped growing. Microcephaly can be present at birth, as in Kirsty's case, or it may develop in the first few years of life. The head of a baby with microcephaly will fail to grow as the child progresses through infancy.

Microcephaly is most often caused by genetic abnormalities that interfere with the growth of the cerebral cortex during the early months of fetal development. It is associated with Downs syndrome, chromosomal syndromes, and neurometabolic syndromes.

Babies may be born with microcephaly if, during pregnancy, their mother abused drugs or alcohol; became infected with a cytomegalovirus (a member of the herpes family), rubella (German measles), or varicella, (chicken pox) virus; was exposed to certain toxic chemicals; or had untreated phenylketonuria, (a genetic disorder that can damage the brain and cause severe mental retardation).

Nothing was found that indicated why Kirsty suffered from microcephaly.

Micrognathia

Micrognathia is a smaller-than-normal jaw, often the lower jaw or chin. This may be part of a syndrome. A syndrome is a pattern of multiple anomalies or birth defects with a single cause, which can be genetic, or hereditary. The birth defects seen in a syndrome involve more than one body system, meaning, for example, there may be a problem with the jaw, heart, or kidneys.

Pierre Robin (Pee-air Ro-ban) sequence, a birth defect in which the jaw or chin is small and recessed, is also associated with micrognathia. If Pierre Robin is isolated, meaning there are no other conditions or anomalies, it is referred to as a sequence. A sequence is more than one defect that occurs as a result of a single presumed structural problem that starts a chain of events. This chain of events will result in changes in development of another organ or body part. Pierre Robin fits this definition of sequence if there are no other birth defects except those related to the small chin, tongue, and cleft palate.

Usually when the child is older, orthodontic treatment might align the teeth correctly, though there is no guarantee of success. Kirsty had this teeth defect, but there was no success with treatment.

Osteoporosis

Osteoporosis is a disease of the bones that leads to an increased risk of fracture. In osteoporosis, the bone mineral density (BMD) is reduced, bone microarchitecture is disrupted, and the amount and variety of noncollagenous proteins in the bone are altered.

Osteoporosis can be prevented with lifestyle changes and sometimes medication; treatment for those with osteoporosis may involve both. Lifestyle changes include preventing falls and exercise. Medication should be taken as prescribed, and a sensible exercise regime carried out on a regular basis.

Polyarticular Junior Chronic Arthritis

Polyarticular junior chronic arthritis (PJCA) is the inflammation of the synovium, the lining tissues of a joint. It is a subset of arthritis seen in childhood, which may be transient and self-limited, or chronic. It differs significantly from arthritis seen in adults (osteoarthritis, rheumatoid arthritis) and other types of arthritis that can begin in childhood and are chronic conditions (e.g., psoriatic arthritis and ankylosing spondylitis).

Symptoms of PJCA are often nonspecific initially, and include lethargy, reduced physical activity, and poor appetite (often due to medication). The first manifestation, particularly in young children, may be limping, or as in Kirsty's case, a painful and stiff neck, with severe rotation problems. Children may become quite ill, with persistent flulike symptoms. The cardinal feature is persistent swelling of the affected joints, which commonly include the knees, ankles, wrists, and small joints of the hands and feet. Swelling may be difficult to detect clinically, especially for joints such as those of the spine, shoulders, hips, jaw, and sacroiliac joints, though ultrasound and MRI are very useful for diagnostic purposes.

PJCA usually affects five or more joints in the first six months of the disease. Kirsty's disease eventually affected every joint of her body. This type of PJCA is more common in small girls than boys. However, the disease does occur in both sexes. Symptom onset is often dependent on the subtype of PJCA, and is active from preschool years to the early teenage years. The disease is extremely painful and debilitating and needs to be treated with urgency. Valgus is a deformity of the bone as a result of the debilitating effect of arthritis, a bending inward of the knees (genu valgum) or at the ankle, as occurs in flat-foot (pes Valgus). This was another of Kirsty's problems and made walking both painful and very difficult.

Pulmonary Oedema

Pulmonary oedema is a buildup of fluid in the lungs. Normally on breathing in, air is sucked downward through the main respiratory passageways into the tiny air sacs, which are distributed throughout the lung tissue. The oxygen in the air is then absorbed through the air sacs, called alveoli, and transported into the bloodstream for distribution around the body. Carbon dioxide, in turn, passes out of the bloodstream and into the air sacs to be expelled when breathing out again. This process is known as gaseous exchange.

Pulmonary oedema can occur for a variety of reasons but usually is due to a buildup of pressure in the circulation as a result of relatively weak heart function.

Since the heart is unable to pump blood around the lungs adequately, the pressure builds up and fluid leaks out of the blood vessels into the lung tissue itself, eventually spilling into the air sacs.

Quite often pulmonary oedema is caused by left ventricular failure, as Kirsty suffered, or mitral stenosis and is known as a waterlogging of the lungs.

Pulmonary oedema is a very serious condition that can lead to acute respiratory distress (ARDS) and result in the patient dying if not treated in the appropriate manner. ARDS should be treated in intensive care units to give the patient every chance of surviving a very dangerous situation. Kirsty was not treated in the appropriate manner and consequently paid the ultimate price.

Raynauds Disease

Raynauds disease, named after Maurice Raynaud, the Paris physician who published a thesis on the subject in 1862, is a condition in which circulation becomes suddenly obstructed in outlying parts of the body. It is due to spasm of the smallest arteries in the affected part, as a result of nervous influences, and its effects are increased both by cold and various diseases involving the blood vessels. It is predominantly a disease of women, the majority of cases occurring before the age of forty. The condition is most commonly confined to the occurrence of dead fingers or the toes, ears, or nose becoming numb and waxy-looking. This condition may last for some minutes or may linger for several hours, even for a day or two.

Retinal Detachment

Retinal detachment is movement of the transparent sensory part of the retina away from the outer pigmented layer of the retina, the moving away of the retina from the outer wall of the eyeball.

There are three layers of the eyeball. First is the outer, tough, white sclera. Lining the sclera is the choroids, a thin membrane that supplies nutrients to part of the retina. The innermost layer is the retina, which is the light-sensitive membrane that receives images and transmits them to the brain. The retina is made up of several layers. One layer contains the photoreceptors, the rods and cones that send visual messages to the brain. Between the photoreceptor layer, which is also called the sensory layer, and the choroids is the pigmented epithelium.

The vitreous is a clear, gel-like substance that fills up most of the inner space of the eyeball. It lies behind the lens and is in contact with the retina.

Retinal detachment usually occurs because of the development of a hole in the retina. Holes can occur because of degeneration of the retina, traction of the retina by the vitreous, or injury. Fluid from the vitreous passes through the hole, causing a split within the retina. The inner part of the retina becomes detached from the outer part; the latter remains in contact with the choroids. The detached retina loses its ability to detect light, with consequent impairment of vision.

Retinal vasculitis

Retinal vasculitis is an inflammatory disease of the retinal blood vessels of the eyes that may be associated with primary ocular conditions, or with inflammatory or infectious diseases in other parts of the body.

The clinical symptoms of retinal vasculitis include blurred vision, altered colour perception, metamorphopsia (distortion of images, especially straight lines), floaters, and blind spots. Some patients may suffer without any obvious visual symptoms, as with multiple sclerosis. Most patients with the vasculitis do not have an associated serious systemic disease. However, it is critical to evaluate each patient fully if he or she is suspected of possibly having this problem.

In the most serious cases of retinal vasculitis, it is a sight-threatening eye condition that involves the retinal vessels.

Active vascular disease is characterized by exudates around retinal vessels, resulting in white sheathing or cuffing of the affected vessels.

The prognosis for patients with retinal vasculitis is variable. Some that have treatment are fortunate to have preservation of both vision and visual function.

Unfortunately for Kirsty, though, she had therapy and aggressive treatment but still lost the vision in the right eye and continued exudates in the left.

Transient Ischemic Attack

A transient ischemic attack (TIA) is a stroke that lasts generally for only a few minutes. It occurs when the blood supply to a restricted area of the brain has a temporary disturbance, resulting in a brief neurologic dysfunction that persists, by definition, for less than twenty-four hours.

Symptoms include a sudden one-sided paralysis of the body (hemiplegia) and may be accompanied by a tingling in the affected arm or leg. There may be loss or impairment of speech, disturbance of vision in one or both eyes, sudden confusion, trouble with speaking or understanding or even walking, dizziness, loss of balance or coordination, and sudden headaches.

The short duration of these symptoms and lack of permanent brain injury is the main difference between a TIA and major stroke. TIAs are considered extremely important predictors of a stroke.

Vasculitis

Vasculitis is inflammation of the blood vessels. In Kirsty's case, the disease affected her small and medium blood vessels, including renal arteries, which impaired kidney function. This problem may, as in Kirsty's case, be caused by damage to the lining of the vessels and cause narrowing or blockage, causing blood flow to be restricted. This, in turn, may harm or destroy the tissues supplied by the affected blood vessels.

Vasculitis is probably caused by small particles called immune complexes circulating in the blood that adhere to the vessel walls and provoke inflammation. Normally these complexes are consumed by white blood cells.

LAST WORDS TO KIRSTY.

From her dad, with deepest love.

> How do I find thee?
> How do I see thee?
> How do I touch thee?
> How do I hear thee?
> How do I smell thee?
> How do I sense thee?
> How do I know thee?

You are always there, you never left.

You are forever in my heart.

Thank you for who you are.

Rest in peace, little angel.

Kirsty Jayne Pearce

22 February 1986-29 August 2003

ABOUT THE AUTHOR

CHARLES PEARCE LIVES IN THE COUNTY OF ESSEX IN ENGLAND, United Kingdom.

He was born in London, England, within the sound of Bow bells, and so is known as a true cockney. He is married to Peggy, who was born on the beautiful island of Mauritius, in the Indian Ocean. Peggy presented him with two beautiful children, a son Tim and a daughter Kirsty. Sadly Kirsty passed away 29 August 2003; she is missed terribly by everyone who had the privilege to know her.

Charles has been involved with the medical profession all his working life, first in general nursing serving in the Royal Air Force for fifteen years, and then as a registered psychiatric nurse, both at home and abroad, serving in Valetta, Malta, the Royal Air Force hospital in Akrotiri, Cyprus, and with the Second Allied Tactical Air Force in Germany. After leaving the air force with sixteen years of service behind him, he immigrated to Australia and worked in hospitals in Melbourne, Adelaide, and Darwin. The latter part of his career was spent with four years in alcohol and drug detoxification in Essex, England, and finally three years as the manager of an elderly people's home also near his home in Essex.

This is the first attempt that Charles has made to write a book, but he feels it has been well worth it because of the subject matter. Having some knowledge of medicine made it easier to write this book, and it has been both pleasurable and sad, but he feels it had to be done.

In March 2007, Charles was elected onto the board of governors of the hospital where Kirsty died and was actively involved in meetings and decision making in regard to future policies within the hospital. He stood down in October 2010.

Charles feels that the best medical situation he ever found himself in was that of caring for his beautiful, though severely disabled, daughter, the care he shared for over seventeen years with Peggy, his wife. Charles feels that it was both a privilege and honour to have had the opportunity of assisting with the care of his daughter, Kirsty; if he could have the chance to once again repeat that experience, he would grasp it with both hands.

With regard to the very poor care given to Kirsty on the night she died, Charles remains very bitter and just cannot forgive the events of that night.

He visits Kirsty's grave every day with Peggy and spends time talking to her. He feels that this is the only way he has of being able to speak to her; he knows she can hear him.

Another way that Charles has for getting closer to Kirsty is to remember and explore once more the lovely times they all had as a family. These memories do not fade, and writing this book helps to recall all those moments of joy.

To Charles, caring for Kirsty was a total labour of love, as is this book.

He states that it has been a privilege for him to have written this book about his charming and extremely brave daughter. Though she has now gone home to God, he always senses her near him, and the tears are always there.